TONGS,
GANGS,
AND
TRIADS

TONGS, GANGS, AND TRIADS

CHINESE CRIME GROUPS IN NORTH AMERICA

PETER HUSTON

PALADIN PRESS
BOULDER, COLORADO

Tongs, Gangs, and Triads:
Chinese Crime Groups in North America
by Peter Huston

ISBN 0-87364-835-8
Printed in the United States of America

Published by Paladin Press, a division of
Paladin Enterprises, Inc., P.O. Box 1307,
Boulder, Colorado 80306, USA.
(303) 443-7250

Direct inquiries and/or orders to the above address.

CONTENTS

V

PREFACE

This book is intended to present a great deal of information on Chinese crime, secret societies, and criminal organizations. However, it also includes material on Chinese history and culture. This is because when Westerners try to understand Chinese crime groups, they often find the complexities of the culture and the history of the Chinese people to be just as big an obstacle as the secretive nature of the groups themselves.

By attempting to describe Chinese culture, I have run the risk of stereotyping. This risk is particularly high when writing a book about crime, a decidedly negative subject in any culture. I hope that I have also managed to share in this work the respect and appreciation that I have gained for the Chinese. My life has been enriched and made more interesting because of the time I have spent interacting with, living among, and studying the Chinese.

Those who are familiar with my publisher, Paladin Press, may know it for its unique and unusual variety of books. Paladin Press readers should be able to appreciate that the Chinese a) survived all manner of disaster and adversity for 5,000 years, b) published the world's first manual of military strategy, c) published and wrote the world's first forensic manual, d) invented not only gunpowder but also the world's first repeating crossbow, e) invented organized martial arts, and f) have a notorious reputation among the nations of Southeast Asia and elsewhere for exploiting loopholes in the local legal codes and business regulations of innumerable nations. Further study of Chinese culture, secret societies, and organized crime will reveal much more of interest.

I studied about China for several years at a state university and received a B.A. in Asian studies, a field I chose because of my natural interest in the subject as well as a stubborn refusal to give in to the realities of the workplace. Following this, I spent time living abroad and bouncing around Asia, where I supported myself teaching English while attempting to make heads or tails out of what was going on around me (something people often tell me I have trouble doing even in America). Intrigued and confused, I read as much as possible about Asian and Chinese cultures, and I have no plans to stop.

In writing this work, I was especially fortunate to be able to draw upon my stints in Asia as an undocumented and illegal worker and English teacher. I read everything I could on the subject of Asian secret societies and gangs and drew upon the occasionally frightening, always illuminating contacts that I have had with Chinese gangsters. I also relied upon the experiences that I have had among the many fine, good, law-abiding Asians whom I have known both here and abroad. The Chinese, like people everywhere, have good and bad individuals among them. Their culture has many great strengths and assets. I hope that I have managed to share some of my appreciation of these as well.

Good luck on life's journey to all,
—Pete Huston, 1995

ACKNOWLEDGMENTS

I would like to thank the following people and organizations for their assistance: Mark Shamon, for computer assistance, help with writer's block, and encouragement; Lewis Treadway, for much of the same and his friendship; Daniel Forrest, Carolyn Touchette, Daniel Nardini, and Tim Holmes, for assistance with research and their valuable opinions and insights.

In addition, I wish to thank the following people for their help and encouragement with my writing career: Keith Houghton, Ed Rotendaro, and the other fine folks who lovingly put together the *Armadillo Droppings* amateur "zine" every few months; Barry Karr, Ken Frazier, Robert Baker, and Doris Doyle of the Committee for the Scientific Investigation of Claims of the Paranormal and its excellent journal, *The Skeptical Inquirer*; Michael Shermer of the Skeptics Society and its journal, *Skeptic*; Jon Ford of Paladin Press, who provided many materials and much advice, and Karen Pochert, my editor, who did an excellent job.

Don McLean of *Soldier of Fortune* magazine provided help above and beyond the call of duty by providing some valuable leads and a surprisingly large pile of back issues relating to Burmese resistance groups and related subjects. A war-torn nation run by a backward dictatorship, Burma manages to be the world's leading opium producer.

The *Penthouse* magazine editorial desk was generous enough to contribute a copy of the article "Getting Oriented," an exposé of the problems of Korean-staffed brothels and the sexual exploitation of Korean women in America today. (Lest anyone ask, they kept the pictures, so I really did read the article.)

I am grateful to the following organizations for contributing information that was included in this work: Lisa Matte at Borders Books for handling the special orders and patiently learning who the Hmong are, Caesar's Casino in Atlantic City for information on its *pai gow* games, the U.S. Drug Enforcement Agency, the Canadian Embassy, the national and New York City offices of the U.S. Customs Service, the offices and staffs of New York State Senator Hugh Farley and U.S. Rep. Michael McNulty, the U.S. Immigration and Naturalization Service, the Royal Hong Kong

Police, and, finally, the Federal Bureau of Investigation and the Treasury Department Bureau of Alcohol, Tobacco, and Firearms, both of which answered requests for information in their own bureaucratic manner.

The following people contributed information that was helpful, and without them this book could not have been completed in its present form: Grace and her family; Michelle and her family; Morgan and his family; Hank, Vic, Knoll, and Ray and their families; Ko-lin Chin; the entire staff of one of Taiwan's greatest machine factories; Nigel and Michelle for showing me the dirty side of teaching English illegally (sorry about the phones; just remember all's fair in love, war, and illegal language instruction); Felicia, best of luck with your situation; Dawn Huston; Leon Huston; Richard and Doris Kersten; Will Kamishlian; Eric Krauter and his fantastic, left-leaning vegetarian housemates—all treated me wonderfully while I visited to do research in their cities; Victor and Fabriana; Tonya and Achmed; and the many, many others who may have been forgotten in the hustle and confusion of putting this work together.

I simply must thank my sister, the accountant, for providing me with the wonderful advice that Chinese restaurant meals were a tax-deductible business expense, especially since I always do make a point of snooping around in such places to see whether I can determine if the workers are legal or not. (Surprisingly often the answer is no, by the way.) Furthermore, she contributed the secondhand coffee maker that kept me going while I was hunched over the word processor. (Of course, these two things may have wreaked havoc with my health, but that's not her fault.)

I thank you all. All mistakes in this work are, of course, my own, but these people did what they could to keep them as small as possible.

For many people throughout the world, living in the United States, the "land of opportunity," has always been something to strive for. Despite its many problems, America continues to be a haven for large numbers of immigrants.

For better or worse, when people from other cultures come in they bring their own ideas and ways of doing things, and along with the good comes the bad. Every immigrant group brings with it not just doctors, engineers, artists, and musicians, but criminals as well. Those interested in understanding certain types of crime and its patterns in North America must consider such immigrant groups as the Chinese.

Although many have called the Chinese in America—and Asian immigrants in general—a "model minority group," it is important to understand that traditional Chinese culture and modes of behavior are very different from our own. When victimized by crime, for instance, a citizen of traditional China would act very differently than the "average" American. Similarly, when those in traditional China committed crimes, they were often different than those of modern Americans. Likewise, Chinese crime groups and secret societies are organized differently than their American counterparts. All these traditions continue to varying extents among the Chinese immigrants in North America today.

Crime is a human behavior. Although all people must eat, have sex, reproduce, and somehow take care of the resulting children, it is "culture" that determines how a group of people does these things. This work focuses on Asian crime and is not an elementary social studies text, but it is impossible to understand crime in a

CHAPTER 1

AN INTRODUCTION TO CHINESE CULTURE

given group without some understanding of the broader culture in which to place the human behaviors that are considered criminal.

In every culture there is a certain amount of individual variation. In describing our own, for instance, most of us would agree that the common morality and religion teaches Americans to be honest, be kind to other people, and avoid committing theft or violence except in extreme cases. However, we all know these ideals are followed by only some. Yet when we are told that in Chinese culture children should honor and obey their father at all times and a wife should be subservient to her husband, many of us assume this is how all Chinese people behave. Being human, the Chinese do not always think or do as they believe they're supposed to.

Similarly, there are varying degrees of Asian-ness. When we speak of Chinese culture or Asian culture with reference to an immigrant group, we must use common sense. Some Asians, particularly recent immigrants and those who spend the majority of their lives surrounded by other immigrants, behave virtually the same as they would in their homelands. They often find the behavior of mainstream Americans exceedingly strange and difficult to understand. Often such people will try to avoid them whenever possible and associate almost exclusively with other members of their culture.

On the other hand, there are many individuals of Asian descent who live in the United States or Canada and have a perfect understanding of American culture and have assimilated to it fully. I'm immediately reminded of two brothers who attended school with me. Although their parents were from Taiwan, the brothers essentially refused their mother's attempts to keep them sinicized: they would not study for the Saturday morning Chinese-language class she had enrolled them in, preferring to play baseball instead. Of course, one should not assume that just because someone seems completely Americanized that he has no connections with Chinese culture.

Keeping individual variation and cultural assimilation in mind, it is a good idea to be familiar with the following key factors and to keep them in mind when trying to understand Chinese behavior. Culture is generally an outgrowth of a people's need to adapt to a set of circumstances or conditions. These factors simply describe the conditions under which Chinese (and some other Asian people) live and the resultant life-style and traditions that have developed over the years.

CROWDING

The population density in China is much higher than in the United States or even Europe. To visit China is to find oneself in a sea of people. China's greatest strength, its greatest resource, and its greatest weakness are one and the same—its population. There are more Chinese on earth than any other nationality.

Finding food for all who live in China has always been a struggle. Although China is a large country, only a small portion of its land is suitable for growing food crops. As the population has increased, the amount of land available for agriculture has shrunk. Today in China, there is virtually no unused land left that could be cultivated for agriculture.

Many Americans wonder why the Chinese don't just grow more food by farming in underutilized areas. The answer simple: such development has already been done; almost every scrap of land that can be used has been, and little else is wasted. For example, for centuries human excrement (so-called night soil) has been carefully saved and utilized as fertilizer. The hills have been terraced to increase farm land, and the level areas have been cultivated for years. It is not uncommon to see such domestic animals as water buffaloes grazing on even the smallest plots of land, including the thin walkways that separate the everpresent rice paddies. There are few simple solutions to the problems posed by overcrowding in Asia. If there were, the Chinese undoubtedly would have discovered them years ago.

Under such conditions, the people are forced to live very close together. In much of urban China today, the crowding is simply amazing by American standards. For example, most homes and apartments share public rest rooms and toilets with their neighbors. There are people in cities such as Shanghai who have literally never been alone in a room in their lives.

Americans are familiar with the stereotype of excessive Asian politeness. Although, like all stereotypes, this one is exaggerated and not universally followed, there is some truth to it. Such politeness is simply an outgrowth of the need for people to get along in close quarters for long periods. In fact, many of the decidedly "foreign" aspects of Chinese culture can be seen as a natural outgrowth of living under unrelentingly crowded conditions.

American law enforcement often uncovers large numbers of illegal Chinese aliens living in shockingly crowded quarters. It's important to understand that although such conditions are worse than those under which many Chinese live at home, due to their experience in living this way, most Chinese find such a situation more tolerable than an American would.

POVERTY

With so many people living together in one place, it's only natural that resources get stretched and that there's little to go around. Sadly, while many Americans take their own comparative wealth for granted, few in China today feel secure about having a guaranteed supply of food throughout their lives.

In many areas of China, the standard greeting is not "How are you?" but rather "Have you eaten yet?" Food and its sharing are a major part of courtesy, hospitality, and politeness among the Chinese.

When it comes to illegal immigration there is one important motivation to consider. Although illegal immigrants and workers are often lied to and tricked, the majority come to North America with the understanding that they will probably receive sub-minimum-wage jobs that will pay considerably better than those in their home countries. They are willing to undergo a great deal of risk and hardship in order to gain such opportunity. Since they are used to having very little, they can save a great deal of money by their standards while working for exceedingly low wages.

HARD WORK AND MONEY = FOOD; FOOD = LIFE

When one has few resources, the choices are to work hard or starve. In traditional China, the bulk of the population was forced to toil day after day simply to grow the food needed to maintain a subsistence-level diet. Most people worked long hours, seven days a week, month after month. Their only vacation would be when Chinese New Year came. During this five-day holiday, most stopped working, held a feast, and celebrated their only vacation of the year. Today, Chinese New Year is still the biggest and most important holiday for most of the Chinese population. (Like the Jewish holidays, Chinese New Year is based on a lunar calendar and therefore shifts its exact dates from year to year; it usually arrives sometime between January and March).

In much of the world, the Chinese are known for their willingness to work hard and their desire to earn or acquire wealth. Although many perceive this as greed, it must be placed in a cultural context. To many Chinese great wealth is simply a type of insurance. If you have wealth you can buy food. If food becomes scarce and its price rises, then only the wealthy will eat. Most Chinese see frugality and hard work as signs of good planning. Many of the refugees in America and elsewhere were only able to survive by having enough money to flee their homeland for another country. Other Chinese and Asians recall the experiences of their parents or grandparents who made it through difficult times only because they had enough money to flee ravaging Japanese troops or hostile Communist revolutionaries, or to buy up food when it was extremely scarce and usurious prices were demanded.

To such people, money is not just a ticket to luxury items such as stereos and sports cars but a means to preserve life itself in the face of an uncertain future.

THE IMPORTANCE OF EDUCATION

The picture painted so far of life in China is one of unrelenting poverty and hard labor. There was, however, a traditional way out, even in ancient times: education. In traditional China, government appointments were based on the results of a civil service examination. The candidate was tested on his knowledge of Confucian classics and had to answer lengthy essay questions explaining how the ancient teachings of Confucius might be applied to a given situation. Confucianism is an ancient philosophy of China, and its teachings describe how the Chinese believe people should behave and the sort of manners, courtesy, consideration, and respect that they should show one another. It emphasizes the duty of authority figures to care for those under them and that of their subjects to be respectful and obedient. Since Confucianism was the predominant philosophy of the scholar class of China, a full knowledge of its teachings was believed essential for a potential government official.

According to law, the tests were open to all men (women were excluded), and the Chinese of any social class could, in theory, become officials if they showed the proper skill and knowledge in these examinations.[1] In practice, however, to pass the exams one had to devote most of one's life to study. Normally only the children of important families could afford the time to study; poorer children had to help their parents with the farm work. Similarly, it took a lot of money to buy the books and other written materials needed to pass the tests. Although the wealthy had a major advantage, the tests themselves were egalitarian and open to all. There are cases on record of peasants uniting to purchase the books and spend the time to tutor a particularly talented son from their village so that he could pass the examination.

Today, it is a Chinese belief and tradition that education is one of the keys to advancement in society. The Chinese encourage their children to study hard to get ahead. It brings great shame when a child does not do well in school. Many Chinese youth gangs in America recruit heavily from disillusioned youth who have dropped out of school (often because of language problems).

The test format consisting of long essay questions that were answered by quoting and referring to the Confucian classics created another legacy that is essential to understanding Chinese attitudes toward education. In time, the test answers were allowed to degenerate, and the simplest way to guarantee a high score was to memorize lengthy essays word for word and copy them onto the paper, using no imagination or variation whatsoever. Books of these essays could be purchased, and the examples provided were seen as the ideal. Since the sample essays were considered perfect by both the test subjects and the scorers, no intelligent student would think of changing them. Even today, Asian education places a much stronger emphasis on rote memorization than does the American system. Although Asian-born students often excel in the American schools, they often do so largely through memorizing a great deal of data to which they have given little thought. There is a tendency to stress education as a road to good grades, certificates, degrees, and other outward signs of education, which are often seen as being more important than the less visible, internal aspects of learning.

Fatalism, Tradition, and Concern for Social Order

In America, a relatively rich country, it is said that most people are really at most only one or two months' paychecks away from destitution and homelessness.

In China, often the margin between being properly fed and starving is much smaller. With resources strained and people living under highly crowded conditions, disruption and chaos are to be avoided. Much in Chinese culture is geared to guaranteeing stability and social order.

Since poverty is the norm and people must labor long hours or risk starvation, their only hope for improvement is through education. And, traditionally, this simply was not practical for most. Furthermore, the life of most Chinese is heavily controlled by the whims of a variety of authority figures: parents, employers, the government.

As a result, over the course of some thousand years a heavy streak of fatalism has evolved in Chinese culture. Most Chinese have few naive expectations about what to expect out of life; they don't expect much in the way of the abstract ideal of freedom or the chance to obtain "self-actualization." Many merely hope to survive. Of course, the Chinese aren't stupid. If they can live in a comfortable house, eat only the best food, hold a fulfilling job, have the freedom to speak as they wish, and try to attain their hopes, dreams, and spiritual yearnings, then that's wonderful. But, simply put, many Chinese fully understand that life is often unfair and unpleasant and that these things are luxuries. When one accepts that life is inherently unfair, then it is possible to shrug off a great deal of hardship. For example, many

Chinatown shopkeepers simply accept frequent extortion attempts, paying what is demanded and dealing with it as a cost of doing business. Other Chinese become extortionists themselves—and shrug this off to forces beyond their control. Similar events happen with the trade in and illegal exploitation of illegal immigrants. A great number of things that many Americans say they would "rather die than do" are things that Chinese of this and earlier generations actually have had to do (e.g., eat insects or lizards rather than starve; work 100-hour weeks rather than starve; sell a young daughter into slavery to raise the money to feed the other family members; put up with bandits or extortionists stealing hard-earned wages month after month rather than being raped, killed, beaten, or burned into starvation).

Aside from this fatalistic streak, there's another factor that must be considered: the behavior of most Chinese is heavily constrained by tradition. In China, a nation thousands of years old, with a culture that emphasizes respect for authority, tradition is very strong. If one follows tradition, stability will be maintained from generation to generation. In a traditional society, responses to change are often locked in the past, and thus everyone knows what to expect. Of course, these days tradition cannot always be followed, and not all Chinese or other Asians find it desirable. The world is changing. Furthermore, as foreign-born individuals come to live in America, they and their offspring tend to assimilate more and more. This results in strong generational and cultural gaps within extended families that many Asians find disturbing.

THE IMPORTANCE OF FAMILY AND RELATIONSHIPS TO AUTHORITY FIGURES

One of the fundamental, extremely strong units in Chinese culture is the family. There are many practical advantages to this. In difficult times it pays to have allies, and generally the most trustworthy allies one can have are relatives and family members. In a survival situation, having family to care for one's well-being can make the crucial difference between life and death.

The Chinese concept of family and the expected obligations and privileges of family life are different from what is considered normal in most of mainstream American society. In the Chinese family, according to tradition, the father is the leader. He has extraordinary authority, including the right to make decisions about his children's lives that might be seen as unconscionable in American society. For example, a father can choose his children's schools, the subjects they study, the activities they participate in— and more. If he is a good father, he will make such decisions based on wisdom and his affection for his children, and the children will benefit from his choices. He can punish them as necessary, but if he is an ideal father then there will be little need for this. After all, if his children know that their father is wise and caring, then doing as he wishes is ultimately in their best interests. Of course not all fathers are good. Making bad decisions about his children's lives, beating them frequently, and encouraging them to do things that are only for his benefit are considered bad behavior by fathers. Nevertheless, the children, if they are moral, are expected to conform to their father's wishes. It is immoral in Chinese society to disobey these wishes, and the fact that one's father might be acting like a lowbred scumbag doesn't change this.

This system results in strong and lasting family relationships and provides society with a great deal of stability. If one needs a place to go and is willing to conform to the wishes of one's father or parents, then the family provides such a place for most Chinese.

Women are similarly expected to obey their husbands (and mothers-in-law): younger children are expected to obey older children; and, outside the family, the citizens are expected to obey their government. The system is, admittedly, both sexist and unequal, yet it does have distinct advantages. With clearly designated leaders and followers, there is great stability and little question about how decisions will be made. To survive, the group must stick together, and in emergencies it is very important to have a clearly recognized leader.

Naturally, since the Chinese are only human, the system does not work ideally all of the time. Often, all family members will act in public as if the father is the ideal but behave quite differently behind the scene. This way the family and the father save "face" (more on this later), while still being human and preserving their sanity. For example, although in public a wife might defer to her husband, in the confines of the home she may nag him endlessly to get a better job or buy her a washer and dryer. Similarly, she might connive to manipulate her husband into doing what she'd like, without his catching on.

In the event of a terrible famine or some financial emergency, traditionally the survival of the family unit has overridden the needs of the individuals in the family. In traditional China a father had the right to sell or give away his children if need be. Under normal conditions, this would be done only in the most drastic cases, when the family was unable to feed the child anyway and money was desperately needed to buy food for the remaining family members. In most cases, the father made such a decision after great deliberation and consultation with his wife, but this was not considered necessary. There are numerous stories and cases on record of fathers getting drunk and selling their daughters to stay in a gambling game or for some equally poor excuse. Although this was common, it was considered quite irresponsible behavior—perhaps equivalent to spousal abuse in our own society.

Because the family's survival was determined through the preservation of its name—and this was passed on through male offspring—boys were traditionally considered more valuable than girls. Female children were raised until they reached a marriageable age and then sent off to join their new husband's family. Such marriages were normally arranged, not chosen by the bride and groom.

These days much of this has changed. Although sons are normally considered more valuable than daughters, the difference is not as great as it once was. Daughters remain in contact with their parents under normal conditions throughout their lives. Even though isolated reports of fathers selling their children crop up from time to time in China, Taiwan, and elsewhere, the practice is highly illegal in both China and Taiwan and most certainly is not accepted or common. (Although still illegal, it does occur with more frequency in such countries as Thailand.)

We cannot understand the situation fully without a classic story concerning a conversation between the duke of She, a nobleman and ruler, and Confucius, the famous philosopher who sometimes served as his advisor.

The duke of She told Confucius, "In my country there is an

upright man named Kung. When his father stole a sheep, he testi-fied against him." Confucius said, "The upright men in my com-munity are different from this. The father conceals the miscon-duct of the son, and the son conceals the misconduct of the father. Moral behavior is to be found in this" (Chan 1963, 41).

In essence, what this story says is that the relationship with the family is more important than any relationship with society at large, and especially with an abstraction like the legal system. In other words, if you take care of your family, and if everyone behaves this way, then society will take care of itself—and you.

Although this story dates back to approximately 500 B.C., there is still a great deal of such feeling today. It is naive to expect Chinese to regularly testify or bear witness against family mem-bers. Although such actions do happen, they are very rare, and even then one should look for the reasons why such uncommon events take place. Some reasons might be obvious, but others could be unfathomable and impossible for us to understand.

If a Chinese parent is involved in a questionable activity, then the children might get sucked into it, accepting the situation and, fatalis-tically, repressing any objections. After all, if one's family is involved, one has few moral options but to go along with the cir-cumstances—which might involve engaging in organized crime or exploiting illegal aliens in a restaurant—as they present themselves.

FACE (bay meang)

Although to many Americans the Asian concept of "face" is strange, an exotic aspect of a foreign culture, the basic idea is really very simple. As in all societies, in order to function a per-son must have a certain amount of respect—without which others of his society will not wish to associate with him (after all, associ-ating with people with little face causes one to lose face, while associating with people with a lot of face causes one to gain face.)

Face is an abstract quantity; some people have more or less of it than others. Generally speaking, the more important you are, the more face you have. You can gain face in different ways. Being intelligent, educated, rich, and smart all help. Of course, if you cannot actually be these things, it's quite enough either to appear that you are or to associate with those who are considered to be. Titles help, as do nice clothes and other possessions.

The accumulation of face is quite important to most Asians, and much of Asian behavior revolves around it. As Michael Harris Bond, a Canadian-born psychologist at the Chinese University of Hong Kong, states, "Given the importance of having face and of being related to those who do, there is a plethora of relationship politics in Chinese culture. Name dropping, eagerness to associate with the rich and famous, the use of external status symbols, sensitivity to insult, lavish gift-giving, the use of titles, the sedulous avoidance of criticism all abound—and require considerable readjustment for someone used to organizing social life by impersonal rules, frankness, and greater equality." (Bond 59, 1991).

To those who wish to understand the world of Asian crime, face will become an important factor. Asians' motivations for lying are often different from what we see in our culture. One common motivation is face. Frequently, if an Asian is forced to admit to something that will cause him to lose face, then he will tell a lie. Often, if an individual has been telling lies, then face can be a powerful motivator to maintain the falsehood even after the practicality and believability of the lie has been lost.

Face can be a major factor in many situations. To interact effectively with those who are culturally Asian, you must always take face into consideration, calculating the potential for embarrassment and resulting loss of face before acting. If you accidentally cause loss of face, you will anger and upset people, reducing their desire to cooperate. On the other hand, if you carefully act to "preserve" or even increase an acquaintance's face, it will be considered a generous act. Asian gangsters, loan sharks, blackmailers, and others often get results through actions designed to cause an individual's loss of face. In many cases, these "embarrassing" acts can be of a subtle sort that many Americans would simply shrug off or might not even recognize as worthy of much thought. Such a system can work to one's benefit as well. If one wishes to apply pressure on someone, then the threat of actions designed to cause loss of face can be an effective means of intimidation to obtain a confession. In some cases, Asians will find the threat of loss of face among their family and others close to them to be at least as effective a deterrent to crime as the threat of being caught. It has been my experience that, in circumstances where they don't believe that their family and loved ones will hear about it, many Asians will behave in a manner that would be considered shameful, and to a greater extent than most Americans would.

The concept of face, and its importance, is one of the primary differences between Asian and American cultures. As such, it's a factor that will be returned to again and again throughout this work.

US AGAINST THEM

As stated earlier, China is a very crowded nation. Under such extreme conditions, one's fellow man often comes to be seen as a threat. This potential threat can take two forms: one is when other people become competitors for scarce resources; the other is more direct—when they become more aggressive and actively threaten one's well being.

In traditional China, individuals divided the people they met into various categories and saw each category as needing to be treated differently. This is still true in China today. These categories were family (and other members of one's group), government officials, and strangers. Members of the same family, village, or other important group were expected to work together and exchange assistance and favors freely without thought of reward. Ultimately, it was felt, all would come out more or less even in the end. A person could rely on his family or his fellow villagers for assistance, and they could rely on him; after all, they had all worked together for generation after generation to overcome such threats as famines, bandits, and natural disasters. When it came to government officials, people were expected to respect and obey them or, at the very least, look as if they did. This was done for a variety of reasons, one of which was simply that government officials could wield a great deal of power and influence in a somewhat arbitrary manner, and it was beneficial to be on their good side. Undoubtedly, a sense of deference to the wisdom of the officials was also a factor.

When it came to strangers and others outside the group, there was little in the way of mutual obligation. Strangers could easily be seen as a threat. It is quite easy, particularly under situations where resources are scarce, to develop a mentality of "us versus them." The needs of one's family and other group members tend to be seen as more important than those of a never-ending stream of potentially dangerous strangers.

When dealing with outsiders, a different set of moral obligations is felt to be relevant than when dealing with friends and family. Members of a group work together to help one another. With strangers, things are much more calculated. Normally, people provide for those close to them, then begin to worry about those outside the group. When it comes to providing assistance or favors to outsiders, trust is not assumed at first. If such people do favors for you, then you are often felt to be obligated to provide them with an equal favor in the future. Under such conditions, people do not wish to accept too much assistance from others, because they may be expected to repay it at an inconvenient time in the future. Similarly, when a favor is accepted, it is generally considered a good idea to repay it as soon as possible. If such giving and receiving of favors continues in a positive manner, then a personal relationship will develop between the two individuals or groups in question, and ultimately they can come to rely on each other more and more. (See the following section on *guan-hsi* and interpersonal relationships.) If such a relationship has not developed, there are few obligations to the outsiders in question.

There is a dark side to this attitude. In some cases, it is easy to see outsiders as a convenient and useful resource that can be manipulated for the benefit of oneself or the group. If laborers need to be hired, for instance, there is little need to pay them any more than the barest minimum. To give such hirelings extra out of some feeling of fairness is to reduce the resources available to oneself and one's loved ones unnecessarily.

Face, by the way, is not something that applies just to individuals. It also applies to a group. Individuals in a group will attempt to show concern for its image and preserve its face. For example, family problems are generally hidden from outsiders. To show the weaknesses within one's group to an outsider is seen as being in very bad taste; according to conventional Asian wisdom, the problems of a group should remain in that group.

GUAN-HSI AND INTERPERSONAL RELATIONSHIPS

company

Closely related to the differences in relationships between those in a group and those outside of it is the concept of guan-hsi (pronounced "gwon-shee"). Guan-hsi is a Chinese term that refers to individuals with whom one has established a mutual aid relationship. Such people (or organizations) are not necessarily in one's group, but they do know that if they help you then they can count on you for the same in the future. Guan-hsi is similar to the English term "connections."

As everywhere else, in China and Taiwan the governments are not always responsive to the needs of the citizens. As we shall see in the section of this chapter on Chinese attitudes toward the law, individuals in the government and other bureaucracies often have a great deal of leeway in their decision making. Under such conditions, often the simplest option is to make use of a personal relationship with an individual in the government who can assist with a needed task. If an Asian does not have a personal relationship with an individual in the government, then he will seek out an acquaintance who knows someone in the government who can be of assistance—sort of a friend of a friend. The basic idea is to attempt to establish a personal relationship with someone with the ability to intervene on one's behalf when needed. The state of knowing such an individual is known as "having guan-hsi," with guan-hsi referring to the relationship, not the individual. It's quite similar to, but more important than, the concept of "networking," which is often helpful when doing research or other complex tasks in the United States.

Having good guan-hsi is a source of gaining face. Of course, if one uses guan-hsi, particularly that of a friend, then one owes a favor or two.

Such obligations are not always repaid, but they are taken quite seriously and it is considered immoral not to pay them. In traditional China, if one owed one's guan-hsi a favor then this would normally be repaid by means of either a gift or, preferably, a favor in the future. In modern times, there is a tendency under some conditions for this system to be converted from "favors owed" to a cash basis. Although undoubtedly much simpler, this often degenerates into simple corruption.

As a source of face, it is not at all uncommon for Asians to exaggerate the importance of their guan-hsi, and, as such, guan-hsi has many important influences upon Chinese behavior. One is a tendency to maintain a wide variety of relationships of one sort or another on the off chance that they might be useful. A Chinese acquaintance of mine, a man in his 40s, has, on occasion, bragged about his important ties with organized crime in his home region in Taiwan. These ties consist of having an elementary school classmate who runs a brothel. Such claims may sound ludicrous, but it is highly probable that one could obtain a favor by this route if, naturally, one were willing to pay the proper price. Since it is not a good idea to "owe unnamed favors to be named at a future date" to gangsters (not to mention the ethical issues), I did not ever take this gentleman up on his generous offer of using his "underworld guan-hsi" on my behalf.

Similarly, there is a great preference in Asian cultures for conducting business through people with whom one already has established a relationship. This increases the level of trust in professional relationships. In his excellent book, *Dragons and Tigers,* police officer and Asian crime specialist James R. Badey described how this affects his relationship with informants in the Vietnamese community. Badey states that it is not at all uncommon for an informant he has recruited to continue reporting to him even after being instructed not to. The informants wished to maintain what they saw as a valuable interpersonal relationship rather than establish a new one with someone unknown (Badey 1988, 7–11).

REGIONALIZATION

The people in one part of China are quite different from those in another. They eat different foods and often cannot understand one another when they speak their native dialects. Although programs initiated in both Taiwan and China to make Mandarin Chinese (the dialect of Beijing) function as a de facto second language for all the population have improved the situation somewhat, regional differences are still extreme. In fact, regional stereotypes and prejudices often influence the attitudes among various Chinese groups in North America as well.

Many in America fail to realize that the world is just as complex on the other side of the globe as it is here. Most of us are familiar with both the real and stereotyped differences between the speech, dress, diet, and behavior of groups such as Italian-, Irish-, and Jewish-Americans. To a Chinese immigrant not very familiar with our culture, such differences might not even be noticed. This individual could, however, discuss and explain at great length the real and stereotypical differences in such groups as the Chinese from Canton, the Chinese from Taiwan, Northern Chinese, Shanghai Chinese, and the scattered, wandering Hakka Chinese. (And if you really wish to get a long-winded, opinionated lecture on ethnic tendencies, ask most Chinese about the typical Korean or Japanese!) Naturally, the seriousness and accuracy of such descriptions vary widely according to familiarity with the given group and the education of the individual.

There are wide variances among Chinese groups within the United States, and it is important to keep these in mind when interacting with the Chinese community in North America.

DISTRUST OF BANKS

For a variety of reasons that we need not get into here (including tax evasion and fear of banks closing), many Asians show a distrust of conventional Western-style banking institutions. Instead, such services are replaced or supplemented with traditional means of storing wealth or obtaining needed short-term capital. Some bank with their "family" association (an organization for Chinese with the same last name) or other unconventional organizations.

Like many tradition-oriented peoples, the Chinese like to keep their wealth in easily used forms, such as jewelry. It is not uncommon for Chinese to have outrageous amounts of jewelry on their persons or in their homes, often out of sight.

This distrust of banks and appreciation for jewelry and gold and such has some interesting ramifications. For example, in New York City, the National Westminster Bank has more safe deposit

Russia

Mongolia

Beijing

North Korea

Japan

China

South Korea

Nepal

Fukien (Fujian)

Guangdong (Canton)

Taiwan

India

Bhutan

Yunnan

Burma (Myanmar)

Hong Kong

Macao

Laos

Vietnam

Thailand

National Boundary – – – – – – – –

Provincial Boundary ....
(Only provinces mentioned in the text are shown)

boxes rented out at its Chinatown branch than at almost any other branch in the city. The single exception is in the district where most diamond merchants are located.

Jewelry is not the only sort of wealth the Chinese tend to hoard. In much of Asia, credit is difficult to come by and risky to use. Often, cash is the preferred medium for a transaction that most Americans would handle with a check or money order. For example, in the real estate business in Taiwan, homes are often purchased with outrageously large sums of cash. It's an amazing thing to see a coffee table heaped with Taiwanese bills and knowing that each one is the equivalent of $40 U.S.

To obtain credit, many Asians use an institution known in English as either a "face bank," a cooperative loan system, or a credit union. This is essentially a club, where members have access to loans from the combined funds of the group. (For a variety of reasons, many centered on regulations governing banking, lending, or interest rates, this system is illegal in the United States.)

The basic idea is simple. A group of people get together and decide to form such a credit union. They then each promise to give a certain amount of money to the group each month. Let's say, for example, that a given credit union might have 20 members. Each member pledges to provide a predetermined amount of money at each meeting. The amount is determined before organizing the credit union and remains the same from month to month. A credit union is organized to last for a certain amount of time only (although this may be renewed and restarted at the end.) The number of meetings is generally equal to the number of people participating in the credit union. For instance, if the credit union has 20 members and a monthly meeting, then it will last for 20 months. Some credit unions meet twice a month, in which case the credit union with its 20 members, would last only 10 months.

At each meeting the members contribute their money. This will result in a pool of combined funds. Continuing with the above example, if the 20 members each contribute $500, then the combined pool of the group will be $10,000, which is the equivalent of what each member will contribute by the time the credit union is closed at the end of 20 meetings. At each meeting, one member will get to keep the pool. This individual will be chosen by a simple method. The members have the option of bidding for the right to take home the funds. The member with the highest bid gets to take the funds home and keep them, but he must pay the other members the amount equal to his bid.

Therefore, each meeting members get some "interest" on their contribution, as well as the opportunity to take home the combined funds. Each member, naturally, can only take home the combined funds once. That is, after all, their entire share of the contribution. The interest paid each month can be quite high or quite low depending on how much competition there is in a given month for use of the funds. Variations of this basic idea exist.

This Asian credit union is an informal system capable of raising large sums of capital for its members quickly. Its informality is its primary strength and weakness. Generally, because the members know one another, there are no background or credit checks. Similarly, there is little provision for the many contingencies and problems that might crop up. If a member dies, disappears, or suffers a financial loss making him unable to participate after withdrawing his share of the money, then there is little agreement on the proper procedures. Disputes can break out. In some cases, such credit unions have been organized by an individual who consciously plans to steal the combined funds of the group and then flee the area. Furthermore, because the system is illegal in the United States, if disputes do arise, members cannot go to the police and expect much assistance. As everyone knows, when large amounts of cash disappear in an illegal investment leaving a wide variety of upset people, the potential for resulting violence is quite real.

ASIAN ATTITUDES TOWARD THE LAW

Confucius said, "Lead the people with governmental measure and regulate them by law and punishment, and they will avoid wrongdoing but have no sense of honor and shame. Lead them with virtue and regulate them by the rules of propriety, and they will have a sense of shame, and, moreover, set themselves right" (Chan 1963, 22). For 2,000 years, it has been a tenet of Chinese governance that if the government sets a good example and encourages people to be moral, then the common people should be able to conduct their day-to-day affairs without undue government or police interference. Furthermore, after countless generations of observation, most Chinese have come to the perfectly obvious conclusion, one that every policeman can attest to, that even the best written laws just don't work as intended in all cases. This attitude toward the legal system was also influenced by generations of harsh experience with officials who could be selfish, cruel, and incredibly biased and corrupt.

These experiences have led to two important attitudes toward the law. The first is that those in law enforcement should be avoided except when absolutely necessary. The second is that often in day-to-day affairs the laws are little more than guidelines. If the laws didn't work as intended, then in traditional China an official would simply ignore them; instead, he would use his wisdom and experience to determine the proper course of affairs. Naturally, an official would have to have the powers to enact his decisions, even if they didn't follow the law, but if the official was just, then the decisions would be just and proper as well. In effect, the Chinese came to believe in the superiority of a benign and compassionate "benevolent dictatorship," where caring officials could do what needed to be done. Some have noted the ready comparisons to the Chinese concept of the ideal family where a caring father rules with a firm but compassionate hand.

To the Chinese, it has always seemed both callous and irresponsible for an official or government representative to hide behind the excuse of simply following the law. They often describe those who follow guidelines and regulations, regardless of the consequences, as "lacking in humanity." This cultural difference leads to many conflicts here. Since in many ways, life in the United States is dominated by a wide variety of laws, ordinances, bureaucratic regulations, and other governmental and organizational guidelines, many Chinese describe America as a nation lacking in compassion and humanity. Often, recent immigrants, tourists, and other Asians with little experience or education in American culture assume that the United States is normally run more or less like their home countries. It is not uncommon for these people to be genuinely confused as to why they are being asked to conform to some relatively trivial but uniformly enforced law. For example, in the work *Harmony in Conflict*, Richard W. Hartzell, an American residing in Taiwan, gives the peculiar example of a Taiwanese Chinese-language newspaper piece in which two Taiwanese described their personal experiences with discrimination in the United States. Often their examples illustrated misunderstood cultural differences rather than true discrimination. For example, on one occasion a police officer in Cleveland told them they could not park in a restricted parking zone, "not even for just two minutes while you pick up a package." Since they could see no harm in their request and could not imagine that anyone in Taiwan would really object to such a thing, they assumed his refusal had to be for some strong reason, most likely discrimination (Hartzel 1988 156–158).

In other cases, Chinese will not readily understand just how constrained by policy many in America really are. They will assume that American bureaucrats have powers and abilities to adjust unpleasant situations and regulations that they simply do not have. This, as well as the uniquely Chinese approach to even minor bureaucratic problems, can be illustrated by the behavior of Mr. C., a Chinese citizen of Malaysia who decided to obtain a driver's license in New York state, where he attended college. He set out first to obtain a learner's permit, which requires passing a brief written test. The information needed to pass the test is all in a small booklet available free of charge from the motor vehicle department.

Mr. C. decided there must be a more efficient way to pass the test than to study the entire book and memorize a great deal of information that he would not be tested on. He began calling Chinese acquaintances who had already obtained a New York driver's license. (These people could be considered some of his guanhsi.) He explained the situation to them and said he wished to know as much as possible about the exact questions asked and the answers to them. Then he began studying the assortment of possible questions and their answers, rather than reading the whole book. (This is illustrative of both the Asian tendency to see education as a means of passing tests and obtaining certificates, rather than as something that might actually be useful in itself and value placed on gaining face: Mr. C. would gain face if his friends agreed that his plan was more clever than the conventional method.)

Mr. C. passed that test easily. (It is, after all, a very simple test.) Unfortunately for him, though, he failed his road test. In this case, most people would simply study harder and learn to drive better. Instead, Mr. C. called his acquaintances once again to see if any had guan-hsi within the Department of Motor Vehicles (DMV). Ultimately, one man, Mr. L., announced that he had quite an important friend at the DMV. (By announcing this, Mr. L. gained face for appearing as an important man who associated with important people and knew how to get things done.) Mr. C. asked Mr. L. if his friend would be able to secretly change the results of his road test. Mr. L. assured him that he would look into it and that, due to the importance of his friend, he thought it would be quite possible. Unfortunately for Mr. L., his friend informed him that the DMV is simply not structured in a manner that allows such acts of corruption to be done easily and routinely as personal favors. This left Mr. L. in a quandary. He had told Mr. C. that he could obtain this favor for him. If it were not done as he said then he would lose face. Of course, if he were to simply explain that the DMV regulations are not that easily broken, Mr. C. would not believe him. Finally, Mr. L. telephoned Mr. C. and blamed him for the situation. He told Mr. C. that although his friend was really quite important and could change the results of *most* road tests, Mr. C.'s results were exceptionally bad, a special case, and nobody could change test results that were that horrible. By firmly blaming Mr. C., Mr. L. managed to preserve his own face. Mr. C. found the excuse quite believable and was ashamed. This story illustrates not just the Asian tendency to see bureaucrats as having more authority than they really do, but also that of actively seeking out, hunting down, and exploiting virtually any conceivable loophole. Now, not all Asians, and not even all Chinese, are quite this creative, but it may account for the fact that some of the world's most successful businessmen can be found in the Chinese population.

CONCLUSION

This chapter was intended to provide an overview of the key factors that one should be familiar with in order to understand

Asian behavior with regard to law enforcement, crime, and similar matters. It's important to remember that these are merely guidelines. Asians, like people everywhere, are individuals, and each responds in a slightly different manner to any given situation. What I have attempted here is to explain how culture might affect the responses of a given individual or group of individuals in a wide variety of situations that relate to Asian crime patterns.

Although my intent is to describe Chinese culture in particular, it can be said that many of the cultures of Asia behave, by and large, in a similar manner. There are, however, important differences and one must keep in mind that every country in Asia has its own culture just as the many European nations do. At the risk of stereotyping, it is considered, for example, that women are more equal in the Vietnamese culture than the Chinese. Koreans are known throughout Asia (much the same as the Italians and Irish in Europe) for being emotional and having terrible tempers. The Japanese are different in many ways from the other peoples of Asia, but there are important similarities. To an extent that is probably greater than in most Asian cultures, there is a tendency within Japan to stress the importance of the group and of mutual obligations and the duty to repay favors to outsiders.

These are societies that use many Chinese institutions and have been influenced extensively by Chinese philosophies such as Confucianism. These societies too have flourished under crowded, semifeudal conditions. There are other cultures in Asia, however, that are extremely different from the Chinese culture and in which these guidelines would not apply at all. For example, the Hmong are a hill tribe of Southeast Asia and China. Many Hmong (also known as the Miao or Meo) fought against the Communists during the Vietnam War in their homeland of Laos and have now come to this country as refugees. This culture and people did not follow Confucianism, did not live under as crowded conditions, had no written language, and had a much more primitive government.

When discussing Asian cultures in America, we must remember that they are all in a state of adaptation to a new environment and culture, and that culture is not personality. As stated previously, some Asians residing in the United States and Canada are

TONGS, GANGS, AND TRIADS:
CHINESE CRIME GROUPS IN NORTH AMERICA

almost completely unfamiliar with mainstream American culture, whereas others have partially adapted to their new conditions but may not realize that there are many things that function differently in this country from their homelands. Finally, there are many of Asian descent who are completely Americanized and know almost nothing about their ancestors' cultures.

There is a full range of adaptations to American culture that one might see among the Asians who come here. Behaviors vary wildly from individual to individual. It's important to have some guidelines and some appreciation of the very real differences between Asians and Americans, but it's also important not to stereotype and overgeneralize.

NOTES

1. Actually, this isn't quite true. There was a small class of people who were ineligible to take the exam because of their background. This included people whose parents came from a despised profession, such as prostitution and entertaining. It also occasionally included small groups of people considered "undesirables" in a particular region. For example, in one region there was a group of people descended from a particular general who was considered to have been cowardly. In another region, a certain people who lived on boats and did not spend much time on land was prohibited from taking the exam. Although this meant that the exam was not egalitarian, by definition, the number of ineligible people was relatively small. The overwhelming bulk of the men of China were eligible.

The known history of secret societies in China goes back almost 2,000 years to a period known as the Han dynasty (206 B.C.–221 A.D.).[1] During this time, a secret society called the Red Eyebrows arose and became involved in politics. (The name came from the distinctive red rouge that its members smeared around their eyes.) Like most Chinese secret societies, it was originally created for political reasons. In 9 A.D., the government of China, known today as the Western (or Early) Han dynasty, was violently overthrown by an usurper named Wang Mang. The Red Eyebrows, like so many later Chinese secret societies, was formed as a secret brotherhood of patriots dedicated to overthrowing Wang Mang's government and restoring the old one. Ultimately, he was ousted, and, lacking direction, purpose, or a livelihood, many of the local chapters of the Red Eyebrows turned to banditry and other illegal pursuits. Such behavior was all too typical of the numerous patriotic secret brotherhoods and societies when they were without patriotic causes to keep them out of trouble.

For the next 2,000 years, secret societies and underground sworn brotherhoods were a recurring feature in Chinese society as the succeeding Chinese rulers and dynasties rose and fell and conditions changed throughout the country. Often when dynasties were weakened, villagers were left on their own without protection from the central government. During these periods, portions of the country were controlled by many small states and kingdoms that competed and fought with each other. Many villagers organized themselves into militia-like secret societies for

CHAPTER 2

THE LONG HISTORY OF SECRET SOCIETIES IN CHINA

27

defense against the groups of bandits that roamed the country. Having the local militia meet in secret helped keep many villages neutral from the wider chaotic politics of the time.

During the periods when China was conquered and ruled by foreigners, such as the Mongols (1279–1368 A.D.) and the Manchus, or Ching dynasty (1644–1911 A.D.), secret societies served an important purpose as revolutionary groups devoted to restoring Chinese rule. For example, the White Lotus Society, a superstitious, religious cult-like secret society, was instrumental in ousting the Mongols and founding the Ming dynasty (1368–1644 A.D.), one of the richest and most advanced of the Chinese dynasties. The decline of the Ming dynasty was marked by the same threats to the imperial government that many Chinese rulers had to face: increasingly dangerous raids by the various tribes of northern border nomads, as well as increasingly widespread internal unrest marked by secret society activity. In 1622, the White Lotus Society staged one of the largest revolts that the Ming government had had to cope with. Although this uprising did not overthrow the dynasty, it did weaken it to the point where the Manchus, another northern nomadic people, were able to sweep down and conquer China, establishing a new dynasty, the Ching.

THE CHING DYNASTY AND COLONIAL PERIOD

The new dynasty was not very popular among the Chinese; many resented its undeniably non-Chinese origins. Its rule was marked by many difficulties, chief among these being overpopulation, the resulting economic problems from stretched resources, and uprisings among the non-Chinese peoples within the borders of China (caused to at least some extent by the increasing competition from Chinese settlers for the use of their traditional lands). Another source of serious trouble was the increasing encroachment by foreign colonial powers as they seized Chinese territory and forced the Chinese at gunpoint to allow imports of technology, manufactured goods, opium, and, curiously, Christian missionaries. None of these was universally welcomed by the Chinese.

As economic and social conditions worsened, secret society

activity increased. Unrest spread as it became more and more obvious that the Ching government was powerless to prevent the disruptive acts of foreign companies, governments, and individuals. The list of secret societies active during this time is seemingly endless. One scholarly work lists the names of 267 secret societies that were active in China during the Ching dynasty. This number must be viewed with caution, however. It is undoubtedly incomplete, since it is virtually certain that some groups remained unlisted or even undiscovered. Also, many groups, in an effort to increase secrecy or to hide from authorities, used multiple names or multiple variants of their name, which skew the numbers the other way.

The Taipings were a rebel army that formed as an outgrowth of a secret society organized around Hung Hsiu-chuan. Hung had developed the belief that he was the son of the Christian God and the younger brother of Jesus Christ, and that it was his duty to bring his peculiar version of Christianity to China. It was a sign of the desperate times that such an individual, armed with such bizarre teachings, was soon able to recruit a following. Hung's secret society called itself the God Worshippers. The secrecy paid off, and although the local officials realized that the group was armed and training for war, they felt that its true purpose was to fight off local bandits. Therefore, there was no attempt to suppress the organization until it had openly revolted against the government. By then, the group had many followers, and local officials were unable to stop it.

Significantly, the Taipings were aided in their revolt at one time or another by a wide variety of secret societies, including the Heaven and Earth Society, the Red Turbans, and countless others. To the north, the Nien, another rebel group in some ways similar to secret societies, made some alliances with the Taipings, as did bands of river pirates throughout the country.

The Taiping uprising raged from 1850 to 1864, with great loss of life on all sides. By some estimates, it was the third bloodiest war in recent history, surpassed only by the wars of the 20th century. Ultimately, however, the Chinese government used large armies that included small numbers of troops trained by Westerners to suppress the Taipings.

During the second half of the 19th century, changes in Chinese life caused by foreign incursions became increasingly significant. As railroads and telegraph lines criss-crossed the nation, they disrupted countless lives and caused great concern among local peoples, who believed it was bad fortune to build except in certain sites. The inability of the Chinese government to regulate the sale of opium in its own country led to widespread frustration. Missionaries were treated with outright hostility on many occasions. Resistance to these foreign institutions was organized around a secret society known originally as Yi Ho Chuan, or the Fists of Harmonious Righteousness. (Later, when the Chinese government recognized the organization officially, its name became changed to Yi Ho Yuan, or the Association of Harmonious Righteousness. Due to the fist emblem and the group's frequent martial arts practices and exhibitions, foreigners called members of this group the Boxers.)

In 1899, the Boxers began attacking missionaries and isolated foreigners, as well as destroying churches, railroad tracks, telegraph lines, and other foreign institutions and property. The dowager empress, the de facto ruler of China, secretly hated foreigners and was quite pleased with the activities of the Boxers. In 1900, large numbers of Boxers attacked, surrounded, and laid siege to the foreign embassies in Peking, with the intent of killing everyone inside. When a multinational force consisting of European, American, and Japanese troops went to rescue their embassy personnel, the dowager empress ordered the Chinese military to resist their efforts to enter Chinese territory.

After a great deal of conflict, the foreign troops defeated the Chinese army, invaded China, occupied Peking, and scattered the Boxers. Foreign governments demanded expensive compensation for damages from the Chinese government, and the Boxers were suppressed and disappeared.

The end of the Boxer uprising marked a turning point in Chinese history. In effect, the uprising had been an attempt to deal with the complex demands of the present using the traditional tools of the past. When the Boxers, who believed they were invulnerable to rifle fire, disastrously failed in their attempts to end foreign encroachment in China, it indicated to all concerned that secret societies using traditional martial arts and ancient magical charms were no match for such technology as machine guns and battleships.

Increasing numbers of Chinese intellectuals, both the classical Confucian scholars and the growing number of foreign-educated Chinese youth, sought to improve and protect China by seeking new models and institutions abroad. Many sought a way of government that could be used to incorporate the best foreign ideas and technology into Chinese life, while preserving the moral values and other cherished institutions that Chinese culture had to offer. Some became revolutionaries and plotted ways to turn China into a democracy. Although these revolutionaries would, on occasion, ally themselves with various secret societies, particularly the Heaven and Earth Society, there was not much common intellectual ground. The traditional secret societies had organized with the stated goal of restoring the Ming dynasty, but the revolutionaries recognized that the days of the imperial Ming government were simply gone.

One way in which the secret societies did help to promote the revolution was through fund-raising for revolutionary activities among the overseas Chinese. Such people, scattered throughout the world, had formed secret societies from an early date. Sun Yat-sen, future president of the Republic of China and the most important Chinese revolutionary of his era, spent a great deal of time soliciting donations and promoting his ideas among the Chinese residents of Hawaii and North America.

Because the Chinese government naturally took great pains to suppress the revolutionary groups, it was inevitable that a great deal of political, secret society, and revolutionary activity took place outside China proper. For this reason, among others, a great deal of secret society, revolutionary, and triad activity took place in areas such as the British colony of Hong Kong and throughout the overseas Chinese colonies around the world.

THE FOUNDING OF THE REPUBLIC OF CHINA

Following the disastrous Boxer uprising, the Ching rulers made frequent, widespread attempts at reform and modernization, but these came too late. In 1911 revolution broke out in southern China. The majority of the provincial governments simply seceded from the central government in Peking, and the dynasty collapsed.

Troubled attempts were then made to establish a democracy. The first president of the newly formed Republic of China was Gen. Yuan Shi-kai, appointed president simply because he was the leading military strongman under the Ching. Sun Yat-sen, leader of the revolution, had no desire to see Yuan Shi-kai as head of state, even though it seemed more desirable to have Yuan the appointed head of the republic than to see China thrown into a civil war that the republican forces might lose.

After a few years, Yuan Shi-kai betrayed the republic, just as he had betrayed the Ching rulers, and made an unsuccessful attempt to name himself as a traditional emperor of all China. His proclamation was widely ignored, and the government of China ceased to function. In the absence of an effective central government, China broke into a number of small squabbling states ruled by warlords. The republican government under Sun Yat-sen continued to function in the south, but the actual territory it controlled was small.

During this chaotic period, secret societies in China remained important, even if their role in the new society changed. In some regions, secret society-type organizations developed to resist the warlords' troops and protect the peasantry. Although there were others, the largest of such groups was the Red Spears, who had a curious mix of ancient and modern practices. Although the Red Spears used modern weaponry and firearms whenever they could obtain them (the Boxers despised modern weapons and only rarely used them), they also maintained a wide variety of superstitious practices reminiscent of their origins in religious cults and groups such as the Boxers. They used talismans and lucky charms, engaged in esoteric breathing exercises traditional to Chinese mysticism, and recited powerful protective prayers—and, as with the Boxers, some initiates believed themselves invulnerable to rifle fire.

In small and relatively unimportant cities throughout China, there were some indications later on that traditional secret societies continued to exist. Morton Fried, an anthropologist who did field work in central China in 1947 and 1948, just prior to the communist revolution, stated that several small secret societies of the traditional type still existed in the area where he did his studies. According to him, these sworn brotherhoods claimed to be

TONGS, GANGS, AND TRIADS:
CHINESE CRIME GROUPS IN NORTH AMERICA

exclusively religious in nature but were actually heavily involved in local crime and politics. Since they did not approve of foreign anthropologists, Fried did not study their activities in depth out of fear for his safety but left us with a tantalizingly brief description of such a group.

In major urban areas, the secret societies began to function more and more as gangsters. The most famous of these was the Green Gang of Shanghai, and the most famous member of the Green Gang was undoubtedly Chiang Kai-shek, a man who also became president (some would say dictator) of China and was one of the key figures in 20th-century Chinese history. The leader of the Green Gang was Tu Yueh-sheng or, as he was nicknamed, "Big-Eared Tu." Tu Yueh-sheng was a gangster, plain and simple. He dealt in opium, prostitution, protection, and the usual assortment of vice that Shanghai was notorious for during the 1920s and 1930s. Although there's a great deal of controversy over the exact relationship between Tu and Chiang, the following facts seem more or less certain. Chiang Kai-shek became involved with the Green Gang at a young age and ultimately became a member. Because he was undoubtedly a man of great drive, ambition, and ability, Tu took notice of him and ultimately sponsored him to attend military school in Japan. Upon his return to China, Chiang became involved with Sun Yat-sen and the republicans, who needed a man with his military abilities. Chiang ultimately became head of the republican military academy and finally the commander in chief of all the republican forces in warlord-era China.

In 1927, with the full sponsorship of the republican government, Chiang Kai-shek embarked on the Great Northern Expedition. The republican government, later known as the Nationalist government, contained a number of political parties. Chiang's party, the Kuomintang, leaned toward the right of the political spectrum. Although Chiang gave a great deal of lip service to the ideals of democracy, it soon became obvious that he himself had fascist tendencies. (In the thirties, he would organize "the Blue Shirts," a secret police force modeled closely on Hitler's Brown Shirts and Mussolini's Black Shirts. He accepted a great deal of military aid and training from the German Nazi regime

That's why the chinese had german helmets

until Hitler's Japanese allies asked the Germans to stop this aid.)

Naturally, Chiang did not like the Communists. He disagreed with their goals, and he feared and resented their growing influence among his forces and the peoples of the areas his armies had liberated. His solution to this "problem" was simple, if not entirely moral. In April 1927, beginning in the city of Shanghai, he turned on the Communist units in his own forces and had them massacred. He was assisted in this bloody matter by large numbers of gangsters and Green Gang members provided for him by his old patron Tu Yueh-sheng.

In 1937, two years before the German invasion of Poland and four years before the Japanese attack on Pearl Harbor, the Japanese invaded China. The role of secret societies, as with so much in China, was thrown into a state of confusion. Some societies, particularly in Hong Kong following the Japanese capture of the city, allied with the Japanese and provided services to the occupation forces. Others threw in their lot with the anti-Japanese forces and did what they could to hinder the invaders. Chiang Kai-shek's old friends in the Green Gang, for example, provided his intelligence services with valuable information on Japanese activities in Shanghai and other occupied territories. (Although Tu undoubtedly provided the Nationalists with a great deal of information, many sources state that he also did business with the Japanese occupiers and bought and sold opium in collusion with them.) Many such groups, perhaps the majority, showed little interest in politics and straddled the fence, avoiding them altogether or else hoping to throw in their lot with whichever side that won.

Anti-Japanese resistance came from two sources: the republicans, that is the Nationalist (Kuomintang) government under Generalissimo Chiang Kai-shek and the anti-Nationalist Communist guerrillas under Mao Tse-tung. Both groups hated each other as much as they hated the Japanese. For this reason, the Nationalists' strategy throughout much of World War II was to accept as much foreign aid as possible in money and material, while using as little of it as possible to resist the Japanese forces. Instead, they planned to save their materiel and men for use against the Communists and to gain control of China once the Japanese were defeated. Any Nationalist resistance to the

Japanese army was further hindered by corruption at all levels in the doomed government of Chiang Kai-shek.

The Communists proved themselves more willing to fight the Japanese and pursued an effective guerrilla campaign against the invaders. This gained them a great deal of foreign support, particularly when their efforts were contrasted to those of the Nationalists.

The Nationalists plotted to increase their power and defeat the Communists. In the upper echelons of the Nationalist government, it was hoped that a way would be found to bring more and more secret societies into an alliance with the government. Because both Chiang and the now long-deceased Sun had been involved with secret societies, the creation of a new society came naturally to the leaders of the Nationalist government. They decided to create a sworn brotherhood of their own organized around secret society traditions, hoping to unite the various secret societies and control them. Originally called the Hung Fat Shan, it was later known as the 14K.

SECRET SOCIETIES AND THE CIVIL WAR IN CHINA

When the Japanese were defeated and the war ended, open civil war broke out between the Communists and the Nationalists. Since the Nationalists had little support among the common people, and their activities were still hurt by widespread corruption, the Communists gained more and more victories. Nationalist units often defected to the communist cause en masse, and it became more and more obvious to all concerned that the Communist forces were winning the civil war.

The Nationalists reexamined the efforts to unite the secret societies of southern China. Large-scale ceremonies initiated great numbers of civilians and military personnel into the Hung Fat Shan organization. Many of the new, actively recruited members had little interest in or understanding of the traditions of the group and instead began referring to the association by the nickname "14," after the street address of its headquarters in Canton. Later the name was changed formally to the 14K, with the letter K possibly coming from the first letter of the founder's family name, but more likely from the K in "karat," the common measure for gold. After the fall of the Nationalists, this name became official, and the 14K went on to become one of the leading secret societies in Chinese communities throughout the world.

In time, the Communists controlled China, and the Nationalists and their supporters were forced either to come to terms with the Communist leaders (something the Communists did not always allow) or flee China. The exodus included a wide variety of apolitical individuals the Communists had labeled "enemies of the state," among them many prominent gangsters and secret society members.

SECRET SOCIETIES AND THE AFTERMATH OF THE COMMUNIST TAKEOVER

Only a very small percentage of the population could afford (or meet the legal requirements necessary) to escape to such places as the United States, Canada, or Australia. The three primary destinations for the bulk of the fleeing population were overland to the British colony of Hong Kong, the island of Taiwan, and Southeast Asian destinations in northern Burma or Thailand, where some armies fled en masse. The bulk of the important secret society members who fled China went to Hong Kong, which had been established by the British in the year 1841 in the wake of the first Opium War. Chinese came to the new port seeking work or fleeing circumstances in China.

POSTWAR HONG KONG

In 1945 the British colony of Hong Kong was in a state of chaos. When the Japanese fled, reestablishing British rule was a difficult task. It was not made easier by the fact that large numbers of refugees from the Chinese civil war and the communist takeover continued to flow into the city for years.

Secret societies of one sort or another had been a fact of life in the colony almost from the founding of the city in the 19th century. Since many used the number three or the diagram of a triangle as one of their emblems, the British referred to them as triad societies or, simply, "triads." Some, such as the local chapter of the

Heaven and Earth Society, were officially patriotic in intent, but in actuality much of their activity involved banding together to commit local crimes. Almost identical were other local gangs of criminals united as secret societies. Ultimately, as these groups grew in influence, other, more law-abiding groups, such as the street vendors, were themselves forced to organize for defense against extortion and threats from the first groups. Their members would then arm and train for conflict, as well as recruit members who were skilled in the martial arts. In some cases, in an effort to improve morale, solidarity, and unity among the members, such groups took seemingly drastic steps. Although they had originally been intended as trade unions, they became sworn brotherhoods and took triad-style oaths of allegiance. At this point, ironically, such groups were virtually identical in most ways to the triad groups they had united to defend themselves against.

Because Hong Kong had become a haven for political refugees from China, a wide variety of political groups were active in the city. Although the British discouraged their formation, fearing problems with China, there really was little that could be done to prevent the groups from functioning in secret.

The population of Hong Kong had always contained a mix of the various Chinese regional subgroups. With the great influx of refugees following World War II came a wide variety of representatives from different organized crime groups from all over China. The Shanghai-based Green Gang, for example, set up new headquarters in Hong Kong. It did not do well in this new environment; its leader and many other members were arrested as a result of tips by rivals. By mid-1966, most experts considered the Green Gang dismantled and gone.

Ultimately, the three most important triad-type secret societies became the Wo group, the 14K, and the Chiu Chau syndicates. Although there are others, these are probably the most important today. The Wo group and the 14K were both originally founded for political and patriotic purposes; unfortunately, they have now degenerated into some of the most powerful organized crime groups in the world.

The Sun Yee On, a Chiu Chau group, is different in history and organization from the Wo group triads and the 14K. The

Chiu Chau live mostly on the southern coast of China and have a long history of involvement in such maritime activities as fishing, trading, and smuggling. Like many other coastal Chinese, the Chiu Chau were prominent among those who left China and settled throughout Southeast Asia. Many Chiu Chau became involved in the Shanghai opium trade, serving as local agents for the British opium merchants. With relatives and extended family members strung out through Southeast Asia and a history of trading and smuggling, the Chiu Chau and their ethnic secret societies were in a good position to become heavily involved in the drug trade and other criminal activities. The Chiu Chau triads grew out of this network of maritime Chinese. Following the communist takeover of China, some of the prominent Chiu Chau groups and leaders fled to Hong Kong, while others moved overseas, where their role in crime, particularly in the narcotics trade, continued and even increased.

Today throughout China, Taiwan, and Hong Kong, things are changing, including the role of secret societies. In Hong Kong, the days of the British Crown Colony are numbered. Much of the territory of the city had been ceded by China under a 99-year lease, which expires in 1997, and the Chinese have made it clear that they want the territory back. The British, having little choice in the matter, have agreed to return this important trading port to Chinese rule on that date. Although the Chinese government has agreed not to interfere with the economic functioning or system of the colony for 50 years, there remains a great deal of insecurity in Hong Kong over the threat of possible Chinese actions in the field of human rights. Many, if not most, of the city's prominent citizens are making preparations to flee the colony; the most desirable immigration destinations include Canada, the United States, Australia, and New Zealand.

Among those who want to leave are the important gangsters and triad society members. Having fled the Chinese Communists once, they are preparing to do it again. For this reason, many of Hong Kong's most important gangsters are actively making attempts to relocate their operations to Western cities, such as Vancouver and New York.

TONGS, GANGS, AND TRIADS:
CHINESE CRIME GROUPS IN NORTH AMERICA

POSTWAR TAIWAN

Although Taiwan is not threatened by immediate takeover by the People's Republic of China, the island and its population of 20 million are faced with their own version of chaos and political uncertainty. Approximately 300 years ago, Chinese started moving to Taiwan in large numbers, displacing the native population of primitive headhunters. In 1894, following the Chinese defeat in the Sino-Japanese War, Taiwan was ceded to Japan. It remained under Japanese rule until the end of World War II. At that time, Chiang Kai-shek's Nationalist government became the ruler of Taiwan. In 1949, the Communists had seized the mainland, and many of the remnants of Chiang's defeated armies relocated to Taiwan, where they established a new home for the Republic of China. The Nationalists maintained that the displacement to Taiwan was only a temporary measure and that they would return to their homeland and reconquer it someday.

Although conditions under the Japanese had been repressive, crime and crime groups continued to exist. When the Kuomintang came to the island, it found hundreds of small, loosely organized neighborhood street gangs. The government did what it could to suppress or restrict their activities, but in time, new gangs simply replaced the old and one gang, the United Bamboo, became prominent. Founded in 1956, the United Bamboo rose at least in part because the bulk of its membership consisted of sons of mainland families whose parents often pulled strings to keep them from being punished. (The children of Taiwanese families usually lacked such connections in the government.) In the late 1970s or early 1980s, the group reorganized itself along tong-style lines and grew dramatically in the process. Today the United Bamboo, as well as one of its rivals, the Four Seas gang, have branches in the United States.

At times, Chiang Kai-shek's government, with the assistance of his son Chiang Ching-kuo (head of the secret police and later president of Taiwan) have used members of the United Bamboo to intimidate and silence opposition figures in Taiwan. In 1984, these connections become internationally known when Chiang Ching-kuo sent United Bamboo members to Los Angeles to assassinate Henry Liu, a Taiwanese-born U.S. citizen who had written a critical biography of Chiang Ching-kuo and had been involved in espionage. Although the government of Taiwan did punish those responsible when it was faced with international condemnation, there is no doubt that the secret police of the Republic of China was involved in planning the act.

New secret societies and sworn brotherhoods that were political sprang up on Taiwan. The Kuomintang was, to a certain extent, an occupying force using Taiwan as a base for its operations to overthrow the communist regime of mainland China, but this intended invasion was threatened from two different sources. One was, naturally, the forces of the People's Republic of China. But a second, more subtle threat came from those on Taiwan, usually Taiwanese Chinese, who wished to end the surreal "state of war" (few shots were being fired at this point), improve human rights for those who lived on Taiwan, and explore the possibility of legitimizing the current state of affairs and finding a way to make Taiwan an independent state with no formal political ties to the mainland. The Taiwan Independence Movement went against the Kuomintang's claim that Taiwan was the only province in China to be ruled by its legitimate republican government—until, of course, it invaded the world's largest nation and defeated the Communist government.

In order to conduct operations outside the law and disrupt the plans of Taiwanese dissidents, the Kuomintang needed some loyal but unofficial vigilante groups, the two most prominent of which were the Iron Blood Patriots and the Anti-Communist Heroes. Both were organized along secret society lines and were recruited from social and ethnic groups whose loyalty to the Kuomintang was considered unquestionable.

The armies of the Republic of China that had fled to Taiwan contained many members of the various triad societies. Since the societies served little purpose in the lives of the old soldiers who made up the bulk of their membership, the triads were dormant anachronisms in Taiwan for many years. All this changed around 1980 when democracy began to flourish in Taiwan with the government's easing of restrictions on free speech and political activity. The triads came to be used as an adjunct to political activities in Taiwan, serving in both legal and illegal capacities and participating in violent and nonviolent activities and organizing support for their favorite candidates—as well as doing what they could to intimidate the opposition.

Today the political situation on Taiwan is becoming increasingly controversial. Although the government and the Kuomintang have gained a great deal of popularity due to Taiwan's astounding economic success, they suffer from a serious lack of credibility. The island has a population of slightly more than 20 million. The People's Republic of China has a population of more than 1 billion. A Taiwanese reconquest of the mainland at 50-to-1 odds seems unlikely. More significantly, even if such a military and political coup were accomplished somehow, integrating the Taiwanese and the mainland economies would be extremely difficult. The per-capita income in Taiwan is approximately 12 times greater than that of mainland China. One of the biggest problems in Taiwan today is illegal immigration from the Chinese mainland by workers seeking jobs. A complete and open integration of Taiwan and China would probably be bad for both of them, and nobody anywhere can agree on how this should take place.

As political activity in Taiwan heats up, the role of the triad societies on this island will no doubt increase.

POSTWAR MAINLAND CHINA

When the Communists took over China, they made a point of suppressing as many of the activities of the secret societies as possible. Many, if not most, societies died out and others went deeply underground as their members were forced to disband and become inactive. Nevertheless, secret societies are such an integral part of Chinese society that they never quite disappeared completely. In fact, some new groups were formed in response to the conditions of post-World War II Chinese society.

During the 1960s, China was rocked by the Cultural Revolution, during which there were constant purges of people who were not considered earnest enough in their communist beliefs. The purges were conducted by the Red Guards, bands of zealous, ultrapatriotic young people who took it upon themselves to indiscriminately root out politically suspicious people. Such purges occurred even within the military, and many career officers and NCOs found themselves without a job under the chaos of the Cultural Revolution. Some of these disillusioned and suddenly unemployed military personnel turned to crime to make a living and banded together into an association known as the Big Circle Society. Ironically, as the Cultural Revolution ended, many former Red Guards were also without employment, and many of them joined the Big Circle Society. Many members left China altogether, and today there are chapters of the Big Circle Society in Hong Kong, North America, and throughout the world.

In the People's Republic of China today the situation is changing. Although China has been communist since 1949, faith in the government and the communist system has been in decline for many years. The Tiananmen Square massacre was only one sign of the loss of faith in the stated ideals of the ruling Communist party. (As a note of interest, many of the Tiananmen Square protesters wore red and yellow headbands in a style borrowed from secret societies.) Although nobody knows what the ultimate results of this situation will be, secret society activity is on the rise once again in China.

Although I have not uncovered any evidence that the traditional kind of secret societies are functioning in China for overtly political and revolutionary purposes, there are at least two other types on the rise. The first are those in the narcotics trade. The bulk of the world's opium is grown in the Golden Triangle, a region consisting of parts of Thailand, Laos, and Burma that border on parts of China, particularly Yunnan province. It is now accepted that those border regions of China are also illicitly producing opium, and there is no doubt that opium and opium products are smuggled through this region en route to Hong Kong and the West. With this growth in the drug trade have come secret societies and underground sworn brotherhoods in China itself. These obtain a great deal of wealth from their dealings with international crime syndicates and the profits from the drug trade. Some can afford a great deal of sophisticated equipment, including planes, weapons, and high-tech communications gear. Although the Chinese government wishes to destroy these secret societies, this has been made difficult by the very conditions that spawned them.

In China the line between secret society and religious cult has often been quite fuzzy. Currently, among the disillusioned crowds of modern China, the frenzied, secretive, and sensationalized religious cults of ancient times are making a comeback. They frequently employ all the trappings of their traditional predecessors and use such common props as faith healing, shamanism, strange rituals, magic charms, and leaders with claims of supernatural abilities. The only feature of these cults that is new to modern times is the use of *chi kung*.

In traditional Chinese medicine, *chi* is said to be a person's life force. Developing and increasing this chi, it is believed, can increase and improve one's health. Chi kung is the traditional art of developing and controlling one's chi. In chi kung, as in much of the traditional Chinese arts, the division between reality and the fanciful has always been rather fuzzy. For example, it has traditionally been felt that by using chi kung one can develop invulnerability and master powerful martial arts techniques that seem to defy reality. The growth in China of chi kung cults is a source of great concern to the leadership of the Chinese Communist party today, some of its officials seeing the trend as a rise in dangerous charlatanism and superstition, and others finding the claims quite believable but viewing the groups as a threat to their power.

Exactly what the growth of such groups will mean in the future of China no one can say. What is obvious is that in China, Taiwan, Hong Kong, and elsewhere, traditional Chinese secret societies in all their forms continue to flourish and, for better or worse, will remain a part of Chinese life for the foreseeable future.

NOTES

1. Over the thousands of years of Chinese history, there were many changes in Chinese life, culture, and popular institutions. For this reason, among others, Chinese history is usually measured by dynasties. A dynasty is an irregular period of time during which China had a particular government and certain social institutions and conditions were in effect.

A s in any advanced civilization, the Chinese group themselves into a variety of clubs, societies, religious groups, special interest and nonprofit organizations, and other diverse associations. To outsiders unfamiliar with this culture, it is often difficult to determine the purpose of every Chinese organization encountered. Nevertheless, in order to understand Chinese criminal organizations, it is necessary to have an idea of what some common types of traditional Chinese law-abiding organizations are. Without this knowledge it becomes impossible to tell the good guys from the bad.

Most people with an interest in the subject understand that Chinese criminal groups consist of the tongs, the triads, and various secret societies, but few take the time to carefully define exactly what they are. The first part of this chapter will provide the definitions, followed by descriptions of various traditional Chinese-style noncriminal organizations. American-style Chinese organizations, both legitimate and criminal (including gangs), will not be covered here but will be covered elsewhere as necessary. The Chinese gang, which is essentially an American-style organization with many Chinese characteristics, is covered in its own chapter.

Secret societies are clubs or groups that keep a sizable amount of their philosophies, activities, or membership hidden from outsiders. Some go so far as to keep many of their internal activities and other aspects of the group—for example, some special body of teachings—hidden from even their own members. Often, members have special signs or other signals by which they recognize one another. There is noth-

CHAPTER 3

THE SOCIAL ROLE OF SECRET SOCIETIES

ing inherently evil in being involved in a secret society; although some secret societies work for criminal or political purposes, others are simply social groups.

Defining a *tong* is a little more complicated. *Tong* is an anglicization of the Mandarin word *tang*. This in turn translates as "hall" or "lodge," but it usually refers to the organization itself, not the building it might meet in (similar to the way the Elks, the American Legion, or any group keeps the same lodge name and number even if it moves to another building). This word is used for many things. For example, the Kuomintang, or National Republican Tong, is the ruling party of Taiwan and the late Chiang Kai-shek's political party. Although few would deny that the organization has participated in some pretty shady deals during its history, virtually nobody would go so far as to label the group a "tong" in the traditional sense, in spite of the fact that it uses this word in its name. In fact, almost all the political parties in Taiwan do this; "tang" has no connotations of illegality but simply refers, more or less, to an organized group with common goals.

When we look at Chinese translations from English terms, tang also appears frequently. For example, both the Republican and the Democratic parties have been termed tongs when their names were translated into Chinese. The Italian Mafia—for reasons I must confess I don't know—has somehow had its name translated as "the Black Hand Tong," and the Ku Klux Klan has in turn been named "the Three 'K' Tong" by the Chinese.

Most Western writers who use the term "tong" tend to do so without much thought, or at least without providing a definition. For our purposes, it is defined as an organization that consists primarily of unrelated Chinese people united to assist one another by a bond that includes secret ceremonies and oaths. This definition encompasses many things, but then again, there are a lot of different kinds of tongs. In this book "tong" is used frequently. The term "the American tongs" is used to describe any one of a group of Chinese-style tongs that were founded in the United States or Canada and continue to exist in North American Chinatowns today.

The tongs (also known as sworn brotherhoods or secret soci-

Doorway on left (27-29 address) is Dong An Tong headquarters in New York's Chinatown.

New York meeting place for Chi Kung Tong, aka the Chinese Freemasons.

eties), like family, district, and dialect associations, are one of the primary social organizations in Chinese society and one of the first sorts of groups that will appear when the Chinese find themselves in a new territory. For example, the first Chinese social organization formed in Canada was a branch of a secret society known as the Chi Kung Tong, which was established in Barkersville, British Columbia, in 1862 (Li 1988, 73). (The group also had, and still has, branches in the United States.) As a point of interest, many Americans compared the early Chi Kung Tong to the Freemasons, and it became commonly known as the Chinese Freemasons. The group exists today and has branches in most of the Chinatowns in America. The English-language sign has a Masonic symbol and says "Chinese Freemasons." The Chinese sign underneath says "Hung Men Chi Kung Tong." (Hung Men refers to any of the many southern Chinese secret societies.) Although there's still some controversy over the matter, it appears that the group has never been officially affiliated with or chartered by the Freemasons. Although the group is not officially a criminal organization, it has been implicated in a variety of criminal activities in New York City, Boston, and elsewhere.

Another term frequently heard is "triad." Many of the tongs in Hong Kong use symbolism based on the number three or the use of triangles, because three has mystical significance in Chinese culture. Many British officials in Hong Kong and elsewhere in Southeast Asia seized on this use of "three" symbols and began referring to such groups as "triad societies." Today the term is widely used to refer to some of the tongs. Although it's difficult to define the term exactly, its use is normally reserved for groups from southern China that were organized for the purpose of overthrowing the Ching dynasty or their more recent, related societies that were or are prominent in Hong Kong. (Although there's technically no real reason why one could not refer to "Taiwanese triads," it sounds very strange and is not done in this work.)

OTHER VARIETIES OF TRADITIONAL CHINESE GROUPS

Because the Chinese value family and family ties so greatly, when they are forced by geography to rely on people other than

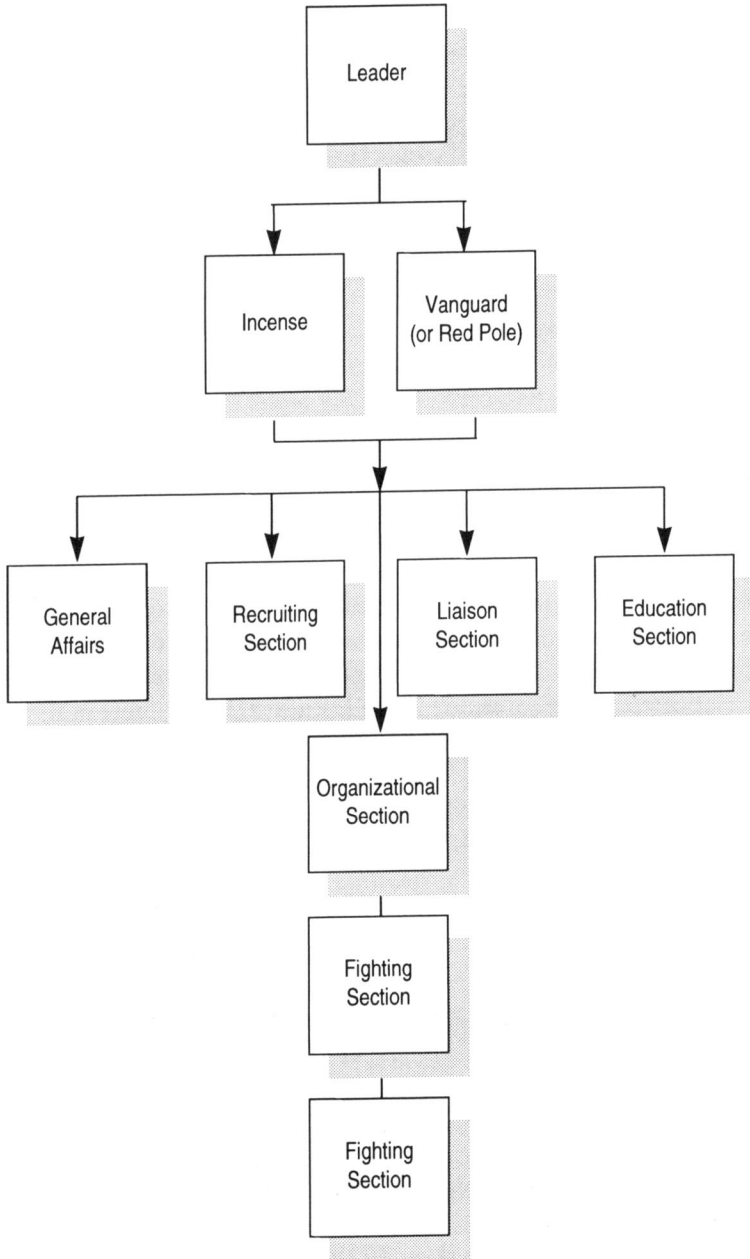

Structure of a traditional tong or triad.

THE SOCIAL ROLE
OF SECRET SOCIETIES

49

their blood relatives, they often seek membership in a group that can serve as a substitute family. The first group of this kind is the "family name association," intended for a wide variety of people with the same surname. For example, anyone with the family name Chang would be eligible for membership in the Chang Family Association. According to Chinese legend, all such persons with the same family name are believed to have a common ancestor—the mythical being who, according to legend, was the founder and first ancestor of the entire clan.

Chinese family name associations exist in large numbers in the major cities of the United States and Canada. There are more than 40 now active in New York City alone. They are generally harmless, law-abiding social organizations, and their main purpose is providing assistance and social activities for their members. Although the exact services offered vary from one association to another, some common ones are making monetary loans available to members (particularly those interested in starting a business) and arbitrating and settling disputes involving members. The associations also hold a variety of social functions, primarily dinners, and serve as places where members can gather to celebrate the important Chinese holidays. One function they serve that is particularly important in Chinese culture is to assist with or provide funeral arrangements for members. In some cases the groups now have their own cemeteries, but before the communist takeover of China, they helped prepare the remains of members for shipment to China for burial.[1] In some cases, they will help raise bail money for members, but this is not considered an important service, and it is not done in all cases for all members arrested for all crimes. Discretion is used by the association in providing bail. The family association also helps newcomers to North America locate cousins and other relatives in the new world.

In the Chinese way of thinking, one's family can also be seen as part of a larger organization known as a clan. Although in modern-day China and Taiwan, the clan really doesn't serve much purpose in the lives of most people, this is the institution that the family association is designed to celebrate. Clans, like most things in China, have legends and traditions. In some cases, two or more clans are felt to have a special relationship based on some real or mythical acts committed by one or more of their more prominent ancestors, and these might form an association together. Such an association functions in a way quite similar to that of the family name associations, except that membership is open to persons with any of two, three, or four family names instead of just one. For example, in many Chinese centers in North America, the Four Brothers Association functions like a family association for anyone with the name Liu, Chang, Chao, and Kuan. These are the names of four of the heroes of a classic Chinese novel, *The Romance of the Three Kingdoms*. Three of these characters are blood brothers, and the fourth is their very good friend and comrade. Their relationship has been a major inspiration for secret society members. The Four Brothers Association was inspired by the relationship of these four heroic comrades, and the organization was designed to emulate and commemorate what was seen as the idealized relationship among these heroes, while serving the role of a family organization among its members. (Although the Four Brothers Association was historically one of the main groups involved in the fighting in the New York City "tong wars" of the 1930s, it is generally not considered a tong but simply an unusual version of a family association.[2] I know of no allegations that it is involved in criminal activities today.)

Among the other early Chinese organizations established in North America were the district associations. These were similar to family associations, but membership eligibility was based on place of origin, not family name. There were also dialect associations for Chinese persons who spoke the same dialect but did not necessarily come from the same place. For example, in the 19th-century San Francisco Chinatown, the majority of Chinese were Cantonese speakers and were organized into a variety of district and name associations (as well as sworn brotherhoods). A minority was the Hakka; its members in America came from Canton too, but they had their own traditions and dialect (in fact, in 19th-century Canton there were open "race wars" between the Cantonese Chinese and their Hakka neighbors.) Since they did not have large enough numbers to form family and district associations, the Hakka Chinese in San Francisco had the Hakka Association, l its membership was open to all native speakers of its dialect.

Although these organizations today might have some meetings in secret or certain traditions, legends, or ceremonies that are not to be shared with outsiders, they are not generally considered tongs or secret societies. Even though they might on occasion become involved in politics or, in extreme situations, unite for the armed defense of their members, this was not their primary purpose.

CHARACTERISTICS OF CHINESE TONGS AND SECRET SOCIETIES

The specific Chinese institutions and traditions that combine to make the Chinese criminal secret societies unique include the sworn brotherhood, a "noble outlaw" tradition—the heritage of traditional knights errant—and organizations whose members have taken an oath of brotherhood and undying loyalty to one another.

THE SWORN BROTHERHOOD

The family association is not the only sort of artificial family that exists in Chinese culture. There is also the institution of sworn brotherhood or sisterhood between unrelated individuals.

Sometimes people decide that it is not enough to be friends and instead choose to become sworn brothers. To do this, two (or more) men normally go to a temple and, in a brief ceremony, promise undying loyalty to one another. On occasion women do this as well, but it is much more common among men. (Bonds of sworn brotherhood and sisterhood would probably never cross sex lines, because intimate yet platonic friendships between men and women are extremely uncommon in Chinese culture.)

Sworn brotherhoods play a significant part in Chinese literature. The adventures and exploits of the heroes of *The Romance of the Three Kingdoms*—united as sworn brothers in ancient China and dedicated to righting wrongs, helping the common people, and aiding each other at any cost—have served as an inspiration for countless generations of Chinese. Sworn brotherhoods such as the tongs see themselves as the direct spiritual descendants of this tradition and strive to follow in the footsteps of characters such as these. The members of the Chinese criminal secret societies are united in oaths of brotherhood. This is true of even the modernized street gangs. Although the members of the groups frequently fight among themselves, this should not be taken to mean that they ignore such oaths altogether.

THE "NOBLE OUTLAW"

In many cultures there is a perception that not everyone who breaks the law is a predator. Instead, many people who live outside society's rules and survive through criminal activity are seen as heroes who help the common people whenever possible. There is a whole genre of Chinese literature dealing with the exploits of Robin Hood types who rob from the rich and give to the poor, traveling the country and righting wrongs. Often, in Chinese tradition these heroes are seen as having been forced to take up a life of crime out of necessity. Some had lost their livelihoods following an unjust lawsuit. Others were avoiding punishment for a crime they did not commit. Still others had taken the law into their own hands to avenge a wrong, often one that was done to a family member, a close friend, or even a sworn brother.

One of the most popular of the many novels and stories of widely varying quality that deal with the adventures of noble outlaws is *The Outlaws of the Marsh.* (The work has also been translated under the title *The Water Margin,* and Pearl S. Buck, the famous author and longtime resident of China, published another version as *All Men Are Brothers.*) This novel describes the adventures of a band of 108 heroes who had been unjustly convicted of crimes or exiled from their homes by corrupt officials.[3] In real life, the members of outlawed secret societies take inspiration from these novels. They don't just see themselves as outcasts hiding in the shadows, but rather as the direct inheritors of a proud and just tradition of noble outlaws. Just as the English have Robin Hood and Americans gunfighters, the Chinese have their outlaws turned heroes.

The classic noble outlaw in traditional Chinese culture is the knight errant who travels throughout the country righting wrongs and fighting for justice and honor. Although there is obviously a strong parallel with the European tradition of wandering knights, there are differences. The Chinese knights had no respect for the traditional Chinese class structure and associated with whomever they pleased, regardless of the shock it might cause in "proper" circles. Many tales tell of Chinese knights who formed close friendships with those who were considered the riffraff (e.g., musicians, dog butchers, others in despised professions). This may be because such knights came from all social classes themselves. In Europe one usually had to be born a knight. In China one simply had to choose to be one and act like one.

The knights errant had their own code of conduct that stressed generosity and altruism; a strong sense of personal justice and the willingness to act on it; individual freedom; loyalty to friends, brothers, and patrons; courage; truthfulness in words and action; concern for personal honor; and contempt for acquiring wealth. Anyone who is familiar with the actions and behavior of Chinese criminals knows this is hardly a description of their behavior. Nevertheless, Chinese crime groups often claim to be following at least some of these ideals, notably personal justice, the desire to help the common people, and loyalty to their friends and brothers in the society. The modern criminals have chosen from among the ideals of the heroic outlaw knights of ancient China and do see themselves as following the traditions.

The strange twist put on these traditions is illustrated in the writing of Aleko E. Lillius, a Finnish-American who spent time among the pirates of the South China coast in the late 1920s and learned much about their lives and motivations. In *I Sailed with Chinese Pirates*, he recounts how the pirate band followed the secret society traditions (Lillius 1930). Its two main sources of income were the extortion from fishermen and their sailing craft and kidnapping of sailors and other travelers. If the captives were rich they were held for ransom. If they were poor and no one could afford to pay a ransom for them they were killed. Torturing the prisoners was routine if the leaders felt it might prove helpful in acquiring wealth. Clearly, such acts were of little benefit to anyone outside the pirates' group of friends and relatives. Despite this, the group claimed to be motivated by a desire to help the poor at the expense of the rich. This was justified to some extent by the group's spreading some of the wealth it acquired among the residents of the poor village it used as a base. The pirates bought things from the villagers, thereby "helping" them. The fact that this was at the expense of other poor people who were strangers to both the pirates and the villagers did not seem to be a major consideration.

A CHINESE CRIMINAL SUBCULTURE

Some say that the noble outlaw and knight errant traditions have combined to form an entire set of patterns and role models for criminal behavior in Chinese society. Ko-lin Chin, a Chinese-American sociologist who has studied Chinese gangs and secret societies extensively, believes that to some extent their members, particularly the "hard-core" members, should be viewed as a subculture of Chinese culture. In other words, they have rejected the values and standards of behavior of the mainstream culture and replaced them with different ones. Hard-core Chinese criminals behave like criminals. Although they are not behaving like normal Chinese law-abiding citizens, they are behaving like normal Chinese criminals. They know how Chinese criminals are supposed to act because of a large number of stories, traditions, and histories of criminals and the criminal life-style.

This is not uncommon; in most cultures, those involved in organized or semiorganized crime behave in similar ways. They might dress similarly, use the same slang, live the same life-style, and so on. Most cultures have a criminal subculture. In Chinese society, those who choose to follow the criminal tradition are sometimes referred to as the *jiang hu* subculture. *Jiang hu* translates to "rivers and lakes," and the term refers to the members' rootless, "floating life-style" and sense of detachment from society at large. For a Chinese to say, "I am jiang hu," is somewhat akin to an American criminal saying, "I am a biker," or "I am a gangbanger," or a Mafia member saying, "I am a 'man of honor.'" Jiang hu have gone through experiences the outside world cannot appreciate or properly understand. The fact that the mainstream society does not approve of their life-style is unimportant to them. Their peers understand and share their life-style, and besides, theirs are the only opinions that count. The attitude of the society at large is not particularly relevant, for they have rejected those values and replaced them with those of their own group. They accept this identification as a secret society member—and the very real risks that it poses to their lives and freedom—with a sense of fatalism. According to one scholar (Chin 1990, 143), a common maxim of those in Chinese crime groups is "I am a jiang hu man. I am not in control of my fate." This countercultural underworld is also referred to from time to time among the Chinese as "the dark society" and its members as "dark society elements."

Although the criminal behavior of such people cannot be excused, we should attempt to understand the way they see themselves. As Sun Tzu's *The Art of War* states, "If you know yourself and you know your enemy, you will never have to fear the result of a hundred battles." The Chinese criminals who are part of the jiang hu life-style see themselves as following a tradition. They might even see themselves as anachronisms—individuals who would be better suited to life in a time when society had more use for warrior knights and heroic Robin Hood-like bandits. Although such groups seem to be more heavily involved in intimidating shopkeepers than fighting for noble causes, a member might justify this as the simple necessity of being born in the wrong place at the wrong time.

CHINESE SOCIETY'S VIEW OF SECRET SOCIETIES

To some extent, Chinese society by and large sees the role of traditional secret societies as being more than criminal (although this does not necessarily apply to gangs). It is more or less true that anyone involved in a civil war who winds up on the winning side is treated as a hero. Therefore, since secret societies were generally involved in most attempts at overthrowing every unpopular government in China during the past 2,000 years, they and their members are looked upon, to some extent, as the descendants of proud bands of idealistic revolutionaries. Although they may have been criminals at times, it is also understood that various tongs worked hard to lead rebellions against the Manchus and to assist the efforts of Sun Yat-sen, Chiang Kai-shek, and even Mao Tse-tung.

The tongs look on this heritage with pride. Even today, among the majority of tongs and secret societies in America and elsewhere, political goals feature prominently. In the 19th century, virtually all tongs gave some periodic lip service to their *raison d'etre*—driving the foreign Ching dynasty out of China. Following the establishment of the Republic of China, the primary threat to the government of China became the Communists. Chiang Kai-shek, coming from a secret society background himself, made a special effort to focus tongs and secret societies into anticommunist activities. As the Communists took over and many people were forced to flee, most of the tongs in Hong Kong became either actively anticommunist or, at the very least, politically neutral. (There are other reasons why the Chinese in America tend to often be actively anticommunist. These will be looked at in the chapter on the overseas Chinese and Chinese immigration.)

Today in North America, the majority of tongs are anticommunist and pro-Kuomintang, or at least claim to be. They see their anticommunist stance as a natural outgrowth of their tradition of idealistic revolutionariness. To many, this itself justifies the existence of the triads today.

The Social Role and Values the Societies Promote Among Their Members

Pledging oneself to the destruction of a government on the other side of the world might provide a nice focus for some unresolved anger, but for most people it's not exactly an everyday activity. The tongs also serve as a social group committed to the moral and spiritual betterment of their members. Like college fraternities, Shriners, Elks, or many other similar organizations in our society, they often were devoted to little more than meaningless socialization under a veneer of brotherhood and self-improvement.

The self-improvement aspect of secret society membership follows certain patterns. The tongs pledged to follow certain values. Chin has identified the following five values as being at the core of the ideals secret societies profess to follow: 1) loyalty, 2) righteousness, 3) nationalism, 4) brotherhood, and 5) secrecy (Chin 1990, 18-19).

Loyalty in this case means loyalty to the secret society. Recall that one of the key aspects of Chinese culture is the concept of "us against them." This is particularly apparent when we look at the idea of loyalty to a secret society by its members. In this case it refers specifically to not exploiting a society too much or exposing its secrets to outsiders. Loyal members will not start another secret society without the permission of the leaders of the society. Similarly, loyal members of a secret society will help their brothers in times of need and not take advantage of either their secret society brothers or their brothers' wives or families.

A secret society member's views of righteousness are not necessarily the same as those of the outside world. Alone in a sea of hostile outsiders and dangerous enemies, he relies on his sworn brothers as his righteous allies. He sees them as the proud descendants of a tradition of bold, heroic Robin Hoods. It is righteous to protect one's brothers from outsiders, even if it means breaking the law. To kill or victimize outsiders when it means living up to the sworn oaths of membership and protecting one's fellow members is righteous behavior. It is considered righteous to steal from the rich to help one's brothers or the common people. Likewise, members are encouraged to destroy or defeat those who oppress or take advantage of the common people. For this reason, secret society members traditionally despise such individuals as landlords, merchants, and public officials, all of whom they see as taking advantage of ordinary people through price gouging and other exploitive practices. Secret society members often see themselves as self-appointed vigilante champions of justice out to attack the corrupt power structure and help the underclass.

Nationalism is the third key value of the traditional tong ideology. The tongs are very devoted to helping China. Their entire stated purpose or existence was, in many cases, their desire to overthrow an undesirable Chinese government and replace it with a more benevolent and patriotic one. In many cases, the members of the tongs tend to despise the wealthier and better-educated classes of China as apathetic and lacking devotion when it came to the needs of the homeland.

The final key value of the tongs is secrecy, which, to the Chinese, has always held great value. One of the classic works of Chinese strategy is Sun Tzu's *The Art of War*. The oldest known guide to strategy in existence, it was written for generals and other military planners in the 4th century B.C. and is a marvelous guide to strategic thinking and planning, not just for military operations but for a variety of other, more common struggles. One theme Sun Tzu stresses time and time again is the importance of obtaining as much knowledge as possible about an enemy before choosing a course of action. Conversely, if you do not allow the enemy to know about you, he cannot plan effectively or win against you.

Secrecy about one's organization is a necessity for a tong that claims to be involved in an on-again, off-again guerrilla-style struggle with the ruling powers. Outnumbered and outgunned, members of a revolutionary society were forced into secrecy for their own survival.

In addition to the practical, there's a spiritual reason for secrecy. The Chinese film star Bruce Lee once wrote, "Secretiveness can be a source of pride. It is a paradox that secretiveness plays the same role as boasting—both are engaged in the creation of a disguise. Boasting tries to create an imaginary self, while secretiveness gives us the exhilarating feeling of being princes disguised in meekness. Of the two, secretiveness is the more difficult and effective."

In fact, in two of the greatest uprisings in Chinese history— that of the Taipings, which lasted from 1850 to 1864, and the Boxer uprising of 1900—a key factor in their initial success was that no one was completely sure what they were up to, so no one could really decide that their activities should be stopped until after they had grown too powerful to be suppressed easily.

TONGS AND CRIME

The traditional revolutionary-type tong, due to its devotion to overthrowing the government, was illegal (at least in China and Hong Kong). One must differentiate between a revolutionary society intent on overthrowing a government for idealistic purposes and an organized crime group intent on robbing people for self-gain. Tongs are not by definition organized crime groups.

The exact relationship between tongs (or sworn brotherhoods) and criminal activity is a matter of not just great debate but also great variation. Some are definitely organized crime groups masquerading as fraternal brotherhoods. At the other extreme, there is an organization in Australia that claims to be a completely legal and aboveboard triad and is a legally registered "Masonic charity" under Australian law. This organization, the Mun Ji Dong, is proud of its idealistic heritage of being a Chinese anti-Manchu revolutionary organization. Despite this, or perhaps because of it, it has made its lodge open to the press and even has a Caucasian member. In most cases, however, the definition is not so clear.

If tong members themselves are not criminals, a number of them will undoubtedly come to know criminals. In some cases, although the tongs claim to be law abiding, they have, for one reason or another, developed strong ties to criminal groups, particularly Chinatown youth gangs. Some knowledgeable people claim that such ties are a matter of self-protection and serve the best interests of the community. (These points will be looked at more in a later chapter.) Other tong members deny, often unconvincingly, that these ties exist at all.

Tong members' primary loyalty is to each other. If one of the fraternal brothers does become involved in criminal activity, the others are pledged not to turn him in to the police. Of course, this doesn't mean such betrayal will never happen, but it would violate the sworn oaths of group members.

In many Chinatowns throughout the world, the tongs were intended as fraternal organizations devoted to assisting their overseas Chinese members. At times, they would turn to violence or criminal acts to defend themselves or to settle serious disputes with rival tongs. These violent disputes became the "tong wars."

The membership of many tongs tends, to some extent, to invite criminal types. The sort of person who is traditionally initiated into a tong is often 1) male, 2) without family contacts, and 3) seeking adventure, opportunity, and novel experiences. When he becomes part of a tong, he finds himself in a situation where a new body of like-minded persons in similar circumstances is pledged to help him in all cases and sworn to secrecy about his activities.

Sociologists often speak of a "deviant ideology." An ideology is a group of ideas followed by a given group of people, normally to provide a moral or other justification or framework for their beliefs, morality, or behavior. A deviant ideology encourages someone to act in a manner that serves to reduce the feelings of guilt one would normally experience when committing crimes or other antisocial acts. Often in our culture, people with a conscious or subconscious desire to commit violent, criminal, or other anti-social acts will be attracted to a variety of racist, occult, neo-Nazi, "survival of the fittest," or similar ideas. They often mix them together into some sort of "deviant ideology" to justify whatever they might feel compelled to do. The tong "ideology" that encourages members to see their brothers as more important than others and the rich as justified targets for robbery and attack could serve this purpose.

The tong places the needs of the group above those of society at large. Loyalty to one's sworn brothers is considered more important than any normal obligations to society. It is considered moral to rob and steal as long as the target is believed to be exploiting the common people. Similarly, due to the strong emphasis on loyalty, it is quite easy for a member to get dragged into crimes or be obliged to cover them up.

CHINESE CRIME GROUPS TODAY IN NORTH AMERICA

In North America today, Chinese crime groups can be divided into broad categories. Contrary to stereotype, the organization of Asian crime groups is surprisingly loose. A Chinese criminal secret society is often more like a "crime club" than an underground army. Although members must be initiated, swear oaths, and promise not to betray the group's secrets, they can nevertheless belong to more than one group at a time as long as they follow certain rules about which groups they join. For example, one obviously cannot belong to two groups that hate one another, but one can usually belong to two different groups that are neutral toward or friendly with each other. It's kind of like belonging to the Elks and the Shriners and being a fully affiliated Boy Scout leader.

There are other reasons why a Chinese criminal secret society can be seen as a crime club. Although the members are expected to follow the orders of the leadership—and this might include involvement in criminal acts—they are still perfectly free to go and commit any crimes they wish on their own, unless specifically instructed not to. Furthermore, secret society members can often recruit from among their fellow members—their "brothers"—to go and commit these crimes. For example, if four members of the On Leong Tong (aka Merchants Benevolent Association) rob a jewelry store and are arrested, this does not mean that the robbery was planned or approved by the tong; the four who happened to be members of it robbed a jewelry store.

To determine links between organizations is often very difficult, if not impossible, for this very reason. Members of different groups meet informally from time to time while socializing in a normal fashion—perhaps while gambling—and might then decide to get together to plan a crime and then implement it.

Such individual crimes can be quite confusing if one mislabels them as organized crime activities committed by a specific crime group. For example, in Taiwan the United Bamboo and the Four Seas are rival gangs. The members of the two groups often fight with each other over control of territories for a given operation. Nevertheless, in the United States members of the two groups have cooperated in kidnappings.

Having emphasized the loose and often overlapping membership of Chinese secret society crime groups, we can now describe the types of groups themselves. There are different systems of classification in use. I choose to distinguish between four kinds of groups: tongs, triads, indigenous North American gangs, and foreign-born gangs.

The tongs are generally old groups that have been in America for 100 years or more. They were intended as sworn brotherhoods where Chinese immigrants could socialize and help one another. Many tongs have been involved in criminal activities, but mostly to provide members with illicit things they desire (e.g., gambling).

In the 19th and early 20th centuries the various tongs frequently came into conflict, and this led to a series of bloody wars between them, notably in San Francisco in the 1890s and in New York in the 1920s, Today, although some tongs are involved in some crime, it is much more common for tong members to strike out on their own to engage in such activities. Nevertheless, important tong members have a network of social contacts throughout the country that often provide them with considerable help in carrying out complex criminal schemes or avoiding justice. Today in the United States, although there are others, the leading tongs with an involvement in criminal activities are the On Leong, the Hip Sing, the Tung On, and, to a lesser extent, the Chinese Freemasons (or Hung Men Chi Kung Tong). Although the Fukien American Association (aka Fujianese American Association) is frequently listed as a tong, this must be differentiated from the others. It is similar in form and structure to the other organizations but is of much more recent origin. The On Leong, the Hip Sing, the Tung On, and the Chinese Freemasons all date from the 19th century; the Fukien American Association is less than 20 years old in the United States.

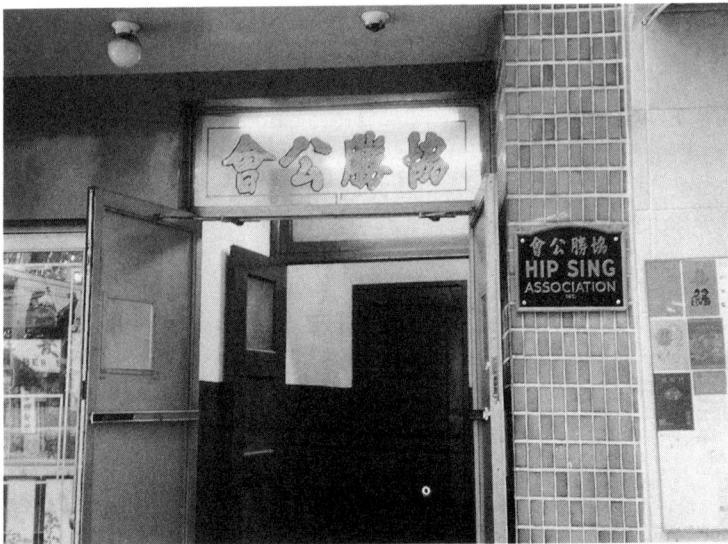

The Hip Sing meeting place in New York's Chinatown.

The triads are generally secret societies that were formed in Asia and exist primarily for criminal purposes. Although the dividing line is very fuzzy, the literature on the subject generally attempts to distinguish between the tongs and the triads. Triads were generally formed for a noncriminal purpose and then became corrupt, but there is really no hard-and-fast rule. Some triads active in the United States are the Wo Hop To, a Hong Kong-based member of the Wo group that has come to dominate Asian organized crime in San Francisco; the Hong Kong-based Sun Yee On, a Chiu Chau triad; and the 14K. Although it is difficult to judge the full extent of involvement of the Sun Yee On and the 14K leadership in Asian crime in North America, nobody denies that members of these groups have immigrated and are involved in criminal activities and that more wish to come here from Hong Kong as the clock ticks until the colony's takeover by the People's Republic of China. As they join other criminal groups or tongs upon their arrival in North America, while still retaining their membership in an overseas triad, the extent of these groups' activities in North America is anyone's guess.

The third sort of Chinese criminal secret society is the indigenous Chinese youth gang. Although "youth gang" is something of a misnomer, many of the gang members being in their 20s or 30s, these groups must be distinguished from the other, more traditional Chinese crime groups. The "gangs" were often started spontaneously in the United States by native-born Chinese-Americans or Chinese-Canadians or by recent immigrants upon their arrival in America. The gangs were formed for either self-defense or crime. Unlike other ethnic gangs in America, many Chinese gangs were started by tongs and tong members in order to increase the "muscle" of the given tongs as they maintained their image as law-abiding groups. However, many Chinese gangs in America were formed without tong sponsorship or aid. The full story of tong-gang relations will be described later in this book.

Although the gangs all started out small, many have grown considerably, as has their level of sophistication, organization, and ability. Today, some gangs have branches in many cities across the continent. The Ghost Shadows have actually spread from New York City overseas and established branches in Hong Kong and Taiwan. Today the Wah Ching is the leading Asian organized crime group in Los Angeles; it used to be the leading crime group in San Francisco before it was displaced by the Wo Hop To. (Many gang members, particularly the older ones, are also members of tongs or triads.)

The fourth category comprises foreign-born Chinese gangs. Although this is not normally broken out as a separate category, it is a distinction I feel is worth making. When law-abiding Chinese immigrate to America and Canada, it is impossible to prevent criminals from coming with them. This results in relatively young but sophisticated crime groups being transplanted from abroad. For example, the Big Circle Gang was formed in China in the 1960s by former Red Guards and Chinese People's Liberation Army personnel who lost their careers and were discharged during the chaos of the cultural revolution. It is now one of the leading Asian crime groups in Canada, active in heroin smuggling, credit card fraud, and importing illegal aliens. Although the group is not a triad, many of its members are members of various triads. The United Bamboo gang was formed as a street gang in Taiwan in the 1950s, as was the Four Seas gang. As both groups grew to power and increased in sophistication, they consciously attempted to model themselves after the older triads. Nevertheless, they lack their traditions and history. Today in the United States and Canada they are active in a wide variety of crimes.[4] The Fuk Ching is a gang from Fukien (Fujian) province that was transplanted with increased immigration. It is heavily involved in smuggling illegal aliens into North America, and one thing that makes the group extra dangerous is the manner in which it smuggles in "soldiers" and extra muscle to further its activities.

NOTES

1. Traditionally in China, funerals and burials were very important and lavish. The Communists, with some justification, ordered the curtailment of many funeral practices because they felt they were a waste of better-used resources.
2. *The Romance of the Three Kingdoms* has had quite an influence on the development of Chinese tongs and secret societies. For this reason, references to this work will appear throughout this book.

3. For those who might wish to read the works mentioned, these classics have undergone multiple translations and printings and there are several different editions and versions.

4. Many people consider the United Bamboo and the Four Seas to be triads. Although I don't, I will be the first to admit that this is just a quibbling matter of definition. In any event, they imitate triads in form and style. I prefer to reserve the term triads for groups that are older and were started for some purpose other than crime but became corrupt. I mean no disrespect to those who use another definition and state what it is up front.

Before the 20th century, the majority of Chinese who left China did so for economic reasons. The majority of those came from two coastal provinces—Canton in the south and Fukien in the Southeast. The Fukienese emigrated mostly to points in Southeast Asia, such as Vietnam, Thailand, Malaysia, and the other areas of the region. The Cantonese also went to Southeast Asia, but many went to North America. The overwhelming majority of those who came to the United States and Canada were from Canton, and a surprising number of them came from the coastal towns—the majority from two counties in particular.

Another group that came to America at this time were the Hakka, who spoke a dialect different from that of the other Chinese and lived a slightly different life-style. A few hundred years ago, they were forced to leave their homes in northern and western China and wander in search of new ones. When they found places to stay, they would settle but make little or no attempt to integrate with the local Chinese population. (The Chinese traditionally refer to them somewhat sarcastically as "the guest people.") A sizable number eventually left China looking for places to settle. Other Hakka fled China after violent conflicts with the local Chinese. (During the mid-19th century, when the Chinese first came to America, there were widespread civil wars in Canton between the Hakka and the Cantonese.) Among the Chinese in America, the Hakka traditionally were the largest non-Cantonese group, and although this has changed, there were a number of important Hakka organizations in America in the Chinese community.

CHAPTER 4

THE OVERSEAS CHINESE AND THEIR HISTORY IN NORTH AMERICA

The countless Chinese who went abroad over the past few hundred years usually intended only to work for a limited time and planned to save money and return home. But many found themselves having to stay in their new homelands, either by choice or from lack of money. The first few generations to leave China went almost exclusively to Southeast Asia. What are now the Philippines, Malaysia, Indonesia, Vietnam, Thailand, and Singapore saw their share of Chinese immigrants arrive in search of wealth and opportunity. Many Chinese still live in these countries today. Until recently, European powers such as Spain, England, Holland, or France controlled many of these nations. These colonial powers actively recruited Chinese laborers, merchants, or administrators to help them exploit the most wealth possible and, in fact, there are cases of European officials kidnapping or commandeering boatloads of Chinese to their colonies for use as forced labor. The Chinese were known for their willingness to work hard—often much harder than the native peoples of the colonies.

Although to this day, large numbers of Chinese live throughout Southeast Asia, those seeking opportunity were soon forced to search farther afield, making their way to Australia, Europe, North and South America, and even Africa. They came as merchants and as laborers.

Today Chinese live throughout the world. In some countries, particularly in Southeast Asia, they have a peculiar status. They arrived many years ago to make their fortunes, and although some failed and died, others succeeded to an astonishing extent. Today in much of Southeast Asia, a major part of the local economy is controlled by Chinese businessmen, many of who come from families that have lived outside China for many generations but have not adapted to any real extent to the local culture. They speak Chinese in their homes, eat Chinese food, and practice Chinese ways. The local populations often resent this, and many of these nations have made a real effort to change the situation. Malaysia, for instance, has laws prohibiting the Chinese minority from discriminating against the Malay majority. For example, by law Malays must hold a certain percentage of management positions in all large corporations in Malaysia. In Indonesia, public education or performances in the Chinese language are prohibited, although a variety of Indonesian dialects and other foreign languages are permissible. In Thailand, all college applicants must have a Thai, not a Chinese, name. Citizens of Chinese descent can attend, but they must use a Thai name to do so, as encouragement to integrate more into Thai society.

Some fear that this hostility might turn violent and have decided to leave before things get worse. Some of these nations, notably Malaysia and Indonesia, have had violence and rioting, spontaneous and officially sanctioned, against the Chinese population.

In the communist nations of Southeast Asia, the highly successful Chinese capitalists did not fare well. Many were killed and others were forced to flee. In fact, a surprising number of the "Vietnamese" or other Southeast Asian refugees are descended from Chinese who had lived in Vietnam for generations but had not assimilated.

THE EARLY CHINESE IN AMERICA

According to some sources, the first Chinese visitors, two men and a woman, arrived in America in the summer of 1848. There is no record of who they were or what motivated them to visit the new territory of California. When word got out that gold had been discovered in a nearby streambed, countless other Chinese followed. Like most men who come to a gold rush, they were desperate, usually single, lonely, and willing to take risks. The overwhelming majority came from the poor villages of the southern Canton coast. Seeking opportunity and the chance to get rich in America, they left a home known for its poverty, frequent peasant uprisings, constant clan feuds, banditry, floods and famines, and disruptive foreign merchants dealing in opium and bibles.

Although it seems that at first the Californians were greatly impressed with the hard-working and colorful Chinese residents of their territory, friction soon developed. Anglos, Mexicans, and others came to resent the competition for mining sites from Asian people who did not speak their language and followed "strange" customs and traditions. If the Chinese had a common role in the crime scene of the California gold rush days, it was as victims. This situation was not helped by the indisputably racist legislation passed in California at the time. When it was made illegal for Chinese (and some other races) to testify against whites in the courts, this effectively allowed any white thug to do as he wished and was able to the Chinese, so long as there were no white witnesses around who wished to get involved (and there rarely were).

F.T.W.

In 1858, the first Chinese wandered northward from California and made their way to Canada. Again, they were lured by gold, and this time the gold rush was in British Columbia. From there on the story of the Chinese in Canada is remarkably similar to that of the United States.

CHINESE LABOR IN THE WEST

When the gold petered out, some Chinese remained, and some continued prospecting on the off-chance that they might strike it rich or get by on the scraps others had missed in worked-out mines. Some did laundry, farm work, or other menial labor. By 1875 the Chinese made up 25 percent of California's male labor market. When continent-spanning railroads were completed, the Chinese spread throughout the United States.

The 1870 census listed 46 states and territories in the continental United States. According to the census, 15 of these had no Chinese and 14 others had only a token population of less than 10 Chinese individuals. Five states or territories had populations of more than 1,000 Chinese. These were California with 49,277; Idaho with 4,274; Oregon with 3,330; Nevada with 3,152; and Montana with 1,949. The 1880 census, which followed the completion of the railroads, showed drastic changes. California had 75,132 Chinese residents; Oregon had 9,510; Nevada had 5,416; Idaho had 3,379; and Washington's Chinese population had increased from 234 to 3,186. Montana had 1,765; and in Arizona the Chinese population had swelled from a mere 20 to 1,630. Similarly, in New York state the 1870 census had shown 29 Chinese, whereas the 1880 census showed 909. In 1880 only two states, Vermont and North Carolina, had no Chinese at all, and only seven had fewer than 10 Chinese workers within their borders.

The general attitude of the majority population toward the Chinese laborers was quite simple. They were, in essence, seen as a cheap, dependable, but apparently subhuman and unassimilable source of labor. When Chinese workers could ease a significant labor shortage they were welcomed. When they presented real or perceived competition with white labor, then the working-class whites would attempt to drive them out. This could be done with legislation; threats; or, straightforward, mindless violence, looting, and rioting. The rich often preferred to hire Chinese because they would work longer hours for lower pay and rarely conducted strikes. According to one source, in 1876 white male laborers in California were paid $2.25 to $5 a day, while white child laborers received $1 a day, and Chinese laborers were only given $.90 each day (Nee 1986, 45).

There were many industries in California (e.g., cigar rolling) whose leaders claimed they simply could not survive without the cheap Chinese labor. That Chinese workers did not go on strike was not due to their enthusiasm for their jobs; it was simply that the white employers controlled their food supply and their wages. The non-Chinese workers were separated from the Chinese by language, customs, and hostility, and would rarely, if ever, assist the Chinese in the event of a strike.

Much of this was contract labor that was controlled by Chinese overseers or contract workers who would recruit and control the laborers and, in return, garnishee their wages, reducing their pay even further. The life of a Chinese laborer was also controlled to a surprising extent by the Chinese merchants' associations, which often made arrangements to bring the workers to America under indentureship. The merchants would promise the laborers jobs and passage, and in return the workers were expected to pay them back with interest. These contracts were often misleading, but the workers had little recourse. The merchants were not too choosy about the places they found for the workers to go or the conditions they might be forced to labor under. Often the merchants hired out Chinese laborers as strike breakers—further increasing resentment of the Chinese among the whites.

Chinese contract laborers, working under hard and often dangerous conditions, were vital to the construction of the continent-spanning railroads that permitted the development of both western Canada and the United States in the 1870s and 1880s. Without this cheap labor, the railroads might not have been built so quickly. Despite this, no Chinese were invited to the dedication ceremony of what was seen as one of the greatest accomplishments ever made by white Americans. The completion of the railroads left many Chinese unemployed and spread throughout the United States.

CHINESE ORGANIZATIONS IN NORTH AMERICA

Although the Chinese of all classes (including merchants) had initially formed family and district associations, the merchants' associations soon dominated the less influential organizations and, in fact, controlled many aspects of Chinese life. They monopolized the import of all luxuries and necessities from China, they negotiated contracts, and they were more educated and wealthier than the laborers. They were often older and hence more respected. As they increased in wealth and gained familiarity with conditions in America, many began to function as spokesmen for the Chinese community.

The merchants' associations instituted a system whereby all Chinese who wished to leave the United States were checked by their family association to ensure that they did not have any outstanding debts to Chinese merchants in America. If they did, they were forbidden to leave and forced to remain in America until they had paid.

For their part, the American authorities were usually quite content to leave the Chinese alone and let Chinatowns govern themselves unless problems (e.g., gambling or prostitution) spilled out into the surrounding city. Although the police would seek to prevent or stop major tong wars or other violence, they only rarely had enough contact with or understanding of the Chinese community to do more than break up the fight and chase after the fleeing combatants.

TONGS, GANGS, AND TRIADS:
CHINESE CRIME GROUPS IN NORTH AMERICA

Today their powers have declined considerably, but the descendants of these merchants' associations continue to wield a great deal of power throughout Chinatowns in America and Canada through a single organization known as the Chinese Consolidated Benevolent Association (of America). Originally referred to as the "Six Companies" (after the six largest members), in 1880 it was incorporated as the CCBA.

TONGS, TONG WARS, AND PROSTITUTION

The Chinese laborers in North America began organizing tongs and secret societies soon after their arrival. The Chi Kung Tong (now known as the Chinese Freemasons) was involved in extortion attempts and violence against other Chinese groups in the United States in the early 1850s (Nee 1986, 68). It established a branch in Canada in 1862 (Li 1988, 73).

Chinese women were scarce in the American West of the 19th century. From 1870 to 1910, the ratio of male to female Chinese immigrants in California (the primary point of entry for Chinese to the United States) was always at least 10 to 1, and a ratio of 20 to 1 to was much more common. From 1881 to 1890, as little as 1 percent of the Chinese in America was made up of women.

Although some merchants brought their wives and attempted to raise families in America, few, if any, of the common laborers could afford this luxury. Besides, most of them planned only to come to America, make their fortune, and then return; having a wife nearby would only complicate things. With such a lack of women, Chinese prostitutes were in high demand. The trade in Chinese prostitutes was begun in the 1850s and, by the 1870s, was described as "the importation of females in bulk." These females were often victims who had been sold into prostitution as girls by impoverished families of 19th-century China. Other women had been kidnapped. Still others came voluntarily seeking money under an indentured labor contract. Some undoubtedly needed to earn money for relatives at home and assumed that, upon their return, the shame of being a prostitute in a faraway country would be forgotten. History records that the white men of the region found Chinese women quite desirable and often visited brothels where they worked despite white prejudice against Chinese. The prostitutes often worked on contracts similar to those of the male laborers.[1]

Although it would be logical to assume that the tongs would spend a great deal of time defending their members from attacks by whites, in reality the situation was quite different. The tongs mostly fought among themselves or with other Chinese organizations.

The first tong war in North America is said to have occurred in the 1860s when a member of the Suey Sing Tong apparently "stole" the mistress of a member of the Hop Sing Tong. The Hop Sings declared war on the Suey Sings. Several men on both sides of the conflict died, and the Suey Sings ultimately gave in and returned the girl (Asbury 1933, 184).

Although disputes over gambling debts or territories were some of the causes of tong wars, if historical reports are to be believed, this affair was typical, and disputes over Chinese women may have been the leading cause of tong wars (Nee 1986, 90-93; Asbury 1928, 301 and 1933, 82, 91-92; Heaps 1970, 62). Part of this seems to have been simply no more than an outgrowth of the high cost of shipping prostitutes and other women across the Pacific. According to one report from a 72-year-old member of the Suey Sing Tong (recorded in 1972) if the person who "took" the woman away from her place of business paid off the cost of her indentureship, there were no problems. If not, the financially injured party would recruit his tong to assist him in recovering either the damages or the woman (Nee 1986, 91-92). Naturally, many of the Chinese living in America could not afford to pay off the women's entire indentureship at one time, so violence would often ensue and the "boyfriend" would ask his tong for assistance. And so the pattern continued. Although many tong wars have been forgotten, some were recorded with great interest by white journalists and others who found fights by Chinese men armed with hatchets to be "good copy."

In 1871 in Los Angeles, a dispute over payment for a woman resulted in violence between members of the Hong Chow Tong and the Nin Yung Tong. After arrests and repeated flare-ups of violence, a white sheriff was shot in the shoulder while attempting to apprehend one of the leading participants. His wound proved fatal. Following the shooting, an angry mob (reported to comprise 600 people—a 10th of the city's population at the time!) formed and a riot broke out. Angry citizens lynched the Chinese man accused of shooting the sheriff, then turned on all other nearby Chinese, looting their property and killing them indiscriminately. In the end, 19 Chinese were reportedly lynched and a large number of others shot or killed (it seems the actual number was too embarrassing to record). Eight white people served short prison sentences for actions committed in the riot.

This incident, where virtually the entire Chinese community was punished for the shooting death of one white man, probably explains why the tongs restricted acts of violence to other Chinese instead of responding to threats from whites (Heaps 1970, 61-71).

In 1875 in San Francisco, the Suey Sing Tong got into yet another fight over the love life of one of its members. A Suey Sing brother named Low Sing attempted to elope with a girl known as Kum Ho ("Golden Peach"). Her "master," Ming Long, a noted fighter and member of the Kwong Dock Tong, split Low Sing's skull with a hatchet rather than lose his valuable investment. As the demands and accusations escalated, the two groups finally agreed to meet in the middle of a Chinatown street at high noon to settle their dispute with knives and hatchets. When fighting commenced, the San Francisco police arrived and broke up the fight. The hatchetmen fled, leaving behind nine wounded, four of whom later died. The police, apparently lacking Chinese informants, made no arrests and were unable to determine the cause of the dispute. Following this the Kwong Docks apologized and paid a small fee to the Suey Sings. Ming Long, fearing revenge from the Suey Sings, then fled to China, and the war was over.

The first tong wars in New York City seem to have started in 1899 and then flared up periodically up to the end of the 1930s. The city suffered recurring conflicts involving the On Leong Tong, the Hip Sing Tong, and the Lung Kong Tin Yee (Four Brothers Association). Although the latter is not normally considered a tong, in the New York tong wars of the 1920s and 1930s, the Four Brothers Association was not only behaving just like the tongs, it was also one of the most belligerent participants.[2]

Above and right: New York Chinatown tongs.

TONGS, GANGS, AND TRIADS:
CHINESE CRIME GROUPS IN NORTH AMERICA

THE IMAGE OF CHINESE AND CHINATOWN VIOLENCE

The periodic outbreaks of tong violence were a very real part of life for the Chinese in America before World War II. Nevertheless, the violence and the dangers of life in Chinatown were undeniably exaggerated to the American public. The stereotyped image of the "slit-eyed, opium-crazed Chinese assassin" directed by an inscrutably fiendish "Fu Manchu-like" secret society leader seems to have taken hold and was encouraged by many.[3]

In San Francisco, there was a licensed Chinatown Guides Association that was under the control of the city government. Exactly, why the city insisted on licensing such guides is unclear—professional ethics, honestly, and preserving the city's image most certainly weren't at issue. These guides would guarantee a thrilling tour through "exotic Chinatown" for their customers and then deliver. Of course, such thrills were guaranteed because they were staged. A good guide arranged a variety of mock opium dens, cheaply hired hatchet-waving "tong assassins,"[4] staged knife fights among Chinese, and carefully dug tunnels. In fact, it was probably through these hokey tours that the myth of large tunnel networks under the Chinatowns of America arose.

THE HISTORY OF IMPORTANT IMMIGRATION LAWS

Despite the fact that, in general, the Chinese were a hardworking, law-abiding people who had much to offer to the United States and Canada, there continued to be a great deal of anti-Chinese sentiment. Many Americans pushed for laws to exclude the Chinese. Their complaints tended to center on a few points. The Chinese, they said, did not assimilate into American society, nor did they even try to. They ate strange food. They had, it was claimed, established their own government in America that had its own jails, judges, and rules. The Chinese brought no women to America except prostitutes. Naturally, there was another side to each of these claims. The Chinese, of course, could not have assimilated to American society even if they'd tried. There was simply too much prejudice and hostile feeling toward them. Although they ate "strange" food, this was hardly unconstitutional. And although the Chinese merchants' association did tend to dominate the other Chinese, the typical Chinese laborer didn't choose or approve this situation, and to say that the Chinese had their own system of government was an exaggeration in any event. They did seek to mediate disputes among Chinese before non-Chinese and the outside government became involved, but they did not have a separate legal system. As for the claim that all Chinese women in America were prostitutes, this too was an exaggeration. Some merchants brought their wives to America, though these women were normally not seen on the streets of the city. Besides, the Chinese prostitutes had large numbers of white clients. Nevertheless, the whites succeeded in pushing through a great deal of anti-Chinese legislation.

In 1868 the Burlingame Treaty, which guaranteed free and equal immigration and travel for both Chinese and Americans in the others' country, was reversed when the Chinese Exclusion Act of May 8, 1882, suspended the immigration of Chinese laborers, skilled and unskilled, for 10 years. (Teachers, students, merchants, and travelers were allowed to travel and move freely.) The law was extended for another 10 years on May 5, 1892, and renamed the Geary Act, and on April 27, 1904, it was made permanent. The Scott Act of October 1, 1888, prohibited the return of all Chinese laborers who had temporarily left the United States with plans to return. The reentry certificates of 20,000 men in this category were summarily declared void. The Immigration Act of 1924 prohibited all Chinese wives from immigrating to the United States. (Ironically, the whites had gone from complaining that the Chinese did not bring their wives to America in sufficient numbers to prohibiting them from bringing their wives at all.) These laws were the only pieces of legislation in U.S. history that excluded members of a specific nationality by name.

The situation began to improve during World War II, when the United States was allied with China against the Japanese and China wanted steps taken to ease the anti-Chinese restrictions. The middle of the war in 1943 marked the repeal of the Chinese Exclusion Act. This allowed for the entry of 105 Chinese persons per year ("Chinese people" being defined as anyone of half or more Chinese blood, regardless of country of origin), and they were allowed to become naturalized American citizens—a first for Chinese immigrants. The War Brides Act of 1945 allowed for easier entry to America by Chinese women who had married American citizens. Approximately 6,000 Chinese brides entered the country in this way.

Other legislative acts allowed more Chinese into the country. Following the war, the Displaced Persons Act of 1948 allowed 3,465 sailors, students, and other Chinese who found themselves trapped in the United States due to problems in China to stay permanently. The Refugee Relief Act of 1953 allowed 2,777 Chinese refugees fleeing communism to reside permanently in the United States, and 2,000 more who already had U.S. entry visas were allowed to enter for the purpose of residence.

Throughout all this, there were often exemptions for the relatives, spouses, and children of those Chinese who had already secured permanent residence in the United States through one means or another. Naturally, a great deal of immigration fraud and misrepresentation took place. Many "paper sons" entered illegally and stayed. On September 11, 1957, legislation was passed that allowed these "paper sons" to become legal residents if they had a spouse, parent, or child who was a U.S. citizen.

Little by little, the situation improved. John F. Kennedy signed the Presidential Directory of May 25, 1962, permitting more refugees from Hong Kong to enter the country. The act of October 3, 1965, legislated widespread change in the previous immigration system by abolishing the previous national quota system and allowing each nation outside the Western Hemisphere 20,000 immigrants. The Immigration and Reform Act of 1986 was designed to reduce immigration fraud. Among its provisions was the requirement that all employers take steps to verify that their employees had a legal right to work in the United States. To counter a backlash, it also gave aliens who had arrived illegally before 1981 the right to remain in the United States. For this reason, many aliens who are caught today insist that they have lived in the United States since before that year.

Although there is a quota that limits the number of Chinese who can enter the United States to work, live, or study, there is nothing in the legal code that is specifically aimed at restricting the immigration of Chinese per se. Under the quota, a certain number of people from each country are allowed to enter the United States for the purpose of establishing residence each year. Priority within this quota is given to people who fit certain categories. Among those favored are relatives and wives of U.S. citizens, those with skills that are in demand within the United States, and those willing to invest large amounts of money to develop industry and create jobs in the United States.

The Canadian situation tended to parallel that of the United States. In general, Chinese immigration to Canada became increasingly restricted up until the second world war. Little by little, anti-Chinese restrictions were lifted until, in 1967, they were removed from Canadian law altogether.

CATEGORIES OF CHINESE IMMIGRANTS
AND RESIDENTS IN NORTH AMERICA

Today, Chinese legally residing in North America can be divided into three broad categories.

THE CHINATOWN CHINESE

The first category is the Chinatown Chinese and their descendants, or those who were admitted to the United States as their relatives. These are the people whose history has been told in this chapter. Their ancestors almost universally came from Canton and the southern Chinese coast. Although they have lived in the United States or Canada for many generations, in some cases their newly arrived relatives lack skills and language abilities.

THOSE WITH VALUABLE SKILLS, EDUCATION, OR INVESTMENTS

The immigration laws of Canada and the United States are designed to allow large numbers of people whose skills or education might benefit the country to enter and establish residency or citizenship. Particularly for non-Caucasians, this tends to be a post-World War II phenomenon, so most Chinese who entered the country this way did so relatively recently. (Members of this category are often seen as highly educated and successful and are described as "model minorities.") Thus there is a disproportionate number of Chinese immigrants today with astonishingly high levels of education. On the other hand, it is still quite rare to find a Chinese firefighter or automobile mechanic.

Although such people do face real prejudice from time to time, they usually find good jobs and become part of American society quickly. It should not be forgotten that that most of them were quite successful in their homelands: they were at the top of the social ladder where they came from, and they simply managed to stay at the top of the social ladder when they transferred to a new country. These immigrants tend to have only a marginal relationship with many of the older Chinese-American institutions and associations. They shop in Chinatowns on occasion for special Asian products that they cannot easily find in America, but few wish to live there if they can buy a nice suburban home.

Given the uncertain future of both Taiwan and Hong Kong, many of the successful residents of these countries have made a conscious effort to arrange for a relative or two abroad to help them leave should conditions become ugly in their homelands. A surprising number of top government officials in Asian countries own property or have relatives in the United States or elsewhere that can help them immigrate if the need should arise.

In addition to having the right education or skills, another way people can obtain an immigration visa for the United States or Canada is to invest a large amount of money in either of their economies. In the United States, the specified amount is $1 million. In Canada, it's $500,000 (in Canadian currency). Such amounts of cash belong primarily to successful businessmen, and many of them manage to create flourishing businesses even when they move to a new location. In Vancouver, Canada, one of the most desired locations for Asian immigrants, such wealthy businessmen are often nicknamed "the yacht people," due to the means by which they arrived.

TRANSIENTS

The third category of Chinese in the United States are transients, such as students or tourists.

The students show a great deal of variation in the extent of their assimilation to American culture. Some have little interest in, understanding of, or appreciation for American culture or society, and it often becomes apparent that their reading comprehension is much higher than their listening comprehension. They spend much more time reading English from textbooks than actually speaking the language. Anyone who spends much time around Asian students in America should be prepared for occasional examples of extreme cultural misunderstanding, stereotypical attitudes toward American whites and minorities, and often a profound lack of experience with American laws and institutions.

NOTES

1. There was a great deal of racism or at least ethnocentrism in the attitude of many whites toward the Chinese of this time. Many white men would pay money just to

look at a naked Chinese prostitute in order to see if there were any major differences in the anatomies of Chinese and white women. See Herbert Asbury, *The Barbary Coast* (New York: Old Town Books, 1933), 174. Others believed that the Chinese were genetically capable of laboring harder under worse conditions because they had fewer nerve endings near their skin and could feel less pain. See Lynn Pan, *Sons of the Yellow Emperor* (London: Mandarin Paperbacks, 1990), 97.

2. These are described in some detail in Herbert Asbury's very readable classic *The Gangs of New York* (New York: Old Town Books, 1928).

3. For more on this stereotype, see Arkon Daraul, *A History of Secret Societies* (New York: Carol Publishing Group, 1961, 1989), 234.

4. The question of why they were called "hatchet men" is answered by Officer Smith in *The Hatchet Men*: "A great many of them carry a hatchet with the handle cut off. It may be about six inches long with a handle and a hole cut in it. The have the handle sawed off a little, leaving just enough to keep a good hold . . ." See Richard H. Dillon, *The Hatchet Men* (New York: Coward-McCann, Inc., 1962), 163.

To the rich, educated Chinese and the students and tourists, a Chinatown is a place to purchase Chinese services and products that are not economical to sell elsewhere in North America.

To the poorer, working-class immigrant Chinese, Chinatown is a place where jobs are readily available to those who lack English-language skills. Most come intending to work hard, save money, and, if things work out, go home. Others plan to remain in the United States but hope to make their fortune and then buy a big house in the suburbs or in a nicer neighborhood. For them, although Chinatown may not be the nicest place to stay, it suits their needs quite well.

Many people have the misguided notion that a Chinatown is a small community where the Chinese live together in a tightly knit group because they find this more pleasant than facing the confusion inherent in American society. The following statistics should demonstrate just how naive this view is.

There are more than 150,000 Chinese living in New York City's primary Chinatown in lower Manhattan. (There is a second and a third Chinatown as well, in the Flushing section of Queens and in Brooklyn, respectively.) According to author Gwen Kinkead, author of *Chinatown: A Portrait of a Closed Society* (1992), 80 percent were born outside the United States, and of these, half have lived in America fewer than five years. Kinkead also states that 1,400 Chinese immigrants arrive each month to seek their fortune in this primary Chinatown alone! These people come from many different regions of China, and

CHAPTER 5

CHINATOWNS IN NORTH AMERICA

85

Chinatown scenes: Roosevelt Market in New York City, mural depicting Chinatown culture.

TONGS, GANGS, AND TRIADS:
CHINESE CRIME GROUPS IN NORTH AMERICA

Many Chinatowns are not small neighborhoods.

Chinatown traditions: bloody angle of Doyers Street, a frequent site of tong war ambushes in the 1930s.

Idol of Guan Di—a popular deity and character in Romance of the Three Kingdoms—*in an American Chinatown.*

virtually all come here to get rich. They normally do not wish to become involved in distracting affairs such as local politics or the problems of people they don't know and probably will never see again. The Chinese in New York's Chinatown speak at least 10 different dialects. Often, the members of one subgroup of Chinese will have a traditional animosity or prejudice toward members of another. As mentioned in Chapter 4, a wide variety of groups, associations, and organizations vie for control of as many people as possible. When citizens of Chinatown gain prominence and wealth, they usually move to the suburbs, thus depriving the community of their potential leadership. Others become successful by exploiting the community, and, therefore, although they might seek a position of leadership, they really have no desire to improve the conditions of the typical immigrant laborer whose sweat helped make them rich in the first place. Some might wonder whether patriotism would help unite the residents of Chinatown, but even here there is a problem. Politically, they are split into various groups, depending on whether they support the rule of the People's Republic of China or wish for the return of the Kuomintang.

A Chinatown is generally a disorganized, chaotic area full of people wanting to get rich fast, often any way they can. It also contains many broken people, long since forced to abandon their dreams of obtaining wealth and glory and hoping merely to survive. Chinatowns are not the idyllic communities many

An all-American establishment in Chinatown; building in back is the Lee Family Association.

tourists like to see them as. They are, instead, a phenomenon unto themselves.

ECONOMIC CONDITIONS

Because Chinatown offers jobs for people with no English-language ability, many Chinese end up working there, mostly in two fields: the restaurant industry and the garment industry. Such jobs pay poorly—often much less than minimum wage. Hours tend to be extremely long, even by Asian standards. When Jane H. Li, a Chinese-American, Cantonese-speaking reporter for the *New York Times* went undercover as a Chinatown garment worker for a week to research a story that appeared in the March 12, 1995 issue, she was hired at a rate of $.65 an hour and expected to work 84 hours a week! Some waiters are paid $200 a month and work more than full-time hours. Others are not paid a wage at all but are expected to live off the tips they receive at their restaurant (and most people tend to undertip in inexpensive Chinese restaurants in Chinatown). Naturally, there are no benefits, overtime wages, or vacations.

In the garment industry, sweatshop conditions are still common. Although many of the workers are unionized, problems exist. In spite of the fact that the International Ladies Garment Workers' Union (ILGWU) has established a minimum hourly wage, workers are usually paid by the piece, and employers take advantage of this by frequently switching assignments and rates. Thus, the workers are often paid rates below the national minimum wage—and much less than the minimum set by the union. The average worker in a Chinatown garment factory labors 10 to 12 hours a day, six days a week, every week of the year.

Working and safety conditions are often horrible. In Asia, safety and sanitation standards are generally much lower than in America, yet in Chinatowns, conditions tend to be dangerous even by Chinese standards. Often fire exits are locked to reduce the chance of theft, kitchen grease filters are in need of replacement, and soap and other cleaning supplies are unavailable in the rest rooms for either employees or customers.

Naturally, the workers have little recourse. Complaints to employers fall on deaf ears, and there are problems with calling for government intervention. First, illegal aliens (as many of these workers are) do almost anything to avoid attention from the government. Second, even if this were not a concern, lack of English and unfamiliarity with the various bureaucracies and government departments make it difficult for workers to file complaints effectively.

Within both prevailing industries, although the pay is generally exploitive, financial incentives do apply. The harder a waiter works, the more he will make in tips. The more pieces a seamstress sews, the more money she makes. This means that workers labor hard in an effort to make more money. It does not mean that they get rich. In fact, they generally must get as much of the extra pay as possible in order to meet their standard low wages.

For their part, employers often claim to be trapped by the conditions. It is not easy to run a profitable business in Chinatown. Although many upscale restaurants make a lot of money for their owners, most new, low-budget Chinese restaurants fail and close in their first year. The market is very tight and shows little sign of changing, because such low-cost restaurants are among the few businesses new immigrants feel they can easily manage with their existing skills. In such a competitive market, costs need to be cut wherever possible, and underpaying workers is one way to do so. Similarly, garment workers must compete hard for contracts.

Surprisingly, land and property costs are quite high in most Chinatowns. There are at least two reasons for this. First, most Chinatowns are located close to the downtown of large urban centers, where property tends to be worth quite a lot. Second, the value of the properties have been inflated by investment from Asia. Chinese investors prefer to buy property in Chinatowns. The investors apparently find purchases in Chinese neighborhoods much easier, and they can invest in businesses or property owned by relatives or acquaintances. Naturally, with overseas investment, the value and cost of the property goes up.

A lot of property is being purchased by Chinese, particularly from Hong Kong, with criminal connections. Again, a reason for this is to facilitate their possible immigration in the future. A second reason is money laundering.

In the excellent work *Yakuza* (1986), Kaplan and Dubro state that Japanese gangsters commonly arrive in the United States, particularly in Hawaii, and purchase hotels and other property in cash—often without even evaluating the prices of nearby real estate carefully. The money they are investing comes from illicit sources; they cannot spend it in Japan in large quantities, because the authorities would prosecute them for having a large and illegal income. By contrast, any income from the property in the form of rents or other profits can be explained to the Japanese authorities as coming from a legitimate source.

This may very well be one reason that there is a great deal of criminal investment in North America's Chinatowns. In fact, with land values so extraordinarily high in Chinatown, almost any piece of property has value. Landlords or storekeepers will even rent out the right to do business on the sidewalk in front of their property to street vendors illegally.

FAMILY LIFE

Recall that in the idealized Chinese family, the father is a wise and benevolent teacher and leader for his children, particularly his sons. The mother provides love and attention for the children and strives to ensure that they have a good home life.

In Chinatowns, among the families of many unskilled laborers this pattern breaks down. Often both parents work 10, 12, or more hours almost every day. The children spend long hours on their own and rarely see their parents. When they do, they find their parents have little understanding of the lives they are leading in America's public schools and on the streets of some of North America's toughest cities. Often when the family has a problem, the children are forced to translate for the parents and try to explain aspects of American culture, life, or government. This erodes the Confucian tradition and upsets the idealized pattern that is the basis for much of Chinese morality and ethical teaching. Many children come to the conclusion that their parents have little understanding of their situation and so have little to offer them in the way of example.

Thus in Chinatowns there is a large community of teenagers who lack supervision and have lost faith in their traditional morality and authority figures. Life is not easy for these teenagers; their only hope for advancement is to attain suitable job skills or education to break free from the cycle of poverty their parents are trapped in. As immigrants, however, they find that obtaining an education in a foreign language is not easy, which often leaves them frustrated and confused as they struggle through their lessons. Other times, the inevitable temptations that unsupervised teenagers and adolescents face cause them to do things other than study, which cause many of them to have trouble in school, ultimately fail, and drop out.

A class of people with little in the way of job skills, low moral training, and no future is thereby created. The option of returning to Asia is not realistic; these youths have no skills that are in demand in Asia either. Such youths are easily recruited into the many Asian gangs in America's Chinatowns. Although many parents are aware of the risks of their children going bad in Chinatown, there are few choices available to them. Some have been known to send their children abroad to study and live with relatives in Hong Kong, Taiwan, or elsewhere, but this is the exception, not the rule.

POLITICS OF CHINATOWN

The events of China's history, as described in Chapter 2, provide a background as to how Chinese politics affect those of any Chinatown. In a Chinatown's politics, two places must always be considered—the People's Republic of China and the Republic of China (Taiwan).

Politics have always centered around events there, rather than in North America. This in itself is not unusual. Many minority groups here maintain an interest in their homelands, for example, the Irish-Americans and the Jewish-Americans. Nevertheless, the depth of a Chinatown's traditional involvement in Chinese politics is unusual. The CCBA, the important Chinese merchants' association, had a chapter in virtually every Chinese community in North America and, because it was composed of the most important and influential members of the Chinese community, became the de facto ruler of Chinatowns. This arrangement was unconsciously promoted by various state, local, and federal agencies that found it simplest to ignore situations and conditions in nearby Chinatowns, or else go to the local CCBA (where a respected businessman could explain it to them in English) and obtain clarification.

Having been established with the support and financial contributions of the overseas Chinese, the Republic of China continued to cultivate their support, which to a large extent was done through the CCBA. The Kuomintang had vowed to return to mainland China someday, and as part of this, it did everything in its power to remain on good terms with the CCBA.

When the People's Republic of China was established, many Chinese in America welcomed the new government. Many also had complaints about the CCBA and thought the change would weaken it. Others hoped the new government would prove more idealistic and less corrupt than the old one. On October 9, 1949, 18 days after Mao established the People's Republic of China, several hundred inhabitants of San Francisco's Chinatown gathered to celebrate the event. A few minutes into the speeches, members of either the Hop Sing or Bing Kung Tongs invaded the auditorium, tore down the flag, sprayed much of the audience with blue dye, and may have assaulted some of the speech makers (reports vary). The next day, a tong-war-style "hit list" with the names of 15 of the prominent speakers was posted, offering a $5,000 award for the death of each one.

Things did not get any better for those who supported the People's Republic. When the cold war broke out, many U.S. citizens began to wonder if the Chinese in America might be spies. Over the next 20 years, the FBI interrogated many Chinese-Americans with leftist tendencies. Others' privacy was invaded and their loyalty brought under scrutiny simply because they had crossed the Kuomintang or the CCBA, which in turn would report them to the FBI as possible communist collaborators.

China's entry into the Korean War raised anxiety among the

Chinese in America even more. Although the bulk of Chinese-Americans were simply apolitical businessmen, most had seen firsthand how the U.S. government had put Japanese-American citizens in internment camps during World War II.[1] It therefore seemed prudent to show as much visible support as possible for the Kuomintang on Taiwan.

In the United States there were two groups of people with a special interest and insight into events in China. These were the Chinese-Americans and the generally non-Chinese scholars and academics who had studied or lived in the region.

The Kumintang and the circumstances had combined to pretty much guarantee support for the Republic of China on Taiwan among Chinese-Americans. As for the scholars, in the McCarthy era of the early 1950s, it was fairly easy for the Kuomintang to aver that those who supported or admired the People's Republic were communist agents, sympathizers, or even spies.

The Kuomintang kept close tabs on the Chinese-Americans in the United States. Spies were hired, organizations were infiltrated, and students and workers were paid to give reports on their fellow Chinese-Americans. The FBI, always anxious during these years to ferret out suspected communist agents, found the Kuomintang and its agents a useful source of reports on the political activities in the Chinese community.

The Kuomintang's close ties with the CCBA, the tongs, and the other elements of the traditional Chinatown elite were carefully maintained, and steps were taken to ensure that the situation remained unchanged. For example, many key people in America's Chinatowns were given seats in the Republic of China institutions on Taiwan reserved for "overseas Chinese" representatives. Similarly, key members of the CCBA were given lucrative commercial concessions, such as monopoly rights on certain imports.

However, this situation could not continue indefinitely. The number of Chinese coming into the United States was growing, with many from Hong Kong and mainland China, who felt little loyalty to the Kuomintang on Taiwan. Simultaneously, a large number of young Chinese-Americans were growing discontented with the self-serving monopoly on power of the CCBA and its allies.

NOTES

1. During World War II, the U.S. government ordered large numbers of Japanese-Americans to leave their homes and live in relocation camps. The stated reason was that such people were a danger to the United States and might prove to be a threat to the internal security of the country. Undoubtedly, however, there was a racist element to this act. For a good description of life in these camps, see Jeanne Wakatsuki Houston, *Farewell to Manzanar* (New York: Bantam Books, 1973). Houston, a Japanese-American woman, grew up in one of the camps.

TONGS, GANGS, AND TRIADS:
CHINESE CRIME GROUPS IN NORTH AMERICA

C riminal gangs are regarded as a growing problem in America. Unfortunately, much of the literature about them is confused and confusing, partly because the definition of "gang" is very broad. At one extreme is the traditional neighborhood band of adolescents who hang out together regularly to play basketball, but might occasionally engage in shoplifting, a little bit of graffiti, or a fistfight with the kids from another neighborhood. At the other extreme are groups whose members range in age from 10 to 40 and who meet regularly to plan and engage in criminal activities, have written constitutions and by-laws, possibly wear "colors," possess formidable arsenals and have established chapters in cities throughout North America. Lumping such vastly different groups together makes it almost impossible to write about what constitutes a Chinese gang in America.

Sociologists, criminologists, and others who study gangs often classify them by different levels, assigning each level a number. Some researchers, however, prefer to use a system of names. Although no standardized system of classification is universally used at present, one such system is given at the end of this chapter as Table 6-3. The system used here provides a more accurate picture of what is meant by "gangs."

When we speak of Asian gangs in the United States and Canada, further differentiations must be made. Not only do they have a wide range of organizational levels, they also differ in some fundamental characteristics. In North America gangs, as opposed to the generally older, more sophisticated secret societies, come from three different sources and grow and develop in three different ways. First are the *indigenous Asian youth gangs* formed by young Asian immigrants or native-born youths of Asian descent. These groups generally are quite similar in form, structure, and development to the gangs formed by other ethnic groups in North America. Second are *those who work with Chinatown tongs*. Many of the most dangerous Asian youth gangs fall into this category. In such cases, the gangs and the tongs remain separate organizations but have overlapping memberships. Often the older, more experienced, and educated tong members serve as advisors to the leaders of the gangs. In some cases, particularly on the West Coast, this relationship has backfired and the gang has grown into a more powerful and influential entity than its sponsoring tong. Third are the *transplanted foreign gangs*. Often, these gangs have developed a high degree of sophistication and organization in their home countries. When members of the group emigrate and establish a chapter in the United States or Canada, they bring their criminal skills and abilities with them.

HISTORY AND DEVELOPMENT OF CHINESE GANGS IN NORTH AMERICA

As already noted, the traditional Chinese criminal group in North America was an offshoot of the societies of adults who had primarily united for mutual protection and self-interest (e.g., tongs). Neither the groups nor the mutual-aid societies had any number of the youths we nowadays associate with urban Chinese gangs.

Even though tong wars had become endemic to many American cities shortly before World War II, the tongs were forced to tone down such behavior. The restrictions on Chinese immigration at that time also meant that there were few Chinese youths to commit any crimes. According to Richard Dillon's Afterword in his 1962 work *The Hatchetmen*, a history of San Francisco's 1890s tong wars, the crime rate in that Chinatown of 1962 was incredibly low, and gang and tong violence was essentially nonexistent.

After World War II, Chinese families started coming to America in large enough numbers for adolescents to form gangs, and the first ones started forming in the 1950s. The best place to study the development of Chinese gangs is in New York City; it has North America's largest Chinese population and well documented information available on Chinese social problems.

In New York of the 1960s, most American-born Chinese youth attended the public schools near Chinatown. The student body of these schools was then approximately 95-percent black and Hispanic and only 5-percent Chinese or white. For the Chinese students, the simple act of attending school could be very dangerous, because they were frequently terrorized and abused by the blacks and Hispanics. Since school and community officials did little to help, Chinese students responded by forming a gang known as the Continentals. First established in 1961, it had up to 100 members at times.

The Continentals were organized primarily for self-defense. Although its members were known to engage in gambling, truancy, and fighting with other gangs, they did not actually commit street crimes against their community (at least not as a group). According to the classification system used in Table 6-4, the Continentals were a level 1 or "emergent" gang.

There were other important differences between the modern Chinese gang members and those of the Continentals. The latter were almost all American-born Chinese, and the majority was reasonably well-adjusted to American society. In contrast to many of the young Chinese gang members of today, they did not suffer from hopelessness and desperation. Unlike many later, more dangerous gang members, their problem was how to get through school without getting beaten up, not how to get through life in a society that had no use for them. Although the tongs still existed, particularly in their public role as social clubs for men, the members generally had little common cause with such groups as the Continentals.

In 1964 the situation changed as two new gangs formed in Chinatown. The first was the White Eagles, which was originally formed by a member of New York's On Leong Tong. He began by bringing local youths together into a group originally called the On Leong Youth Club, whose primary activity was to study martial arts under the leadership of a tong member. The exact motives of this leader remain unknown. Some say he wished to provide a gathering place for youths so they would not become restless and engage in activities that would disturb the community. It may also have been an attempt to improve his reputation as either a philanthropist or a man of importance.

In contrast to the American-born Continentals, the White Eagles were mostly Hong Kong-born. As such, they felt closer ties to the Chinatown community, but a greater alienation from any mainstream American community. They also had an affinity for the concerns of Chinatown residents and rage toward the outside world. For instance, they took great pride in beating up those who tried to leave Chinese restaurants without paying the bill or who harassed and abused Chinatown residents. Their main concern was the situation of Chinese immigrants, not the fate of Chinese students in the public schools. Since the White Eagles recruited mostly from the large number of Hong Kong immigrants rather than the smaller number of American-born Chinese, they grew faster than groups such as the Continentals. Also unlike the Continentals, they had some ties to the older, more established tongs. In the terminology of some sociologists and criminologists, a gang like the White Eagles is a level 2 or "crystallized" gang.

A similar group was the Chung Yee. This gang appears to have formed spontaneously, without outside organization. Like the White Eagles, the Chung Yee recruited and grew among the immigrants from Hong Kong.

By 1965, the Chung Yee and the White Eagles were the dominant groups on the streets of New York's Chinatown. By then the Hong Kong immigrant gangs had developed a new enemy—the American-born Chinese! The foreign-born Chinese took great pride in their nationality and claimed that the American-born Chinese did not really understand Chinese culture. The American-born Chinese resented this sort of treatment from people who had just arrived in the neighborhood. The foreign-born Chinese began dictating to the Continentals

TONGS, GANGS, AND TRIADS:
CHINESE CRIME GROUPS IN NORTH AMERICA

where they could walk and on which sides of the street. Although the Continentals might have resisted, they were outnumbered and they ultimately disbanded. Such friction continues to this day. By 1968 there were five gangs in New York's Chinatown: the Chung Yee, White Eagles, Liang Shan, Flying Dragons, and Black Eagles (an offshoot of the White Eagles). All had much in common. They all resembled martial arts clubs, and each studied these arts under the direction of a kung fu master and instructor, who was invariably a member of one of the neighborhood's tongs. Their self-appointed duties consisted largely of protecting their neighborhoods from unwanted visitors and driving away American-born Chinese youths who wandered into areas the gangs considered off limits.

THE 1970s: THE TONG/GANG RELATIONSHIP SOLIDIFIES

During the early 1970s, violence grew as the gangs began vying for control of Chinatown. The White Eagles and the Black Eagles clashed more frequently and ferociously than was customary in the past. In 1970 the first Chinese youth was arrested for murder following the fatal stabbing of a 17-year-old White Eagle by a Black Eagle on the streets of Chinatown. After that, arrests of Chinese youth increased considerably, primarily on assault and weapons charges.

The early 1970s was a time of radical social change, political questioning and agitation, and great improvements for the civil rights of racial minorities throughout the United States—and Chinatown was no exception. Chinatown's old guard could see its power and influence slipping away as the newer groups sought to establish a new order. Meanwhile, the gangs had become more violent and predatory in their own community. They extorted food and money from restaurants and robbed gambling halls. As their conflicts grew more violent, it became commonplace for gang members to carry guns and knives. Outsiders became worried about entering the neighborhood, and the tourist trade was affected, further hurting the restaurants and other businesses.

Such problems made the tongs, the traditional secret

societies in Chinatown, look powerless and archaic. To combat all the problems in one fell swoop, the tongs began establishing closer relationships with the various street gangs and hiring them as "soldiers." In this way, a tong felt it could not only curb a gang's behavior directly but also dispatch the gang to defend an area of Chinatown from other gangs. This tong affiliation changed forever the pattern of the most important Chinese gangs in North America.

TONG-AFFILIATED GANGS

As the ties between the tongs and the gangs solidified, the economies and behavior of the gangs changed. Gang members were able to live in apartments provided for them or rented to them by their tong. They often ate in restaurants owned by tong members. Gang membership could now be a full-time occupation, and members had little immediate need to attend school or maintain close ties with their families. To sociologists and criminologists, these changes meant that the gangs of Chinatown had changed significantly from being the simple, almost innocent groups they were originally. Because of their adult leadership, their own living quarters, their access to improved weaponry, their increasingly serious violent acts, and the fact that their gang membership could literally now be a full-time profession, the groups could now be easily classified as level 3 or "formalized" gangs.

All of this, unfortunately, did little or nothing to reduce the level of violence in Chinatown. Gangs still fought each other and, in an important change, members of individual gangs fought increasingly among themselves. As the gangs became more powerful and their membership more cohesive, the leadership of a gang became more valuable and hence more worth fighting for. There may be other factors as well. Ko-lin Chin has described how the tongs provided advisors to their affiliated gangs who subtly did what they could to create intragang strife and division, making it easier for the tongs to control the gangs (Chin 1990, 98-100). With only a few exceptions, the overwhelming majority of tongs now have an affiliated gang. With tong-gang affiliation came an escalation of intertong rivalries. As the tongs competed to gain control, money, or respect from their fellow Chinatown residents, one that did not have an affiliated gang would be at a serious disadvantage. Once such arrangements between the tongs and the gangs became commonplace, gang affiliation became more or less essential to being a tong in an American Chinatown. In many cases, a tong with branches in many different cities might ally itself with a gang that does not have chapters in all those same cities, forcing different branches of the same tong to affiliate with different gangs in different cities.

However, this does not mean that a tong controls all of the operations of its gang affiliates. Most of the criminal acts of any given gang are done without the control, approval, or knowledge of its tong. If the crime and extortion became too blatant and disruptive to the community at large, however, the tong's representatives step in and try to curb the gang's activities. The relationship between the two entities is loose, and few wish to tighten it. The tongs want to retain deniability for the acts of the gangs, and the gangs wish to keep their freedom and their own identity.

Tong-Affiliated Versus Unaffiliated Gangs

Not all gangs have a tong affiliation. There are more Chinese gangs than tongs in most cities. Similarly, although many tongs have branches in several cities across the United States and Canada, this is not so for most Chinese gangs. Of the New York City Chinatown gangs that originated in the United States, only the Ghost Shadows and the Flying Dragons have branches in other cities. The Ghost Shadows have branches in Boston, Chicago, Houston, and Toronto, and elsewhere. Unlike many other gangs, all members of the Ghost Shadows are also members of the On Leong Tong, although most members of the On Leong Tong are not Ghost Shadows.

The Wah Ching, a Chinatown gang that began in San Francisco, has spread widely as well. It has branches in San Francisco, has spread to Los Angeles, Portland (Oregon), Dallas, Houston, Denver, San Diego, Oklahoma City, and Rapid City (South Dakota) and is involved in activities as far away as

Arlington (Virginia), Boston, and even New York City. Although the Wah Ching originally had a close relationship with the Hop Sing Tong, the gang grew to where it became more influential than the Hop Sing. Today the Wah Ching is one of the most powerful criminal organizations on the West Coast. Nevertheless, its situation is not necessarily permanent. Ironically, in the Wah Ching's native San Francisco, the Hong Kong-based Wo Hop To triad recently supplanted it as the most important criminal group.

With more and more Chinese immigrants coming to North America, the Chinese population spread from the Chinatowns. At first, the Chinatown gangs had considered any Chinese business that lay outside the staked-out areas of Chinatown as fair game for their extortion and robbery. In time, however, gangs sprang up in non-Chinatown areas with a predominantly Chinese population. Some were indigenous to North America and grew naturally in their own neighborhoods. Often these gangs developed among later immigrants who found themselves threatened by an already existing group or gang of either Chinese or non-Chinese origin. Typically, such gangs do not have a tong affiliation and exist only in one city. Although they can be quite dangerous, their level of organization and sophistication is lower than that of older Chinese crime groups. It is not uncommon for less experienced, sophisticated, and organized groups to be more violent and ruthless than their longer established rivals, acting quickly to intimidate enemies and making a reputation for themselves, rather than being cautious about the law enforcement attention such acts will bring.

TRANSPLANTED ASIAN GANGS

At times, a large number of Chinese would come to North America from a particular site in Asia and bring with them their own gangsters, who would establish a local branch of their same criminal group. Both the United Bamboo and the Four Seas are gangs from Taiwan that have local chapters in Taiwanese communities throughout North America. (Some in Taiwan joke that since it is primarily the most successful Taiwanese who emigrate to North America, the gangs in the new world have too many officers and too few rank and file to boss around.) Although these are not generally affiliated with the older, primarily Cantonese-speaking tongs in the United States and Canada, they might have affiliations with newer tonglike organizations representing people from their region of China. For example, the Fuk Ching gang, a group that came to the United States with immigrants from Fukien province, has a close relationship with the Fukien American Association.

THE UNITED BAMBOO GANG

The United Bamboo is the most famous of all Taiwanese crime groups, yet it dates back only to 1956.

The friction between the native Taiwanese Chinese and the mainland Chinese who retreated to Taiwan in 1949 sometimes turned violent among the students and teenagers of the island, and the formation of gangs occasionally resulted. But these tended to be loosely knit, level 0 or level 1 "emergent" gangs only; there really was no need for anything larger or better organized, and the Taiwanese police probably would not have tolerated anything more serious, in any event.

The United Bamboo became more important as its members grew older, and its members and leaders are said to have taken full advantage of their close family ties with the Kuomintang to shield themselves from police attention. In time, the gang grew to control an extensive share of Taiwanese vice, gambling, extortion, and other rackets, and it became quite influential in the Taiwanese movie and television industry. Nevertheless, it was still relatively small and disorganized.

In 1970 it was estimated to have only about 100 members, a high turnover rate, and only a loose organizational structure as it increased in strength and size and committed more serious crimes, the group found it necessary to improve its organizational structure. Its leader, Chen Chi-li, turned to Chinese tradition for guidance in this modernization. College-educated members of his gang approved of and assisted with this measure. For this reason, the United Bamboo gang is

TABLE 6-1
GHOST SHADOWS ORGANIZATION

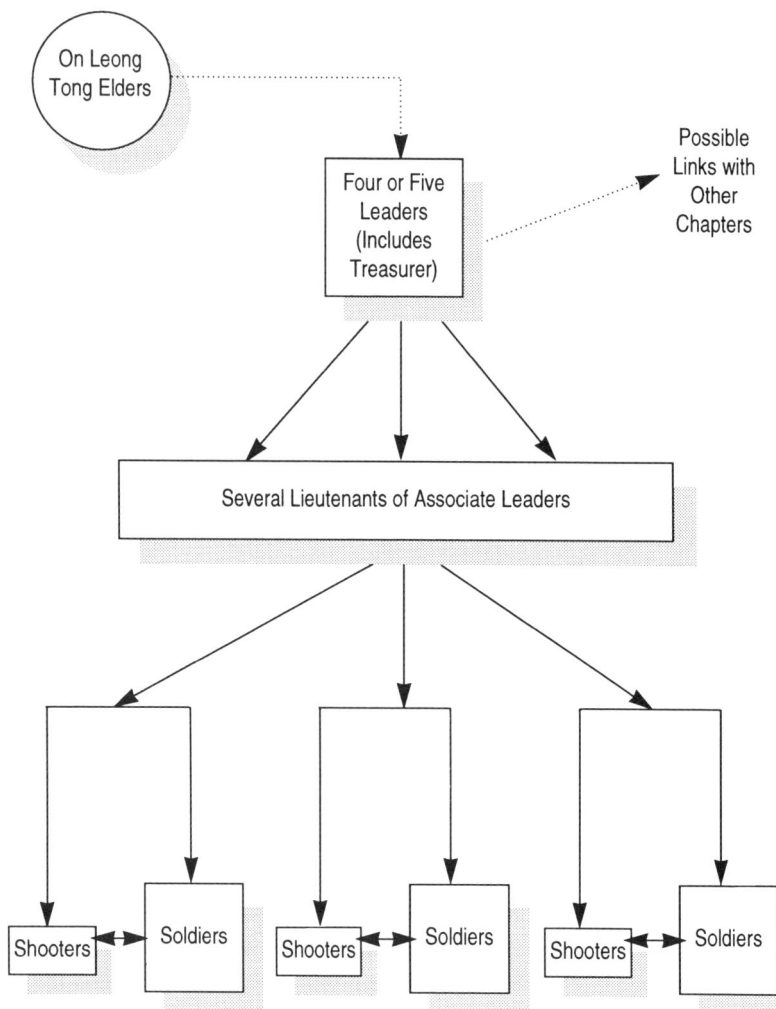

```
  ┌──────────────┐
  │ On Leong     │ .......►  ┌──────────────┐
  │ Tong Elders  │          │ Four or Five │ ........►  Possible
  └──────────────┘          │ Leaders      │           Links with
                            │ (Includes    │           Other
                            │ Treasurer)   │           Chapters
                            └──────────────┘
```

Four or Five Leaders (Includes Treasurer)

Several Lieutenants of Associate Leaders

Shooters ↔ Soldiers   Shooters ↔ Soldiers   Shooters ↔ Soldiers

TABLE 6-2
WAH CHING ORGANIZATION

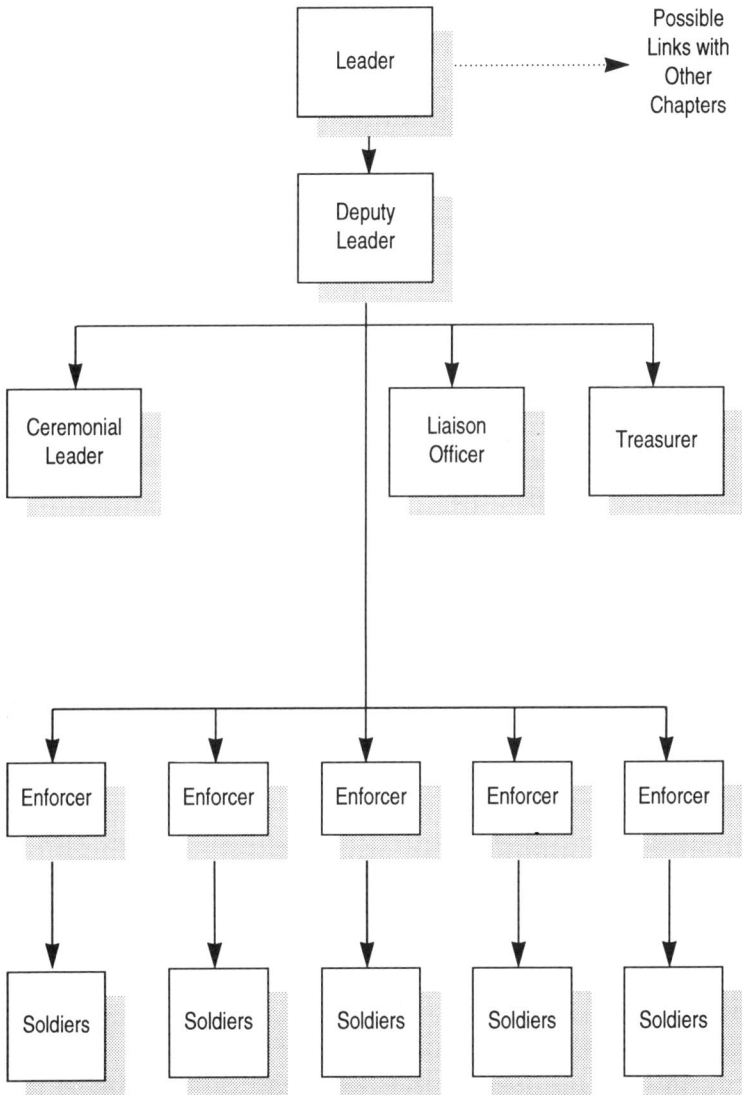

```
                    ┌──────────┐
                    │  Leader  │ ········▶  Possible
                    └──────────┘            Links with
                         │                  Other
                         ▼                  Chapters
                    ┌──────────┐
                    │  Deputy  │
                    │  Leader  │
                    └──────────┘
       ┌─────────────────┼─────────────────┐
       ▼                 ▼                 ▼
  ┌──────────┐      ┌──────────┐      ┌──────────┐
  │Ceremonial│      │ Liaison  │      │Treasurer │
  │  Leader  │      │ Officer  │      │          │
  └──────────┘      └──────────┘      └──────────┘
       │
  ┌────┼────────┬────────┬────────┬────────┐
  ▼    ▼        ▼        ▼        ▼
┌──────┐ ┌──────┐ ┌──────┐ ┌──────┐ ┌──────┐
│Enforc│ │Enforc│ │Enforc│ │Enforc│ │Enforc│
│ er   │ │ er   │ │ er   │ │ er   │ │ er   │
└──────┘ └──────┘ └──────┘ └──────┘ └──────┘
   │        │        │        │        │
   ▼        ▼        ▼        ▼        ▼
┌──────┐ ┌──────┐ ┌──────┐ ┌──────┐ ┌──────┐
│Soldie│ │Soldie│ │Soldie│ │Soldie│ │Soldie│
│ rs   │ │ rs   │ │ rs   │ │ rs   │ │ rs   │
└──────┘ └──────┘ └──────┘ └──────┘ └──────┘
```

consciously modeled after the tongs of southern China both in form and in structure, right down to such details as the initiation ceremony. Today it is the most highly organized and important gang in Taiwan.

As the United Bamboo's crimes grew more serious, family ties could no longer protect its members, and a police crackdown sent many of its members to prison. To escape arrest, many members moved to the United States, Canada, and elsewhere, and the United Bamboo now has chapters throughout North America and the world. Just as the Taiwanese joke goes, in the United States it has too many officers and too few rank and file, which has forced many gangsters to take up occupations in legitimate industries, such as importing oriental food products.

Nevertheless, United Bamboo activities continue in Los Angeles, San Francisco, New York City, Houston, Dallas, Las Vegas, Vancouver, and most other major urban areas in North America. Today the United Bamboo commits the full range of crimes typical of Chinese crime groups: immigration-related scams and smuggling, kidnapping, importing narcotics, gambling, loan sharking, and murder. In the past, the group worked with Taiwanese intelligence sources, notably in the assassination of Henry Liu, a U.S. citizen from Taiwan who was working as a double agent for Taiwanese and Chinese intelligence groups while simultaneously writing a critical biography of the life of Chiang Ching-kuo, president of Taiwan (the Republic of China).

Like many other Chinese crime groups, the United Bamboo has links and alliances with other criminal groups. In Southern California, it has established a working relationship with many Chinese and Vietnamese youth gangs, which provides muscle for its activities as it exploits the reckless, violent tendencies of these younger, less organized groups, including the Black Dragons and the Vietnamese V-Boys and Hung Pho.

Another Taiwanese organized crime group active in the United States is the rival Four Seas gang, a group with a similar history. Although not as large or widespread as the United Bamboo, it conducts the same activities and is known to cooperate both with members of the United Bamboo and the Taiwanese intelligence authorities.

THE BIG CIRCLE BOYS

The Big Circle Boys is a Chinese criminal group that grew out of the chaos of the Cultural Revolution that convulsed China in the 1960s, when Communist ultranationalism gripped China, and bands of paramilitary Red Guards roamed the country. Its members acted as a traveling inquisition to judge the loyalty and degree of Communist belief of the citizens of China, and in the process many whose loyalty was found wanting were punished, humiliated, or had their lives destroyed or their careers ruined. This situation crossed all fields of service, including the military.

Left without an income, some of these purged military officers formed a criminal group, the Big Circle Boys, and applied their skills to crime, particularly armed robbery of jewelry stores and banks. When the Cultural Revolution died down, many of the Red Guards had difficulty adjusting to civilian life, and some joined the Big Circle Boys. This group, also known as the Big Circle gang, the Big Circle Brotherhood, and the Big Circle Society, soon expanded its operations outward to Hong Kong, where greater wealth meant an increased take.

A typical Big Circle Boys operation was for a few gang members to illegally enter Hong Kong and execute a series of carefully planned robberies, obtaining as much loot as possible. When satisfied with their profits from the crime spree, the robbers would then sneak back into China, where prosecution and punishment for the crimes was much more difficult. In time the group grew more sophisticated and established, and as its members matured, the style and type of crime it became known for changed. Key members grew wealthy, emigrating to places such as the United States, Canada, and South America. The group began to shift its operations from high-profile, attention-getting crimes, such as armed robbery, to credit card fraud and counterfeiting and alien and drug smuggling; these attract less attention from law enforcement, thus being more profitable in the long run.

Today the Big Circle gang is one of the largest and most powerful Chinese crime groups in the entire world. It is particularly successful in Canada. Although the group is apolitical, it is organized in cells, like an underground revolutionary group. (Some of these cells have their own names, such as the Flaming Eagles.) Members must go through an initiation ceremony and swear oaths that are considered to be stricter and more binding than those of a traditional triad society. Although the Big Circle group is not considered a triad society or tong in the traditional sense, many of its members are also members of such. The group seems to be shifting its activities to less violent crimes but is still heavily armed, dangerous, and capable of acts of extreme violence.

COMMON CHARACTERISTICS OF GANG MEMBERS

The majority of Chinese youth gang members have similar characteristics. The following provides an overview of some of these.

SOCIOECONOMIC BACKGROUND

The majority of Chinese youth gang members come from the lower socioeconomic levels. Few have marketable job skills. Many, if not most, of the hard-core members have a poor working knowledge of English. Of course, the majority of hard-core gang members would not have become so enmeshed in gang life if they had seen other opportunities available to them. Few have much concept of a worthwhile future outside of the gang. If they did, they would not have become involved in a "profession" wherein their lives were routinely threatened.

GENDER

The members of Chinese gangs are all male. Although women or girls do associate with, hang around, or even live in the apartments of gang members, they do so in a subordinate role and are not initiated. They might carry guns for gang members or become caught up in gang-related violence, but it is extremely rare for them to take active roles.

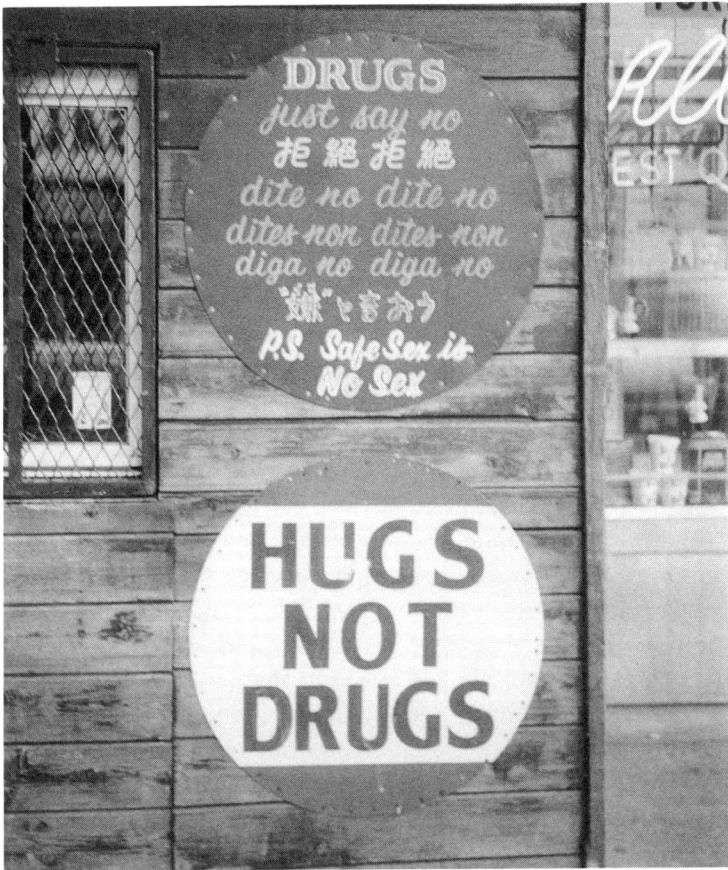

Internationalized "War on Drugs" message near New York City's Chinatown.

In her work *The Girls in the Gang,* Anne Campbell states that even though women are frequently involved in gangs and gang crime, they generally do so in two roles: as "sex objects" and as "tomboys" (the terms are hers). The primary distinction is whether the women take on a "feminine" or "masculine" role. In Chinese gangs, it seems, the women are normally forced into the former, taking a subservient position (Campbell 1984, 8). Although all-girl gangs are a growing problem among Southeast Asian communities in the United States, all-girl

Chinese gangs do not seem to be much of a threat. Nevertheless, my research did uncover an account of one all-female Chinese gang, the Sio Gi Ho, in Singapore in the 1970s (O'Callaghan 1978, 58). Members were young, poorly armed with only knives and sharpened files, and apparently loosely organized and only locally based (what some sociologists might call a level 1 gang). Despite a history of tonglike sworn sisterhoods in Chinese society, Chinese girl gangs do not seem to exist at present. At one time, Chen Chi-li, founder of the United Bamboo, discussed the possibility of setting up a women's auxiliary in Los Angeles to do social and charitable work, but it is not known what came of the plan, if anything.

AGE

Stereotypes notwithstanding, the members of Chinese "youth" gangs are often quite old. A 1983 report by the New York City Fifth Police Precinct indicates that out of 192 Chinese gang members, the mean age was 22.7. Because the report included active, inactive, suspected, and imprisoned gang members, who had already come to the notice of the police, seasoned gang members quite possibly were overrepresented. Nevertheless, many in law enforcement argue that the use of the term "youth gang" is inappropriate in referring to the well-organized and established gangs that dominate Chinese-American crime today.

Some hold that the members of Chinese gangs can be divided roughly into two groups based on their age and their role in the group. The older, more seasoned members are more business oriented and anxious to obtain financial gain; they tend to be the leaders, being in their late 20s or early 30s. These older members tend to increase the integration of the gang into society. The younger, newer gang members are more concerned with establishing a role and an image for themselves within the group. For this reason, as well as others, they are often the most likely to be called upon to perform acts of violence. These more macho members are most likely to be involved in spontaneous, unorganized street violence between gangs. In general, the younger members are the most dangerous to the general public.

Using the newer members for serious acts of violence serves more than one purpose. One is cementing them to the group; once they start shooting people or committing other violent acts, they often feel that they have crossed a point of no return. As accomplices or perpetrators of a crime, they have great difficulty leaving the group, being open not only to prosecution by law enforcement but also blackmail by other gang members in the event of a rift. Having committed acts that are seen as immoral outside the gang but highly acceptable or respectable within it, a young member is likely to develop a firmer commitment to gang life and the values of the Chinese criminal subculture, or jiang hu. Also, using new members for dangerous jobs shields the older, more experienced gang members from both the legal and physical risks. This allows the gang to maintain a seasoned core of the cooler headed, more business-oriented, older members, while "using up" the more plentiful, younger ones.

The majority of the crimes committed by Chinese gangs are characterized more by a willingness to assume risks and intimidate witnesses and victims than by particularly high expertise. For example, in the typical Chinese gang shoot-out, many bullets are fired with very few hitting their targets. Extortion of a restaurateur does not require the same level of skill as, say, international diamond thievery.

The young members are generally more willing to take great risks, both to obtain thrills and to prove their "manhood." It is well known that people who have already been shot at or wounded are less eager to repeat the experience than are those who have never been in such a situation. Older gang members have less desire to take risks and less to prove. Nevertheless, one should not make the naive assumption that "youth" gangs are run by youths.

COUNTRY OF ORIGIN

Although American-born Chinese youths were once quite active in gangs in many cities here, their role has diminished significantly. In fact, many, if not most, gang members are foreign-born Chinese who feel a great deal of antagonism toward American-born Chinese.

TABLE 6-3
GANG CLASSIFICATION

The levels of organization and the structure among different gangs vary widely. Unless this is recognized and understood, much of the available literature on gangs will be meaningless and often appear contradictory. Although no single system of classification is universally accepted, this is one such system and should help clarify some of the descriptions used in this text.

LEVEL 0 PREGANG	LEVEL 1 EMERGENT	LEVEL 2 CRYSTALLIZED	LEVEL 3 FORMALIZED
GROUP SIZE			
Very small	"Pack"	Multiple groups	Large—interstate
WEAPONS USE			
Fists, clubs, rocks, etc.	Knives, improvised weapons	Stolen small arms handguns, etc.	Military arms, shoulder arms, etc.
CRIMINAL JUSTICE IMPACT			
Not labeled as a gang	Recognized as a gang or group by police/community	Social institutions and media label group as gang	Members often in correctional system and on probation
MEETING RESOURCES			
Typically meet only on street corners or in hangouts	Typically meet as a group as "squatters" at host site	Group may have pooled its resources to rent a site	Gang or a member may own real estate or property used for public meetings
LEADERSHIP FORMS			
Unstable and shifting	Charismatic	Tiered and shared to some degree	Stable—usually an older, experienced adult member
CODE OF CONDUCT			
Situational loyalty	Developed by oral tradition	Usually enforced by disciplinarian	May have written constitution/by-laws

LEVEL O PREGANG	LEVEL 1 EMERGENT	LEVEL 2 CRYSTALLIZED	LEVEL 3 FORMALIZED
INCOME SOURCES			
Personal only	Limited	Specialized	Diversified
CRIME INVOLVEMENT			
None	Passive	Proactive	Organized
LEADERSHIP INSULATION			
Does not apply	Usually visible	Somewhat shielded	Very insulated and buffered
INTERNAL ORGANIZATION			
Ad hoc, no role structure loosely knit	Usually a two-level hierarchy— leaders and followers	Usually has multiple levels, including a middle manage- ment structure	Very centralized hierarchy which may extend across jurisdictions
MEMBERSHIP COMMITMENT			
Adjustable	Low (can quit fairly easily)	Medium	High (cannot quit easily; often members for life)

Source: *An Introduction to Gangs,* by George W. Knox (Bérrien Springs, MI: Vande Vere Publishing Ltd., 1991).

Gangs tend to have similar origins and speak a particular dialect. For example, the Ghost Shadows and the White and Black Dragons are mostly from Hong Kong and speak Cantonese. The Fuk Ching are almost exclusively Chinese from Fukien province and speak the Fukienese dialect. The members of the United Bamboo are almost all from Taiwan and speak mostly Mandarin (or possibly Taiwanese). The members of the Tung On group are traditionally Hakka Chinese, primarily from Hong Kong and China, and Hakka is their dialect.

Recall that many ethnic Chinese who immigrate to North

America come from other nations throughout Southeast Asia. The United Bamboo, for example, has been known to recruit overseas Chinese from Thailand. Although there are separate and distinctly different Vietnamese gangs in North America, a surprisingly large percentage of Chinese gang members are overseas Chinese of Vietnamese origin. There are several reasons for this. First, the Chinese in Vietnam were largely of Cantonese stock, and therefore many speak the same dialect as the members of the leading Chinese gangs. Second, Vietnam is a nation that has been rocked by a series of wars and conflicts, the last one, with Cambodia, ending in the late 1980s.

Many Vietnamese, including the Vietnamese-Chinese, were hardened and made ruthless by war. Of those who lost their livelihoods or wound up on the wrong side, many landed in refugee camps in Hong Kong, Thailand, or elsewhere. Life in the refugee camps was itself harsh, competitive, and unpleasant. These are some of the reasons that there are many Vietnamese and Vietnamese-Chinese refugees throughout the world who have little education or legitimate job skills; have a great deal of experience living under harsh and violent conditions; are ruthless, violent, and quick to anger; and have little optimism about their futures; and are willing to take great risks for little gain.

A few Chinese gangs have Korean members. Although the Korean and Chinese cultures are distinctly different in certain aspects, they also share much in the way of moral and cultural background. Although many Chinese find Koreans overemotional and quick to anger, the two cultures share views on what is proper or normal behavior and thus can understand one another easily. It is not at all uncommon to find strong friendships between Chinese and Koreans in North America. In Queens in New York City, there is a mixed Taiwanese and Korean neighborhood. There, the Queens-based White Tigers and Green Dragons have inducted some Koreans into their otherwise exclusively Chinese gangs.

So far, there is no evidence that any Chinese gangs have inducted members of non-Asian origin.

The following tongs have the following gang affiliations. Please note the inclusion of the Fukien American Association, which is not a traditional-style tong but a newer organization founded after World War II. Many would not even consider it a tong because of its much later origin. Also, some say its ties with the Fuk Ching gang are not as strong as the ties between the older tongs and their gangs.

TABLE 6-4

TONG	AFFILIATED GANG
On Leong	Ghost Shadows
Hip Sing	Flying Dragons/Wah Ching
Hop Sing	Hop Sing Boys
Tung On	Tung On Boys
Fukien American Association	Fuk Ching

NOTE: At least one of the major tongs, the Chi Kung Tong (aka Chinese Freemasons), has no affiliated gang.

T he weapons Chinese secret societies use are, naturally, quite different from those of past centuries. Nevertheless, the old weapons still hold some interest due to their prominence in tradition and ritual.

Many scholars believe that today's secret society members are, at least in their own minds, members of the jiang hu subculture and, as such, the spiritual descendants of the wandering knights who roamed China righting wrongs, helping the oppressed, and getting into fights at the drop of a hat. They carried swords, spears, bows and arrows, and shields; wore armor; and usually rode horses—just as depicted in *The Romance of the Three Kingdoms* or *The Outlaws of the Marsh* that popularized the institutions of the wandering outlaw knight and sworn brotherhoods.

Today these weapons—particularly various kinds of swords and spears—figure quite prominently in various styles of the Chinese martial arts. In Taiwan, where gun laws are strict, many law-abiding people keep a sword around their house for home defense. Furthermore, many of them practice various styles of t'ai chi ch'uan or kung fu for exercise. As these styles use both open-handed and sword exercises, many of these people actually have training in swordsmanship. Nevertheless, swords are hardly ever used in criminal activities, because in Taiwan, the criminals—and only the criminals—seem to be able to obtain handguns quite easily.[1]

The staff is another weapon frequently featured in martial arts classes. Among its advantages as a weapon are

CHAPTER 7

WEAPONS AND STRATEGIES OF SECRET SOCIETIES AND GANGS

its low cost and easy availability. Furthermore, it is legal virtually everywhere to carry and own a long pole, as long as it is not actually used as a weapon. Its disadvantages are its conspicuousness and its unwieldiness inside a building or other enclosed space. Nevertheless, in the 1970s, when the Kuomintang clashed with Taiwanese demonstrators outside of its San Francisco headquarters, large numbers of Kuomintang supporters attacked the demonstrators with long bamboo poles brought just for this purpose. Bamboo poles can also be sharpened at one end and turned into spears; Hong Kong kung fu/gangster movies occasionally feature the use of such spears in conflicts. Unlike many plot elements of such movies, this happens in real life as well.

Most of the curious-looking weapons that Americans associate with the martial arts are Okinawan, not Chinese, in origin and were originally farming implements. In the 17th century, when brutal Japanese conquerors outlawed the ownership of all weapons by the common people of Okinawa, these tools were used for fighting. For example, the *kama* was a small scythe for cutting grain and other plants; the nunchaku was separating edible grain from hard chaff. The *tonfa*, which resembles a club with a handle, was actually a handle to turn a grinding stone. The martial uses of these tools were incorporated into the Okinawan forms of karate and eventually came to be known among martial artists everywhere.[2] When Bruce Lee began to use such weapons in his movies, his fans began trying them out as well. Today throughout Asia, many associate the nunchaku with Chinese kung fu, although this is inaccurate.

As the nunchaku became popular, police became apprehensive. Although most Bruce Lee fans and/or martial artists are, of course, law-abiding, peaceful people, law enforcement became concerned when these weapons, particularly the nunchaku, were used in crimes and to commit acts of violence. Soon a wide variety of state and local laws were passed that banned the sale or possession of nunchaku in many locations, including Hong Kong, and in most of the more densely populated states of the United States. In my often repressive home state of New York, it is a felony to own a set of nunchaku under any circumstances, and there is no provision for its ownership by legitimate martial artists. Of course, it is impossible to effectively prohibit the ownership of two sticks connected by a piece of flexible material. Such weapons are easily constructed from scratch and are occasionally sold in kit form or in pieces, sold under the table, or simply brought in from states where they are legal.

Although in China the common people continued to use swords, spears, shields, and farming implements as weapons until surprisingly late in their history, outside China there were adaptations to conditions.

In Herbert Asbury's fascinating description of a tong "soldier" in San Francisco's "Barbary Coast" of the late 19th century, he describes these men as follows: " . . . their queues wrapped around their heads, black slouch caps drawn down over their eyes, and their blouses bulged with hatchets, knives, and clubs" (Asbury 1933, 188). Others carried revolvers. In New York City's tong wars, members reportedly even used dynamite in attempts to blow up each other's buildings. Some tong leaders are described as having worn "chain mail" imported from China under their coats and sometimes a thin sheet of metal inside their hats to protect their heads. Most such tong leaders had a variety of bodyguards—usually "hatchetmen" from the tongs, but white gunfighters were occasionally hired as bodyguards as well.

Today, the use of traditional weapons is still stressed in some tongs but mostly as part of the Chinese martial arts traditions, not for any pragmatic reason. As can be seen from the excerpt on page 128, in the full, traditional initiation ceremony of the triad societies (rarely practiced today), the initiate is pledged to study the use of a variety of weapons and implements of warfare. They are all traditional in nature, and the majority of them are rarely used today.

Martial Arts

There is a long-standing history of ties between the martial arts, Chinese crime, gangs, and the jiang hu subculture. As noted in the last chapter, many of the Chinese gangs in North America

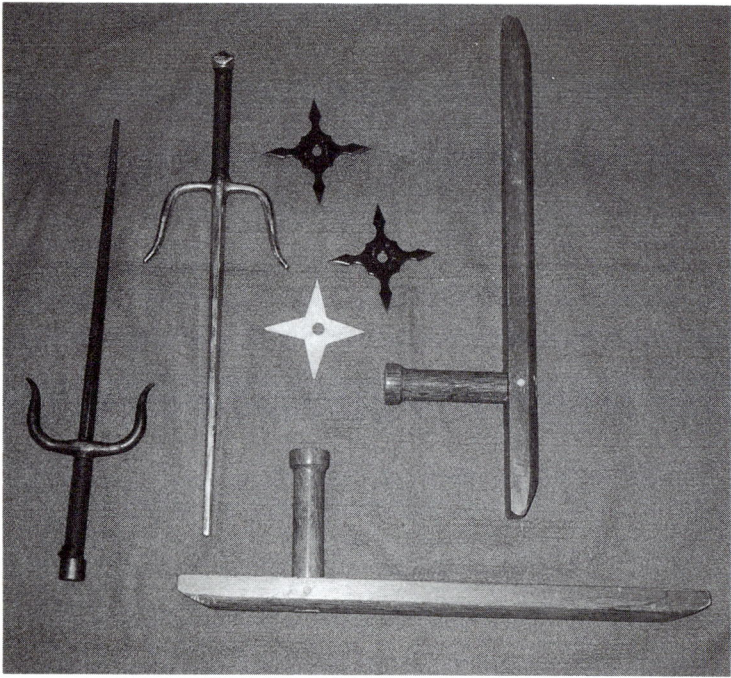

Miscellaneous martial arts weapons: sai, tonfa, and shuriken.

have either grown out of tong-organized martial arts youth clubs or else masqueraded or labeled themselves as martial arts clubs at some point in their development. Other times, martial arts practice has been an activity that has tied together the members of a Chinese gang.

The martial arts are, by definition, an activity that involves practicing the techniques of violence. Yet, seemingly paradoxically, a martial art is not necessarily a violent activity. The martial arts, and Chinese kung fu in particular, comprise a wide spectrum of different styles, all of which differ from one another in some way. Some are designed to be taught and practiced as a system of hand-to-hand combat or self-defense, and others are intended to be practiced as a sport similar to kick boxing. T'ai chi ch'uan is a particular style of kung fu that is famous for its slow-motion exercises and graceful movements. Although some t'ai chi experts claim that the style is quite

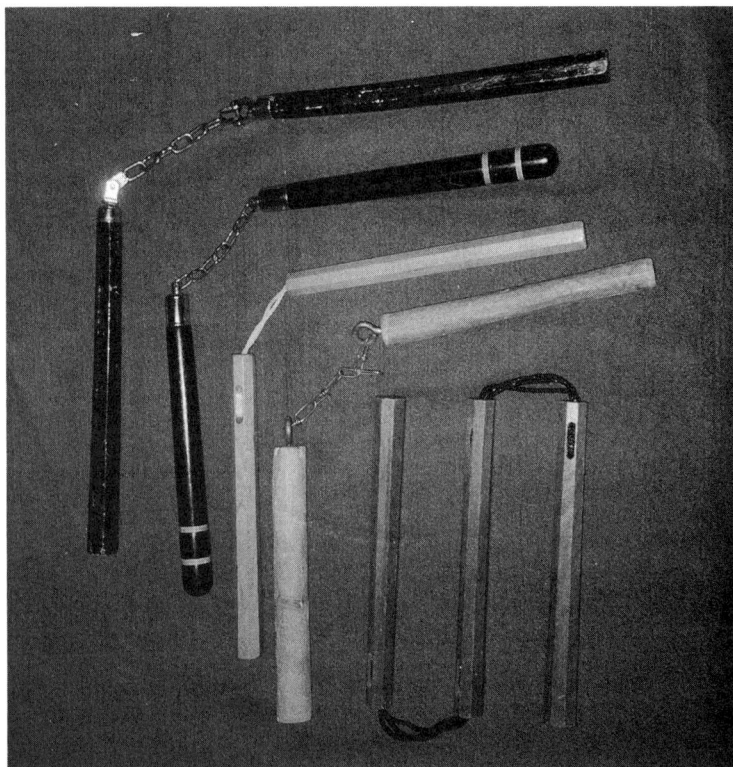

The nunchaku has been banned in many places.

useful for self-defense, others who study it deny this or simply show no interest in this aspect of it. The latter prefer to see it as, like yoga, a series of flowing, leisurely exercises that keep the mind and body limber and working in harmony. Another art, wushu, is useful for fighting, but at its highest levels (as demonstrated by the People's Republic of China's national wushu team), it is practiced more for its value as an awe-inspiring and highly acrobatic performing art.

The martial arts have a well-deserved reputation in some circles as a character-building exercise; sometimes, however, if approached from the wrong angle by an instructor who glorifies violence and encourages aggressive tendencies among his students, they can easily become harmful.

WEAPONS OF MODERN-DAY
CHINESE SECRET SOCIETIES AND GANGS

Modern Chinese gangs are decidedly practical when it comes to choosing weaponry. They generally use the best they can obtain based on their finances and the legal obstacles in their regions. In virtually all Asian nations today, there are strict weapons laws in effect. Furthermore, in some places, such as Taiwan, one of the easiest ways to get the attention of the local police is to deal in or possess weapons. In such places, it often seems, the local police really don't care what you do, so long as you do not possess a firearm (thus putting them in danger).

In their home countries, many of the loosely organized, younger Asian gangs (the "emergent" gangs) essentially carry improvised melee weaponry. Knives of all sorts and sharpened files and screwdrivers are common among such groups in urban areas, where concealment is important.

In Taiwan and Hong Kong, the weaponry often includes machetes (used for sugar cane harvesting in Taiwan) or homemade machete-like choppers. These are often crudely made affairs less than a foot long, although they can be much longer. In their least expensive version, the choppers are made from a single piece of metal with a handle formed by bending or hand-working the end of a sheet and then wrapping it a few times with a suitable material. One edge of the blade is sharpened by either machine or hand file. Sometimes, manufactured knives are used instead of homemade cleavers.[3]

Reports indicate that many gang members are highly skilled in the use of such weaponry. Some practice with them constantly and claim the ability to attack an enemy and "merely" slice a tendon in his arms, leaving him alive but unable to use his arms. He then serves as a living and crippled example of what happens when one crosses the gang that attacked him.

Of the traditional kung fu weapons, the fighting chain is the one that has remained prominent. A fighting chain, also known as a whip sword or a chain knife, is series of connected metal rods, links of chain, or a mix of the two. Its length can vary considerably, but between three and six feet or more is probably most common. At one end of the chain is a handle that is gripped with one hand; at the other end is a heavy knife blade that is dangerous when swung, both for its weight and its sharpness. Like many martial arts weapons, the fighting chain is designed to be flashy and is often twirled in elaborate patterns as it flies around the wielder's body. Also like many such weapons, in the hands of an unskilled user, it is probably more dangerous to the person holding and swinging it than to those he is trying to fight.

Cruder weapons, such as metal rods, pipes, and iron bars are undoubtedly used much more often than fighting chains in gang clashes. Such weapons are not only easy and effective to use in an enclosed urban environment, they are also simple to acquire and conceal. Unlike with a beautiful fighting chain, a criminal generally feels no remorse in disposing of a simple piece of metal in order to conceal the evidence of a criminal assault.

Many people associate the *balisong* knife with Asian gangs. This flashy weapon is featured prominently in *Year of the Dragon*, the controversial motion picture about Asian crime groups in New York City. A balisong knife is a quick-opening folding knife with two free-swinging handles. The person wielding it will grab and hold it by one handle, allowing the blade and the other handle to swing freely. A well-practiced flick of the wrist causes the two handles to swing together, forming, in effect, a single handle that can be gripped. An experienced user can do this in less time than it takes to pop open a switchblade automatically. The balisong knife has a sizable following among martial artists and others who enjoy flashy weapons. A well-practiced user does not simply flick open the weapon. Instead, he also gives it a twirl or twist, followed by a quick opening and shutting maneuver, resulting in some very flashy moves. The idea is to intimidate an opponent before you actually get anywhere near him with the sharp blade.

Unfortunately, the weapon also seems to have intimidated most of the governments in places where it developed a following. In Hong Kong, Taiwan, and China, it is now against the law to sell balisong knives. In North America, many state and local governments, including those of California and New

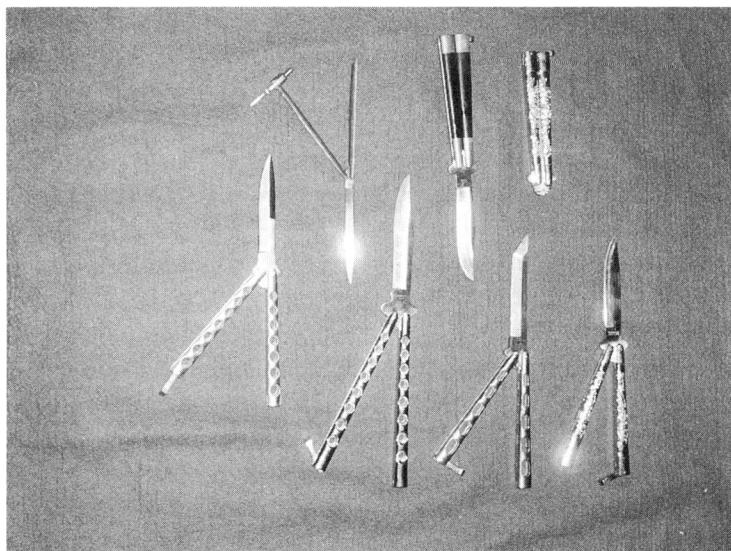

The balisong knife.

York, have also prohibited possession of the balisong. Prior to this balisongs were fairly easy to buy in New York City's Chinatown. The United States has banned the balisong's importation, and few in this country make one of suitable size to be used as a practical weapon.

Throughout the world, firearms are the weapon of choice among those likely to find themselves in the midst of a serious conflict, and Chinese criminal groups are no exception. In parts of Burma, and at times in isolated sections of China's Yunnan province, Laos, or northern Thailand, these groups have literally been small, covertly funded and equipped armies run by the various warlords and former Kuomintang military officers. These armies were often equipped with the assistance or facilitation of CIA, the government of Taiwan, the government of Burma, or other influential outside groups.[4] Some have full military arsenals with automatic weapons, grenades, and other heavy weapons, including .50-caliber machine guns, 75 mm recoilless rifles, and sometimes even hand-held antiaircraft missiles. They often purchase such weapons and supplies on the black market with profits from the opium trade. In other cases, they use what they have captured from the Burmese armed forces who periodically attack them. For this reason, these armies tend to use a hodge-podge of rifles, including Vietnam- and modern-era M16 rifles and M1 carbines, Chinese-made AK-47s, and Burmese-made copies of the German G-3 rifle (also known as the HK 91). Although M1 carbines seem to be particularly common, everything, including British-made Lee Enfield bolt-action rifles and carbines, has been known to be used.

Naturally, these military and paramilitary armies of the opium warlords are, for all intents and purposes, the acting governments in the areas they control. Few governments will tolerate the existence of such a well-equipped force within their borders if there is any way to prevent it.

In fact, Taiwan and Hong Kong, have very strict laws regulating the possession of firearms by private citizens. The police in these territories do everything they can to track down and stop the flow of illegal arms. The Royal Hong Kong Police keep track of all incidents involving firearms or "pistol-like objects." Prior to 1988, a wide variety firearms had been smuggled into the country from various sources. Then there was a significant change. The predominant firearm in Hong Kong became the T-54 handgun, the standard military-issue firearm of the People's Republic of China. There are several possible reasons for this.

One is increased unrest and corruption in China, which leads to the theft of government firearms by means ranging from the quiet theft of warehouses to the armed robbery and holdup of transport trains by bandits. In Guangzhou, (also known as Canton), the Chinese province bordering on Hong Kong, Macao, and the southern coast, there have been reports of frequent government crackdowns on crime.

Another reason is the higher prices the weapons fetch in areas where incomes are higher and pistols are scarcer. Also, there is a great deal of illegal immigration into both Hong Kong and Taiwan, where the standard of living and wages are higher than in the People's Republic of China. These illegal aliens often bring along some valuable contraband, including not only pistols but also opium and heroin, that they can make a profit on.

Another reason Chinese weapons are smuggled in may be the

activities of criminal organizations such as the Big Circle gang. Frequently when these groups enter Hong Kong, engage in a series of armed robberies, and then sneak back out and return to the People's Republic of China, they bring their own firearms from China rather than attempting to purchase or steal them in Hong Kong.

Excerpt from the Triad Society Initiation Ritual

Incense Master: *As a vanguard are you versed in civil and military matters?*
Vanguard: I am wel l versed in both.
Incense Master: *Where did you learn these things?*
Vanguard: Incense Master: *What classical books did you study at the [Red] Flower Pavilion?*
Vanguard: *The books of Hung Man Cheung.*
Hung children study Man Cheung's poems.
On the15th of the first moon the school is opened.
"Hung waters flood everywhere" is the first line in the book.
Hung brothers declare their aims in the imperial palace.
Incense Master: *Name the 18 kinds of military arts you learned at Shao Lin.*
Vanguard: *First I learned the use of the rattan shield.*
Second the use of metal darts.
Third the use of the trident.
Fourth the use of the metal rod.
Fifth the use of the spear.
Sixth the use of the wooden staff.
Seventh the use of the sword.
Eighth the use of the halberd.
Ninth the use of the fighting chain.
Tenth the use of the iron mace.
Eleventh the use of the walking stick.
Twelfth the use of the caltrops.
Thirteenth the use of the golden barrier.*
Fourteenth the use of the double sword.
Fifteenth the use of the duck-billed spear.
Sixteenth the use of the tsoi yeung sword.
Seventeenth the use of the bow and arrow.
Eighteenth the use of the lance.

Incense Master: *Prove what you say.*

Vanguard: *Tactics taught at Shao Lin were a military art. The old traditional teaching remains the same.*

Learn all 18 types of tactics.

In order to protect our lord with sincere heart.

Incense Master: *Your report is indeed correct. I now appoint you to be a Vanguard. If mountains bar your way you should build roads over them. If rivers bar your way you should bring bridges over them.*

Vanguard: *I obey.*

* Unfortunately, neither the Hong Kong Police nor I have any idea what is meant by "the golden barrier." No further details of this weapon (or shield?) are available.

Source: *Triad Societies in Hong Kong*, by W.P. Morgan (Hong Kong: The Government, 1960).

THIRTY-SIX STRATEGIES TAUGHT AND USED BY CHINESE SECRET SOCIETIES

---

1. ***Cross the Sea without Heaven's Knowledge.***   *E.O.S*

   This strategy basically teaches that although it is difficult to hide your actions from those who might be watching, it is often possible to hide or disguise the *purpose* of those actions. By so doing, you can surprise an enemy quite easily.

2. ***Besiege Wei to Rescue Zhao.***

   This strategy teaches that if an enemy is attacking a friend, then one way to rescue the friend is to attack the enemy's home base. By doing this, the enemy is forced to return home to defend his property. Your friend is then left unattacked.

3. ***Murder with Borrowed Knife.***

   This strategy teaches that one way to harm an enemy is to induce a third party to attack him. By convincing an ally to attack the enemy, you conserve your strength and avoid the consequences if the attack is unsuccessful or costly.

4. ***Wait Leisurely for an Exhausted Enemy.***

   This strategy teaches that if you wait for an enemy to attack instead of attacking him first, then often his forces will become tired and exhausted by the act of traveling or laying siege to your home base. Also, although he will have the initiative, you will be able to choose the site of the conflict so that conditions suit you.

5. ***Loot a Burning House.***

   This strategy teaches that if you attack an enemy while he is preoccupied with a crisis of his own, the better your chances of success in the conflict.

6. *Make Noise in the East and Attack in the West.*
This teaches that you often stand a better chance of success by misleading your enemy. If you make it seem that you are attacking from one direction but actually attack from another, the enemy will often be surprised and easily defeated. The strategy further teaches that a wise enemy will be wary of such tricks and not easily deceived.

7. *Create Something Out of Nothing.*
This strategy elaborates on the uses of deception in warfare. As every competent strategician knows, a ruse is a movement or action designed to deceive an enemy. Of course, if the opponent is competent as well then he expects you to try such deceptions. This strategy teaches that, despite this, you can attain success in unexpected ways by using such obviously false attacks and movements. If it becomes obvious that the enemy has dismissed an action as an obvious false movement, then a skilled leader can turn it into a genuine movement or attack, thus taking an enemy by surprise.

8. *Advance Secretly by Way of Chencang.*
This strategy teaches that in order to make a surprise attack successful, it is often helpful to make it look as if you will be attacking in a different, usually more expected way. In a military situation, this could be done by stockpiling boats and/or other vehicles in a place where the attack is expected to come from while actually planning to attack from another direction.

9. *Match a Fire from Across the River.*
This teaches that if your enemies are fighting, often it is best to simply wait and bide your time while judging the best time and method of attack. You should let your enemies fight among themselves and do nothing to interfere.

10. *Hide a Dagger in a Smile.*
The teachings of this strategy are pretty obvious from the name. If you pretend to seek peace, it will often give you a special opportunity to discover the weaknesses and divisions among the enemy's forces. In this way, you can defeat them more easily.

11. *Sacrifice a Plum to Save a Peach.*
This strategy teaches that a leader should be prepared to strategically sacrifice a small part of his force if such an action will ensure victory.

12. *Lead Away a Goat in Passing.*
This strategy teaches that, while engaged in a conflict, you should be prepared to take advantage of the slightest weakness of an enemy or an opportunity to inflict even a small defeat. Through such small victories, you can often obtain the advantages needed to utterly defeat an enemy.

13. *Beat the Grass to Frighten the Snake.*
This teaches that it is good to make a move or attack, even a small and seemingly unimportant one, in order to observe the reactions of your enemy or opponent. By doing so, you may learn about hidden strengths or weaknesses of your enemies.

Tongs, Gangs, and Triads:
Chinese Crime Groups in North America

14. *Find Reincarnation in Another's Corpse.*
    This strategy has a double meaning, the general and the specific. The general one is that you should strive to find uses for things considered to be useless and to employ them if it will help obtain success or victory. The specific meaning is that in the constant uprisings and civil wars that characterized traditional China, it was often difficult to obtain a following and to establish a reputation that your cause was just. Often the simplest way to do this was to claim to be the long-lost descendant of a famous personality. If this was not possible, you could often find a small child or infant who would be assigned the role. For example, when Ming loyalists were trying to overthrow the Ching dynasty, such uprisings would often involve the "discovery," seemingly from nowhere, of a long-lost heir to the Ming throne. This would give the uprising an immediate sense of legitimacy among those who wished to see the Ming dynasty restored. If it was impractical or undesirable to claim descent from an heir to the throne, then a rebel could take on the role of the justice-seeking descendant of some famous person who had been greatly wronged by the current dynasty. One interesting modern reinterpretation of this strategy is to simply take on the role and identity of a deceased person.

15. *Lure the Tiger Out of the Mountain.*
    This strategy teaches that if the enemy is holed up inside a stronghold, you can obtain an advantage by finding a means to lure him out. If he leaves a well-defended base, then you can defeat him more easily.

16. *Leave at Large, the Better to Capture.*
    Although it is usually important to win a battle quickly, this strategy teaches that sometimes it is best to wait. In these cases, a delay will cause the enemy to become nervous or to think about escaping rather than fighting to the death. For example, if your enemy is trapped in a stronghold where you could defeat them but only at great cost, sometimes it is best to let them escape so that you can defeat them later and more easily.

17. *Cast a Brick to Attract Jade.*
    This strategy teaches the importance of utilizing unimportant knowledge or forces as bait to attract larger or more important prizes. A small body of men can sometimes be sufficient bait to lure out an enemy.

18. *To Catch Bandits, First Catch the Ringleader.*
    This teaches that, often, in order to defeat an enemy it is merely necessary to defeat the leader. In many cases, with the leader gone, the enemy forces will crumble and disperse.

19. *Remove Firewood from Under the Cauldron.*
    This strategy teaches that in order to defeat a strong enemy, you should often undermine his sources of strength and power rather than attack him directly. By weakening him before attacking, you have a better chance of accomplishing your goals.

20. *Muddy the Water to Seize the Fish.*
This strategy teaches that you should find a way to confuse the enemy and put his forces in disorder to more easily obtain victory.

21. *The Cicada Sloughs Its Skin.*
This strategy teaches that you should use retreat as a surprise action. While appearing to be inactive, you should secretly make preparations for a retreat or other action.

22. *Bolt the Door to Seize the Thief.*
This strategy has two closely related teachings. The first is that in order to defeat a small mobile force, you must surround and capture it, cutting off the means of escape. Second, it teaches that on occasion it is beneficial to create an ambush site with attractive bait (i.e., the "house" whose door gets bolted) in order to more easily capture the enemy.

23. *Befriend Distant States While Attacking Nearby States.*
This strategy is more or less self-explanatory. It teaches that in order to defeat your enemies you should fight them one by one, starting with those most easily available. While doing so, you should take steps to ensure that you remain on good terms with potential enemies far away so that you do not find yourself overwhelmed.

24. *Attack Hu by Borrowed Path.*
This strategy is intended for a situation where there are two large powers with a smaller power stuck in the middle. If one of the larger powers threatens the smaller power, the other large power may easily conquer and gain control of the small state while pretending to come to its aid. This is, of course, how the Soviet Union captured the nations of Latvia, Lithuania, and Estonia during World War II. It seems the Chinese thought of this tactic long before Stalin ever did.

25. *Steal the Beams and Change the Pillars.*
This strategy teaches that you can obtain success by attacking the key points of an enemy's force with select troops.

26. *Point at the Mulberry and Abuse the Locust.*
This teaches that one way to attack, subdue, or intimidate a powerful enemy or group of enemies is indirectly. For example, although it might not be possible to defeat a large group of enemies, by choosing the most powerful one and defeating him, you might be able to intimidate the entire group. Similarly, if you wish to embarrass a very important person, you might criticize his subordinates' action in order to make him look bad.

27. *Feign Folly Instead of Madness.*
This strategy stresses the importance of hiding the purpose of your actions from enemies so that they will be unable to respond accordingly. There are various ways to do this. One is to behave in a manner designed to imitate the actions of an insane person and make meaningless actions. A weakness of such a plan, though,

is that it is often quite difficult to act insane without giving away some of the purpose of your actions. A preferable method is to simply behave like a fool and do nothing whenever possible. Similarly, your subordinates and troops should not be told the purpose of your actions except when absolutely necessary.

28. *Climb Up the Roof and Remove the Ladder.*

This strategy deals with cutting off troops' means of retreat. It has a double meaning. One is that if you are ambushing the enemy, then it is often desirable to cut off their means of retreat if you wish to destroy them completely. A second variation on this theme, like many Chinese strategies, deals with manipulating the morale of your own troops. If you wish for your own troops to fight with the fury of desperate and trapped men, then cut off their means of retreat. This way they will realize that their only chance of survival lies in victory over their foes. A historical example of this sort of thinking is when the Spanish conquistador Cortez conquered the entire Aztec empire with a small force of men, having first burned his own ships, thereby placing all his troops in a situation where they were forced to choose between victory or death.

29. *Flowers Bloom in the Tree.*

This strategy teaches that you should try to use natural forces and conditions to your advantage. Plan your strategy so that your attacks will be in harmony with natural forces. This will make your forces appear more powerful. It also teaches that at times you may be able to change the conditions of nature to obtain benefit. For example, you could redirect a river or stream or direct water onto a cold field to create icy ground.

30. *Reverse the Positions of Host and Guest.*

This too has a double meaning. The first simply teaches the importance of being prepared to reverse the positions of the defender and the attacker. It teaches that one of the worst situations a commander can find himself in is under siege and surrounded, defending in the middle of enemy territory. The "guest" (the invader) is now the "host" (the defender). A more complicated meaning, though, is that if you are called upon to assist an ally that is very weak, then sometimes the best thing is to subvert its leadership and gain control of its forces.

31. *Beauty Trap.*

This strategy teaches that you can manipulate and undermine the enemy's ability to lead and the morale of his troops by sending agents into his territory. Male agents could be sent to cause unrest and promote dissatisfaction. More subtly, you could send a particularly beautiful concubine or perhaps an entire troop of dancing women to the enemy's general, leader, or troops. The job of such women is not to serve as spies and obtain information, but rather to be so alluring, charming, and seductive that the enemy leader will become distracted and negligent in his duties.

32. *Empty-City Scheme.*

So far, the strategies taught have emphasized the importance of using deception and false appearances in order to confuse an enemy. Of course, a skilled commander will expect such things. Therefore, this strategy hinges on this expectation. In desperate situations, when your forces and defenses are weak and the enemy has overwhelming superiority, sometimes the best thing to do is to simply show him how completely superior his forces are to yours. Since under normal circumstances this would be a completely stupid thing to do, it is quite possible that the enemy will suspect that it is part of a trap or scheme to ambush him.

33. *Turn the Enemy's Agents against Him.*

This teaches that if you uncover an enemy spy or information about a secret enemy plan, you should be prepared to pretend that you know nothing. On the other hand, it might be best to feed the enemy spy false information, fool the enemy leader, and then work to take advantage of the situation.

34. *Self-Torture Scheme.*

This strategy has both a specific and a general meaning. Specifically, it teaches that you may gain the trust of your enemy by inflicting wounds or punishment on yourself or your agent, spy, or assassin. In a more general sense, it teaches that you should be prepared to sacrifice a portion of your forces if it will lead to victory. Another example is that if you wish to make an enemy think he is safe from a surprise attack from your forces, you may publicly punish those among your forces who advocate such an attack. When the enemy takes this as a sign that you do not wish to attack him and relaxes his defenses accordingly, then it is a good time to launch an ambush.

35. *Interlaced Stratagems.*

This strategy teaches that often it is best to use two or more different ruses or strategies in combination in order to succeed. Often it is best to use one strategy to reduce the enemy's mobility and then follow up quickly with another strategy designed to reduce his strength.

36. *Running Away as the Best Choice.*

In essence, this strategy teaches that "he who fights and then runs away lives to fight another day." A good leader chooses the time and place of battle and fights only when it is in his best interests.

NOTES

1. In Japan today, however, the yakuza gangsters do actually use swords in the commission of crimes. Samurai swords are the traditional weapons, although their actual use is declining.
2. There may be an exception to this. The sai, a small trident held with one hand, was probably developed specifically as a weapon. Although some claim it was used to poke holes in the mud to plant seeds, this strikes me as unlikely, since a long, pointed stick would probably work better for the same purpose.
3. In Chinese culture, knives and cleavers both often have long rectangular blades, no

point, and one sharp edge. The difference is that knives are used for slicing while cleavers are used for chopping.

4. For years, the CIA supported the Kuomintang's dreams of eventually invading China and toppling its government. For this reason, it supported the establishment of well-equipped Kuomintang armies in northern Burma near the Chinese border. It also helped arm, train, and equip such armies and turned a blind eye when these groups dealt in opium to obtain necessary operating funds. Although on a few occasions these armies actually did invade Yunnan province and China, they never got any farther than a few miles inward before being driven out with heavy losses.

Naturally, there is a great deal of variation, modification, and innovation in crime committed by different groups. Some of the crimes and crime techniques that are unique to or characteristic of Chinese or Asian gangs in North America will be discussed here.

It will become apparent that Chinese and Vietnamese gangs have much in common. Although there are important differences in the gangs themselves, they frequently commit crimes in similar ways. Not only do Vietnamese gangs frequently behave in a fashion similar to Chinese gangs, Chinese organized crime groups frequently use Vietnamese gangs for their own purposes. For this reason, some information on the behavior of Vietnamese gangs is included in this chapter. The relationship, and Vietnamese gang structure in general, will be described in detail in another chapter.

EXTORTION

One of the most common crimes among Chinese gangs, particularly the Chinese youth gangs, is extortion or "protection." Because most Chinese not only tend to have a rather fatalistic attitude toward crime groups, but dislike trouble and disorder as well, if a crime group such as a youth gang demands payment, they often accept this as just another unpleasant but inevitable cost of doing business. Many Chinese feel that taking steps—such as vigilantism or agitating for increased police action—to remove the threat, would only be a temporary measure. If one group of extortionists is stopped, then inevitably, a second group will come

CHAPTER 8

COMMON CHINESE ORGANIZED CRIME ACTIVITIES

Stores and restaurants in Chinatown are frequent targets of extortion by members of Chinese youth gangs.

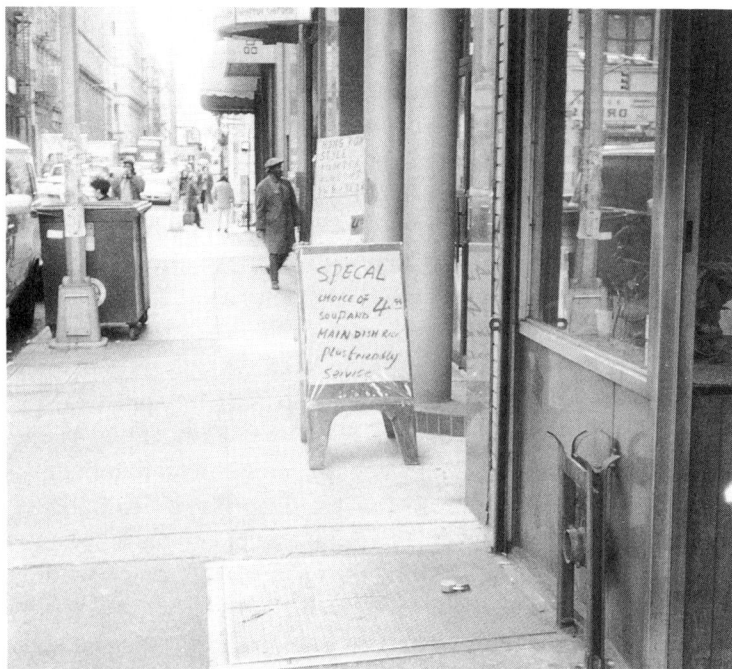

along, and a businessman will find himself right back where he started. In the meantime, according to conventional wisdom, he will have wasted a great deal of time and effort that could be devoted to more profitable activities, such as working and managing the business. Furthermore, such agitation, particularly against Chinese criminals, makes the community look bad and causes a great deal of disharmony. Often it seems easier to pay one group of extortionists and hope that they, in turn, will protect one's business from extortion by their rivals.

Although this attitude might be distasteful to many people, there may be some wisdom in it. In traditional China, the common people had to make many arbitrary payments under threat of violence to a variety of officials or face devastating consequences. Corrupt officials might, for instance, take advantage of their position to request extra "taxes" from the lower classes. This was particularly common during the 1920s and 1930s, when the feuding warlords seemed to constantly request "just one more" special tax in order to build up their armies before the next of their constant conflicts with their many rivals. Greedy landlords often raised the rent to outrageous levels when they thought they could get away with it. Bandits frequently demanded payments from villagers in areas where they could. In coastal areas, there was generally at least one fleet of violent pirates who would insist on payment of "tribute" from fishermen who worked in the areas under their influence.

Finally, when the early Chinese came to America in the 19th century, the rich merchants began imposing a variety of fees and "taxes" on the poorer laborers.

Aside from history and tradition, there are cultural factors at work as well. Most Chinese see themselves as very practical and realistic and dislike unnecessary trouble, an attitude that carries over into gang activities and other violent and potentially violent acts. As one of the axioms in *The Art of War* says, "To fight and conquer in all your battles is not supreme excellence; supreme excellence consists in breaking the enemy's resistance without fighting." With this thought in mind, one sees that there is really no advantage in robbing or mugging someone if you can merely ask them for the money and stand a reasonably good chance of receiving it.

If there is a characteristic difference between the extortion patterns of the Chinese and those of other ethnic crime groups in America, it might lie in a tendency to employ more subtle methods. In some cases, unless law enforcement personnel were familiar with Asian patterns of extortion, they might not even recognize a crime in progress for what it is.

Extortion by Asian gangs can have several goals, which can be either separate or overlapping. One is to gain profit and money for the gang members. The second is largely symbolic and is aimed more at establishing the gang's claim to its "turf" and letting local businessmen and residents know exactly who they are and that they control the territory. In such cases, the members might demand free cigarettes from shopkeepers or an occasional free or heavily discounted meal from a restaurant owner. A third goal can be revenge upon rivals for a previous action or perceived slight. The fourth is to intimidate victims into doing something they otherwise would not do or vice versa. For example, Chinese gangs commonly demand that small businessmen install illegal video games for gambling on their premises, whether they wish to or not. Although the gangs will frequently split the profits of the games with the store owner, the store owner is liable for all fines and penalties if he is caught.

Asian gangs use a variety of standardized extortion techniques. One common method is the "six tables" approach, wherein gang members enter a restaurant during a mealtime, sit down, and order food. They may enter as a group or separately, but each will sit down at a separate table. They will then enjoy their meals at an extremely leisurely pace.

To an outsider, it would be difficult to imagine that anything wrong is taking place. To the restaurant manager, however, the situation is quite bad. If six individuals monopolize six tables, this limits the other customers who can enter his establishment and sit down during peak hours. In some cases, the gang members will go out of their way to be boisterous, loud, and rowdy, further discouraging customers from coming in. They might even break dishes or cause further problems for the restaurant owner. In other cases, they will be perfectly polite and calmly enjoy their meal, but still stretch out the time and monopolize the tables. In some cases, their behavior is perfectly reasonable, except for the matter of their seating.

After the meal, the gang members will discuss the matter of their seating with the owner and make a "suggestion." If he conforms to their demands, they will all sit at the same table when they eat at his establishment and not otherwise scare his customers or interfere with his business. They might demand cash payments, but in many cases, all they demand is a free meal on rare occasions. The demand can be made in a forthright and threatening manner or politely, in an almost friendly way. For example, they might suggest that these "poor boys" are new in this country, and he, the restaurant owner, "as a fellow newcomer to America," should understand their situation and have pity on them.

Only the most naive restaurant owner will miss the threat, no matter how it is phrased. In many if not most cases, the cost of the meals will seem like a small price to pay to prevent further disruptions of his business.

Another common approach to restaurant extortion is the so-called honor guards technique, which is known to be employed by Vietnamese gangs in Texas and elsewhere, but is undoubtedly employed from time to time by Chinese gangs as well (since these ethnic gangs often have close ties and overlapping membership). Gangs post a pair of members outside each entrance of a targeted restaurant at dinner time, in order to maximize the financial damage to the target. They advise potential customers to stay away because, they claim, "some trouble is expected in here tonight." The vast majority of prospective customers will decide to go someplace else. Ultimately, the restaurant owner will come to see why his business is so slow on a particular evening, and although he can't prove that the gang members are responsible, he is quite able to put two and two together. Here too the owner will seek to negotiate a solution, particularly if the gang members are polite, as they often are. If the demands are not too exorbitant, a solution can soon be reached.

A variation on this theme is when some gang members, normally the younger and wilder ones, order meals, refuse to pay, and become argumentative and disruptive. In many cases, the restaurant owner will be unsure of what to do and become quite upset at all this trouble in his small business. At this point, a senior member, having "noticed" the trouble, arrives on the scene, appearing concerned about the owner's situation. He intervenes, chastises the youths, settles the situation, and sends the trouble-makers home, thus ending the immediate problem.

Unfortunately for the restaurant owner, soon after this incident he will be approached by a gang member who will inform him that the gang has offered to "protect" his establishment from future disruptions and problems of this sort . . . for a small fee, of course. This technique is known in Mandarin Chinese as *hei bai lian,* or "white and black faces," obviously referring to the "good" and "bad" gang member roles the extortionists take.

In future dealings, gang members will simply enter the restaurant, order food, and leave without paying, instead, simply writing the name of their gang on the back of the bill. Needless to say, they rarely, if ever, pay their "tab."

Many other common methods of extortion utilized by criminals among the Chinese community depend on Chinese customs concerning money and gift giving. For instance, it is customary at certain times of the year to give *hong-bao*. These red envelopes contain money, and they are normally exchanged on Chinese New Year and for weddings, birthdays, the birth of a boy child (girls are given clothes instead), and other special occasions. The amount of money varies according to the event, the income of the giver, and the relationship of the giver and the receiver.

Although such monetary gifts are customary only on special occasions, there really are no fixed rules. They could, in theory, be given for no other reason than that one person likes another. Thus, gang members might approach small business owners and request such a gift (or a larger one than expected) when there really is not enough of a relationship between them to warrant such an act. It is very difficult to prove legally that one individual felt intimidated into giving such a gift to another, particularly when all the threats used were implicit. (Red envelopes are also often used to transmit bribes.)

At other times, gang members sell goods to shopkeepers at inflated prices. Often, these are festival-related items, such as fireworks or plants that are normally sold to shopkeepers, not individuals. There is a Chinese holiday called Moon Cake Day, on which everyone eats a special holiday "moon cake." Gang members frequently take advantage of the holiday by forcing storekeepers and others to purchase moon cakes from them at outrageously inflated prices.

Chinese gangs solicit extortion money by requesting "loans" or "investments" in some generally nonexistent projects, or they may solicit "donations" to help one of their brothers who has been arrested. In many such cases, youth gang members will attempt to protect themselves legally from prosecution by providing their extortion victims with worthless IOUs In some cases, attempts at subtlety are forgotten, and gang members simply insist that someone give them money "or else."

Gang members extort money from shopkeepers under the guise of friendship. In such cases, gang members flatter a victim by calling him "big brother" and treating him in a highly respectful manner. If the potential victim responds favorably to this treatment and takes to his new role as "elder brother" to the group, then they will soon begin treating him slightly differently. "Surely," they will soon say, "an elder brother should provide assistance to his younger brothers." They will then suggest that an appropriate form of assistance would be monetary donations. This technique is referred to as *tai jiau tsi* (in Mandarin), or "carrying the sedan chair." (A sedan chair was a fancy chair on a platform that was used as a common method of transportation by aristocrats in traditional China. An upper-class person would ride on the chair while a number of servants carried him.)

All such extortion techniques are difficult to prove. Many Asian businessmen in North America are reluctant to report these crimes since they do not expect that much action can or will be taken. (And, sadly, they are often correct.) When they do report the crimes, it is a lengthy and difficult process and involves many court appearances. Often, the complainant's peers and neighbors will not approve of his actions, feeling that they provide no real long-term benefit to anyone and that they make the community look bad. Whether this point of view is valid is not relevant. What does matter is that extortion is theft and it increases the cost of doing business in Chinatowns across America for immigrants who are trying to make an honest living and get ahead through hard work. According to a 1990 study conducted by a New York criminal justice agency, 81 percent of the restaurants and 66 percent of the other businesses in New York City's Chinatown are victimized by gang extortion.[1] Among those who don't have to pay extortion money, many escape such demands through personal contacts among the gangs or, more commonly, tongs that have close connections with such gangs.

When business people do find the demands of youth gang extortionists unreasonable, then they often work to stop them through traditional methods outside of American or Canadian legal systems, including appeal to important institutions such as the tongs.

Even though much of the extortion is to gain free meals in restaurants and establish a permanent relationship between themselves and local citizens based on control of the "local territory," and the penalties for initial noncompliance are, usually, the loss of a day's profits or some other relatively small financial injury (such as supergluing locks shut), the gangs are tending more toward violence against those who refuse to comply with extortion.

Extortion is not confined to Chinatowns or the working class; the upper class and upper middle-class Chinese in the suburbs also face a serious problem with extortion. These attempts at extortion are more sophisticated and better planned because the targets are wealthier. In the suburbs, the efforts often involve direct threats against family members of the targeted victims. In one such case, for example, a New Jersey Chinese businessman was forced to pay $36,000 in response to threats from his own countrymen. Before acting against a target, a gang will have a member go "undercover" and obtain a job or other position at the victim's business to learn all that he can about its owner. This technique is used not just for extortion attempts, but also for robberies. In some Chinese-owned stores, this sort of problem has grown so severe that owners absolutely refuse to hire strangers.

KIDNAPPING

There is a long and unpleasant history in China of taking individuals prisoner and holding them for ransom. Among the pirates of the Chinese coasts and the bandits of the interior, such activities were a prime source of income. In *I Sailed with Chinese Pirates*, Lillius describes how pirates captured large numbers of Chinese sailors and others and imprisoned them in coastal buildings or below decks on Chinese junks until their relatives or friends could raise the large fee required for their release. Of course, not all prisoners were held as captives. As one pirate explained to Lillius, "Hens that do not lay eggs are not worth their keep," that is, those prisoners who were unable to raise a suitably large ransom were simply killed outright (Lillius 1930, 212).

In some cases, prisoners were sold as slaves. This was a particularly common fate for women, often in demand as either household servants or prostitutes. During the Taiping uprising, for instance, looting was considered to be a natural part of the reward for a victorious soldier. Among the booty following a hard day's pillaging and plundering might be young boys and girls who could be sold later for a profit.

In China in the 1920s and 30s, bandits found that kidnapping had certain advantages over other forms of theft. First of all, although loot was often difficult to sell or dispose of profitably, it could generally be assumed that the families of kidnap victims would pay to get them back. Second, if the bandit gang had to hide or run, it was often difficult to carry large amounts of valuable loot, but kidnap victims could be forced to move themselves.

Naturally, bandits preferred to kidnap the very rich, but unfortunately, there were only so many rich people to go around. So they began kidnapping those from middle class, then the working class, and, finally, the poor. Ransoms went down until, eventually, impoverished peasants were kidnapped and ransomed for nothing more than a small bag of wheat or two.

Kidnappers would frequently stake out and observe victims and their households in order to not only better plan the operation, but also to determine the maximum ransom that could be demanded. Then a gang could often make a profit by simply threatening the victim or the family with kidnapping. Here again, the population simply accepted such extortion attempts as a fact of life. (Today, the very rich in Taiwan still receive such threats periodically. Some emigrate for this very reason.)

Often, a small disorganized group of kidnappers found it more profitable to sell prisoners to another, larger group of kidnappers that could collect ransom more efficiently. This was especially true in cases involving foreigners or other important victims whose ransom and return entailed both special profits and special risks. Prisoners were normally tied together and deprived of sleep in order to reduce their chances of escape, and many were forced to act as servants for their captors.

The fate of female captives was traditionally unpleasant in male-dominated Chinese society. Women were considered inherently less valuable than men anyway, but when made captive, their value as potential brides fell. Any woman held prisoner by bandits was generally assumed to be a virgin no longer, and this caused a considerable reduction in the bride price her family would be paid if and when she married. Therefore, families were often unwilling to pay large sums for the return of unmarried daughters, and the women were often simply sold into slavery or prostitution. An entire clandestine network of groups dedicated to this practice existed in ancient China.

Even today, in both Taiwan and China, it is not uncommon to hear of women and teenage girls kidnapped and sold into prostitution. In America, the kidnapping, imprisonment, and holding for ransom of ethnic Chinese is a growing problem and, in a sense, a unique form of extortion. Criminals receive from extortion what they want by making threats. Kidnappers do the same thing, but also retain physical control of their human victims until they are satisfied with the compensation. In Asian kidnappings, the prisoners are generally seen as nothing more than a particularly interesting commodity.[2]

In some cases, kidnappings are elaborately planned and only one wealthy individual is targeted. In others, Asian burglars might enter a home intent solely on robbery but happen also upon the homeowner's children and their baby-sitter; they then tie up, abuse, assault, or kill the sitter and take the children away.

Rather than kidnap one rich person, criminals might try for profit by kidnapping a number of poor people. In bulk, poor people's ransoms can add up to quite a hefty sum. Kidnapping large numbers of people is generally avoided, however, for obvious reasons: it is difficult to hide and care for a large number of people (even prisoners must be fed and given water occasionally); also, kidnapping many people at one time (or even in sequence) attracts attention from law enforcement.

Criminals can avoid both of these problems to some extent, however, if they kidnap illegal aliens, and they frequently do. Sometimes illegal aliens are kidnapped from their places of business and their employer threatened with ransom demands. If their employers refuse to pay a ransom, their relatives can be forced to pay. In other cases, criminals kidnap large numbers of illegal aliens who have recently arrived in this country planning to land illegal jobs. In effect, they "hijack" a shipment of illegal human cargo and demand ransom from any relatives or other concerned parties. In the meantime, they put their captives to work without pay in a different sweatshop of their own choosing, until the payments are made.

In one such case in Baltimore, 63 men, women, and children—a mixture of kidnappers and kidnap victims—were taken into custody by police from one small three-bedroom house. The victims had been transported to the premises at night in rented U-Hauls and had made little attempt to escape. As illegal aliens in a strange country with no money, no papers, no food, serious language problems, no potential employers, and "nowhere to go" in general, they really had no viable options. The Fuk Ching gang was implicated. The Fuk Ching, originally an urban youth gang composed primarily of persons of Fukienese descent, is now an international organization often said to be involved in the smuggling, kidnapping, imprisonment, and enslavement of large numbers of illegal Chinese aliens in the United States.

HOMICIDE

Although Chinese gang-related killings might be taking on a more sophisticated tone in recent years, traditionally, a typical gang homicide consisted of a lot of poorly aimed shots fired at close range in the general direction of the target. Even when the killing was planned, this seemed to be the standard pattern. For example, when Nickie Louie, then leader of the Ghost Shadows, was shot by enemies in 1977, his would-be assassin fired five shots at him from behind at arm's-length (Chin 1990, 86-87). Louie survived.

Much of gang warfare and gang-related killings are spontaneous and revolve around disputes for territory or prestige between rival gangs. Since most gang members carry guns and are poor shots, these public shoot-outs often result in casualties among innocent bystanders.

In some cases, the gangs do carefully plan assassinations of rivals. The gang leaders dispatch a group of members to a site where they have learned that rival gang members will be, and normally arrange an alibi for themselves. Leaders do not participate and are virtually never present when the shooting takes place.

On September 4, 1977, Chinese gangs gained a reputation for extreme violence when, in San Francisco, three members of the Joe Boys gang burst into the crowded Golden Dragon restaurant.

Inside, there were small groups of clientele, which included members of the Wah Ching gang, the Hip Sing Boys, and more mundane types, such as a group of vacationing Japanese students and many ordinary Chinese-Americans enjoying a night out on the town. The Joe Boys, small in size and aged 17 and 18, were carrying shotguns and an automatic rifle. Almost indiscriminately, they began firing into the crowd in an attempt to eliminate the Wah Ching members. Mistaking the Japanese students for Wah Ching, they made a special effort to shoot as many of them as possible. As his shotgun ran out of shells, one of the youth pulled out a revolver and emptied it, taking special care to hit a Japanese girl as many times as possible. When it was all over, five people were dead and 11 were wounded, none of them Wah Ching. The shooters escaped into a waiting getaway car. The crime was only solved six months later when one of the gunmen confessed, providing evidence that ultimately led to the conviction of 10 other Joe Boys members.

This sort of random shoot-out was not unique. In 1982, four men believed to be connected with the Tung On Boys burst into the Golden Star Bar on East Broadway in New York City and began firing automatic weapons into the crowd, killing three people and wounding eight more. The incident was believed to be part of a dispute between the Tung On and the Chi Kung Tong (Kinkead 1992, 84-85).

In July 1990, Vinh Vu, the second in command of the Vietnamese Born to Kill gang, was shot on Canal Street in New York City's Chinatown, allegedly as part of a war with the rival Chinese Ghost Shadows. His funeral was disrupted when three people believed to be Ghost Shadows began firing wildly into the crowd of mourners with automatic weapons they had carried under their coats.

One disturbing aspect of gang-related homicides among Chinese is that more and more of them involve victims who refuse to comply with extortion demands. In the past, those who refused to comply were frequently harassed and their businesses vandalized or disrupted. Now things have escalated from squirting superglue into someone's locks to killing him.

Recently, cases involving Chinese being killed in their cars, offices, or homes have shown an increased level of sophistication compared to previous gang-related murders. The victims have been shot in the head or at close range by gunmen who get into their homes or offices. What the motivation of these crimes was remains unclear, and it is not even known whether they were gang-related. Because the crimes do not seem to involve the usual extortion, robbery, or gang rivalries, one theory is that they are related to heroin trafficking in some way.

POLITICAL TERRORISM AND ASSASSINATION

One result in the United States and Canada of political problems in Asia is that occasionally there is a political motive to Asian crimes carrying over to the Asian community.

For example, in the dispute between Taiwan and the government of the People's Republic of China, both sides have planned or carried out assassinations within the borders of the United States and elsewhere. The Kuomintang is alleged to have planned the assassination of Chou En-lai. This was to have taken place in Paris, employing Italian fascists and a kamikaze dog with a bomb tied to its back. When Chou canceled the trip for unrelated reasons, the assassination was called off (Kaplan 1992, 146-148).

As stated earlier, the tongs have been known to use gangs to further their own political ends. Since the tongs are closely linked with the CCBA and the Kuomintang, it should come as no surprise that, on at least one occasion, the Kuomintang has managed to convince gang members to disrupt and attack pro-Taiwan independence demonstrations in the United States (Kaplan 1992, 277).

Undoubtedly, the most serious act of political terrorism committed by the Kuomintang in America was hiring and recruiting members of the United Bamboo to assassinate Henry Liu, the Chinese-American journalist who had been critical of Chiang Ching-kuo, president of Taiwan and the Republic of China. Although Liu also served as a double agent for both the Kuomintang and the Chinese Communists, which undoubtedly contributed to the decision to assassinate him, the final straw was the publication of his book *Jiang Jing Guo Zhuan*, published in 1984 under the pen name Jiang Nan. Interestingly, although the United Bamboo members involved were experienced organized crime figures in Taiwan, they were new to the United States. Many of those involved were under the false impression that because there were so many killings in the United States, the police would not have much interest in just one more.

Taiwanese independence activists have also been suspected of mailing letter bombs to Kuomintang officials in the United States, as well as planting explosives in their offices in New York and Washington. In one such attack, a Kuomintang official lost his hand. Taiwanese independence groups have also claimed responsibility for arson attempts, shootings, vandalism, and at least one aborted assassination attempt on Kuomintang targets within the United States (Kaplan 1992, 276-277).

In the Vietnamese community, politics play a similar role in crime. Right-wing Vietnamese target those they suspect of "communist sympathies" with assassination, assault, extortion, or arson. It is impossible to determine the degree of sincerity behind these acts of political terrorism: it is strongly believed that many are simply opportunistic acts of extortion in which the criminal uses the alleged goal of soliciting funds to defeat communism to intimidate people into giving him money.

REVENGE

Revenge has a long and honored place in traditional Chinese culture. It can be seen as a motivation for virtually any crime, including assault, homicide, vandalism, extortion, or kidnapping. Often it can actually provide leads to the police.

Among the Chinese customs that underlie revenge is one stating that, ideally, all debts, both good and bad, should be repaid before Chinese New Year. For this reason many Chinese attempt acts of revenge at this time. One prominent assistant U.S. attorney in New York's Eastern District who had made her reputation prosecuting Chinese criminals received a booby-trapped package in the mail shortly before Chinese New Year (Kinkead 1992, 129). (Other, law-abiding Chinese citizens simply make a special effort to ensure that their rent is paid before the holiday.)

According to the traditions of the triad subculture (the jiang hu), one should not gain revenge by harming an enemy's family or family members. Instead, honorable revenge should be obtained by harming an enemy or member of an enemy's gang. (This does not mean that Chinese will never get revenge on an enemy's family, simply that it is not honorable according to the traditions of the gangs and the tongs.)

ROBBERY

In Asian communities in America, generally common targets for robberies include jewelry stores, gambling halls, and private gambling games. There are others. In New York City, robbing patrons in Chinese movie theaters has reached a point where attendance has dropped significantly. Massage parlors seem to be a growing target too. Some of the mobile Vietnamese gangs have been known to target rural gun stores during a series of armed holdups as they cruise on a cross-country "road trip."

When Asian gangs target jewelry stores, they usually go in quickly, seize control fast, and wave a lot of firearms and weapons. One member of the gang will then generally smash the glass on the jewelry display cases with a hammer, and the gang will seize a variety of convenient jewels and gold and then flee. Due to the speed of such robberies, cash and most of the jewelry are left behind.

Most gangs committing these robberies are young, heavily armed, and very excited and nervous. Most often, those in the store are strangers to the gang, and none of them are harmed.

But due to the increasing threat of such robberies, many jewelry stores in Asian communities have improved their security procedures.

Gambling games and halls are frequent targets for gangs as well. This seems inevitable when one realizes that not only is the presence of large sums of cash and valuables a necessary part of such games, but that such games are generally illegal. For this reason, gamblers hesitate to involve the police if there is a robbery. In some cases, the players may report the robbery but attempt to disguise the fact that they were gambling. In his book *Dragons and Tigers,* Jim Badey provides one interesting example where the police were called to the scene of a robbery at a "child's birthday party." Upon arrival, police were told that the party had been invaded by a gang of well-armed youths who robbed all present of their cash and jewelry at knife- and gunpoint. The losses of the 10 guests were reported to total approximately $10,000 to $20,000. Based on the large sums of cash claimed to have been taken and the lack children present, police suspected the guests had actually been engaged in a high-stakes gambling game when they were robbed. Apparently, such a scenario, with such an excuse, is not uncommon (Badey 1988, 3-16, 3-17).

Illegal gambling halls flourish throughout America's Chinatowns and are often guarded by members of Chinese youth gangs (who also serve as lookouts for police raids). Such protection is usually not very heavy, however, and the halls and their customers are often robbed. On occasion, the customers inside are shaken down and robbed by the very gang members who have been hired to provide them with protection from robbery.

Although triad tradition views robbery as a means of redistributing the wealth among the rich and the poor, it can be assumed that most Chinese gang members simply keep the bulk of their loot.

BURGLARY AND HOME INVASIONS

Residential robberies, of which there are two versions, are greatly feared by many Asians.[3] In a burglary, the criminals sneak into the house and then sneak out, taking some valuables with them. In a home invasion, the criminals make no attempt at stealth. They merely barge in, take the occupants prisoner, and terrorize and torture them into giving up their valuables, relying on fear and intimidation to keep them from reporting the crime to law enforcement. The line between the two can turn fuzzy. Many burglary attempts become assaults and kidnappings when residents are found inside. Sometimes, residential and business burglaries and home invasions are extensively planned and involve employees or other sources of inside information. A local criminal gang might plan a home invasion but arrange for a group of out-of-town criminals to carry it out. The loot is then split between the two groups, which naturally makes capture and punishment of those involved more difficult.

Asian gangs generally prefer to prey on their own ethnic groups. In a few cases, Vietnamese criminals have confessed that they chose burglary victims by selecting Vietnamese names at random from the phone book. The same is true of Chinese criminals. In some cases, Chinese and Vietnamese criminals will drive several hours to carry out a home invasion of a Chinese restaurant owner. When no suitable Chinese seem to be available, there is some evidence that such criminals prefer to prey on other Asians rather than on white, Hispanic, or black Americans. In one unusual case in my area, a group of Chinese criminals staked out and then invaded the home of a Japanese-American restaurateur, making off with many valuables.

In such a home invasion, the level of violence is surprisingly high. Humiliation, rape, torture, assault, and needless killing of family members are disturbing elements of such crimes. Part of this is simply sadism, but there is another reason for such atrocities. By terrorizing and humiliating the victims once, the criminals seek to establish that they can do it again if they wish. Often, they make no attempt to hide their identities, but rather flaunt their identities and the name of their gangs as part of the intimidation. In some cases, they will make off with family pictures and identification documents to use in finding them again and punishing them if they talk to the authorities. Sadly, in many cases such intimidation tactics work, and law enforcement authorities have a great deal of difficulty obtaining the cooperation of the victims.

One unusual element of such residential robberies is the unique list of stolen property. Because Asians tend not to trust banks, they often keep large sums of cash at home and convert valuables into such easily transported and universally accepted forms as jewelry and gold. Similarly, Asians who run stores dealing in jewelry and other valuable items commonly store part of their merchandise at home. Therefore, the list of stolen items often contains the more easily negotiable valuables (e.g., jewelry and gold).

It is extremely difficult to find, capture, and prosecute those who commit home invasions, and they are a growing problem among Asian communities in North America. Therefore, law enforcement authorities have tried innovative tactics to fight the problem. Realizing that the criminals who commit such acts, particularly among the Vietnamese, are generally young, reckless, violent, and loosely organized, some police agencies have implemented "sting" operations.

An informant puts out the word that he wishes to either commit, plan, or suggest a target for invasion. When criminals show up to participate, the planning meetings are recorded on audio or videotape. When enough evidence is collected and the criminals actually set out to commit the act, police stop their car on the way to the "targeted house" and arrest them. Some police agencies have claimed that such tactics have led to a visible decrease in home invasions in their communities.[4]

Despite the fact that burglaries happen among Asians, according to some sources, gang members view burglary as a cowardly form of theft used by those who lack character. Apparently, to rob or extort people in person is seen as having more character. Incidentally, some theorize that there is an extensive network of fences dealing in stolen property in the Asian community.

CAR THEFT

Car theft is particularly common among Vietnamese criminals. Curiously, many Asian gangs prefer to steal Toyotas and Datsuns. Although at first this sounds like just another case of Asian gangs choosing Asian victims, the truth is that such cars are chosen because they are easy to unlock, start, and drive. Thus, these Japanese models are easy targets.

In New Orleans, members of an Asian car theft ring stumbled upon a unique form of car theft. They would first take their own legal cars and sell them to an illegal car theft ring's "chop shop." The cars would then be disassembled, and the criminals would be paid cash for the value of the hot parts. After losing the first car, the thieves would steal one of identical model and year as the first but in better condition. They would then disguise the stolen car as the original one, using the plates, registration, vehicle identification number, and other markings for the first vehicle—thus gaining payment for the first car and the use of the second, slightly better car.

CREDIT CARD FORGERY

In Malaysia, China, Hong Kong, Taiwan, Thailand, and elsewhere there is a serious and growing problem with the manufacture of counterfeit credit cards. Asian criminals and criminal groups frequently use them to make purchases throughout the world.

Information on the credit card is usually obtained from corrupt employees in businesses where foreign cards are regularly used. Embossing the necessary numbers onto a counterfeited card is really quite simple with an embossing machine.

Although creating a suitably encoded magnetic strip, holograms, and other technologically advanced features is more complex, there is an ongoing technology war between the major credit card companies and the counterfeiters. As soon as the card companies develop a new security device or procedure, the criminals in Asia begin devoting resources to overcoming it. For example, for a long time the counterfeiters utilized the same technology as the credit card companies to encode information onto the magnetic strip of a counterfeit card. Then the companies developed a new encoding system that made it extremely difficult for a counterfeiter to create an original code that could pass electronic inspection. Soon after, the counterfeiters simply changed their procedures and found a method to copy the code from a valid card onto the magnetic strip of a number of lost, stolen, or counterfeited cards. Soon after the hologram appeared on credit cards, a crude counterfeit appeared in Thailand, and more sophisticated copies soon followed. It is difficult to keep track of the technology and the machinery needed to counterfeit cards, because much of it has other legitimate uses. However, some sophisticated groups such as the Big Circle have even planned break-ins in order to steal the necessary machinery.

The counterfeit cards are quite sophisticated, but one common flaw is improper use of secret codes used by the credit card company. For example, a counterfeit card that appears to have been produced in Seattle might have an imprinted number that would only be issued by a bank in Japan. Nevertheless, this sort of mix-up is frequently missed by the clerks who process the cards. Curiously, in many cases the cards have the names of non-Asians but are actually used by Asian customers. Stores are hesitant to deny a sale to such a cardholder, especially since the credit card companies will generally compensate them for any purchases made with such false cards.[5]

Using such cards to obtain the maximum number of purchases and cash advances before being detected (and the card canceled by the main headquarters) is a carefully planned affair. Frequently, a small band of criminals will be recruited and taught how to pass themselves off as well-to-do tourists. They will then fly from Asia to a targeted location in the United States, Canada, or perhaps Europe. The cards are frequently delivered separately by overnight express to avoid problems in passing through customs. The criminals will then make a number of purchases of jewelry and other easily sold valuables before returning home.

In other cases, the Asian criminal groups will simply have someone fly to North America with a number of counterfeit cards, distribute them, and then share in the profits. Although members of such groups as the 14K, the Sun Yee On, and the Wo On Luk triads have all been implicated in the use of counterfeit cards, it appears that the activity is normally planned and executed by small bands of Asian criminals without the involvement of large-scale criminal enterprises.

THEFT AND FORGERY OF DOCUMENTS

Identification papers are useful in a wide variety of illegal activities, but they are especially valuable to those involved in illegal immigration scams and smuggling, where border officials frequently check travel documents. During my first trip to Taiwan, I had my U.S. passport stolen. Although replacing it was not a serious problem, five years later, while I was entering the United States, a U.S. Customs official politely asked me if I had been to Amsterdam lately. I had never in my life been to Amsterdam—which happens to be the prime heroin smuggling and redistribution center in Europe!

Finally, Asian gangs frequently steal checks and other financial papers from both Asians and non-Asians and find ways to receive illegal compensation for them. There have been cases where Asians have targeted locations for break-ins where they thought they could obtain financial documents, passports, and other identification papers.

Recently, Asian gangs in North American cities have begun to steal beepers, have them reprogrammed, and rent or sell them to other people. The sorts of crimes committed by such groups are constantly changing. As times and conditions change, the only thing that is certain is that such groups will change with them.

NOTES

1. See U.S. Senate hearing notes, *Asian Organized Crime: Hearing before the Permanent Subcommittee on Investigations of the Committee on Governmental Affairs,* 102nd Cong., 1st sess., 1992, 14.
2. Not only are humans seen as commodities in kidnappings, but it is also typical for commodities to be treated almost like human kidnapping victims. I know of one incident in Taipei where an American businesswoman married to a local Chinese citizen had her car stolen and the thieves began sending notes offering to return the stolen automobile for a suitable ransom. The woman's husband, in typical Chinese fashion, bargained the car thieves down to a lower sum, and the car was returned upon payment.

   Of course, this crime would not work very well in the United States, where many cars are insured and payment of some sort is automatically offered if the car disappears. Although the car in this case was quite nice, it was not a unique or one-of-a kind model and could have been replaced. Paying the ransom was simply more economical than purchasing a new one.
3. In Taiwan, apartments and other residences are almost universally equipped with a wide variety of screens and locked grillwork on windows and doors to help prevent burglaries. Unfortunately, these precautions not only serve to lock people out, but also to lock people in, preventing escape by residents and posing a serious fire safety hazard. By American standards, such precautions are undesirable and illegal.
4. See U.S. Senate hearing notes: *Asian Organized Crime—The New International Criminal,* 1992, p. 105-106 and *The New International Criminal and Asian Organized Crime,* December 1992, p. 36.
5. Of course, the business owners may simply fear charges of discrimination. There are, after all, a considerable number of Asian or part-Asian individuals who have acquired a last name that is not normally considered Asian. Many of them grow very weary of being questioned about this and can be quite sensitive to perceived slights and peculiar treatment.

The differences between Chinese and American culture have some important ramifications when it comes to law enforcement. First, Chinese people often continue to do things they did in their old country in their adopted one, although these might be illegal. Two outstanding examples are gambling and fortune-telling—both perfectly legal in most of Asia, but often extremely restricted in North America. Because of cultural differences, to be efficient law enforcement often needs to handle and investigate the crimes discussed in this chapter differently than it would with members of the North American culture.

GAMBLING

Most Chinese readily admit that gambling is one of the most prevalent vices in their culture. It is not uncommon for Chinese men to lose one or two months' salary in one night of gambling (although this does not mean it's approved of—by either their society or their wives!). Because of its popularity in Chinese culture and the sometimes severe restrictions placed on it in America, a great deal of underground gambling goes on among Chinese immigrants here. This gambling varies widely and exists on several levels. Ranging from friendly ad hoc games among acquaintances to large-scale, multistate underground gambling rings run by the tongs and organized crime, illegal gambling has an important place in Chinese society in the United States.

Common games are cards, mah-jong, fan-tan, and pai gow. Mah-jong has somehow gained a reputa-

CHAPTER 9

CHINESE CRIME PROBLEMS UNRELATED TO GANGS

Off-track betting (OTB) in Chinatown.

tion in America as a good game for old ladies, but the Chinese view it as a vice for men only; in Taiwan it is not ladylike for a woman to play mah jong, even if no money is at stake. In fan-tan, buttons are put into a bowl, and the gamblers, who remove them four at a time, place bets on how many will be left in the bowl at the end of the game. A version of pai gow is occasionally played in American casinos (for example, Caesar's in Atlantic City) that cater to Chinese.

The hazards of illegal gambling are many. Compulsive gambling is a very real and common problem in Chinese society. Restaurants and other businesses are often lost or change hands after a night of wild gambling. As people play beyond their abilities, many seek out a loan shark. When they are unable to pay off their gambling debts, these people frequently find themselves owing large sums to gangsters or other dangerous or influential people. It is not unheard of for people with gambling debts to pay them off by undertaking dangerous or illegal "jobs" for organized crime figures, such as becoming couriers in the heroin-smuggling business.

Large amounts of cash being gathered in one place and used in an illegal enterprise simply invite theft, and the victims of such theft can hardly call the police. As described in the previous chapter, gang members often rob illegal gambling dens. On occasion, gang members hired to guard the games will themselves turn around and rob the patrons and players.

In some states, notably California, there has been a trend toward legalizing and licensing gambling operations in order to minimize crime problems. Despite this, both legal and illegal gambling still serve some purposes for Chinese organized crime. First, for the tongs and Chinese organized crime groups, gambling is a major source of income, which they reinvest in a variety of other illegal and legal activities. Second, gambling operations frequently serve as money-laundering tools for the tongs and gangs.

There are at least two ways this works. In the first, a person will purchase a large number of chips at a legal casino or "card club" and gamble with only a small portion of them, say 10 to 20 percent, at several games at several tables for a few hours. When finished, he will then cash in the chips, including the unwagered portion. If anyone asks he will claim that he won the entire amount of chips rather than merely purchasing them. Since few legal gambling places keep track of all chips sold to all customers, it is often impossible to prove the "gambler" wrong, except in the unlikely case that someone has actually been recording his progress at each and every table. Casinos or card clubs make money off the 10 to 20 percent gambled in any event, so careful recording is not in their best interests. In some cases, they will allow patrons to deposit money in their clubs to draw on later for gaming use. If the customer draws from this account, he can often

On Leong Tong—long view from side and close-up of the tong's sign.

simply claim that he won the money at the club. Unless club records are searched and examined, it is impossible to prove otherwise. A second technique is to simply have different people purchase a number of chips below the legal limit that requires

TONGS, GANGS, AND TRIADS:
CHINESE CRIME GROUPS IN NORTH AMERICA

reporting their purchase. If these chips are then cashed in by one or several people, there is no way to prove they were not won in a game of chance.

None of these activities are particularly clever, yet they are effective; it is quite difficult to monitor them at all casinos and card clubs, particularly if the owners are actually assisting an organized crime figure in laundering money. The entire purpose of most money-laundering operations is to provide a criminal an excuse for having large amounts of cash that could not otherwise be accounted for legally. Often, a clever accountant can do much to launder money through creative use of the books of a casino or card club. After all, most patrons in such institutions arrive only to lose money.

Many would argue that Chinese gambling should really be thought of as a large-scale organized crime activity. As evidence of this, they might cite incidents such as the August 29, 1990, indictment of 29 individuals and four organizations as part of a multistate gambling ring run by the On Leong Chinese Merchant's Association in Chicago (aka the On Leong Tong or, as it is now known, the Merchant's Benevolent Association).

FIREWORKS

In much of the United States and Canada, fireworks are illegal or highly restricted. In Chinese culture, however, they play an important role in the spiritual lives of many people. When a business is opened, fireworks are frequently set off since the noise is believed to scare away ghosts and other undesirable spirits. On such holidays, as Chinese New Year, fireworks are set off for the same reason. The Chinese enjoy them on other occasions as well to add to the excitement.

There are often extensive black markets among Chinese in places where possession or sale of fireworks is restricted. For example, despite strict New York state restrictions, I have seen them sold openly on the streets of Chinatown in New York City. (Of course, many illegal things are sold openly on the streets of New York City.)

CODE VIOLATIONS

In Asia, there is not the proliferation of restrictions on the conduct of businesses, restaurants, or rental properties that exist in

America and Canada. Of course, most of these restrictions are intended to ensure the safety of the public, but noticeably increase the cost and difficulty of doing business. Most of the nations of Asia feel that the burden on small businessmen or restaurateurs simply does not make myriad regulations worthwhile; furthermore, their enforcement is often a problem. Those charged with enforcement frequently feel that the punishment of business owners is "lacking in humanity" if it poses a severe burden on them when they are merely trying to make an honest living and take care of their families. Rather than enforce what they see as a "miscarriage of justice" and close the business, code inspectors are frequently willing to turn a blind eye, particularly if a business owner expresses an interest in repaying the the favor and perhaps giving them a consideration. Although it is easy to see this situation as simple corruption (which in one sense it is), it should be recognized that in the eyes of the enforcement people, it really is immoral to put someone out of business, perhaps putting their family at great financial risk, simply to enforce "minor" regulations. The potential tragedy posed by, say, a health risk does not outweigh the very real and established danger of forcing a small businessman to shut down.

Many codes are aimed at reducing hazards that most Chinese people simply don't worry about much. Based on my experience, Chinese are less concerned with accidents, sanitation, and fires than are Americans but worry more about theft, starvation, and being exposed to sick people and catching illnesses from them. It's simply a cultural difference, based largely, no doubt, on historical differences. Many Chinese will, for example, quite willingly block a fire exit to reduce the risk of thieves breaking in. Similarly, a surprising number show little interest in having well-equipped fire extinguishers or first aid kits, taking a fatalistic approach instead.[1]

The problems arise when Asians set up businesses in the United States and begin violating codes. In many cases, they make no effort to research the relevant codes in question and thus do not comply with them. Many times, the underlying attitude is that any problems that exist can be fixed easily if and when government inspectors point them out. Cultural clashes emerge when inspectors begin to fine or even close down businesses for non-compliance. The Asians feel the code inspector is being quite unreasonable when he enforces the laws as written without at least giving them a chance to comply before being punished. The inspectors normally feel that the business owner should have done the necessary research before opening the business. Such clashes are tragic when, for instance, Asians who have quit their jobs and invested a great deal of money in a business without researching regulations lose all of their savings when bureaucrats close them down. Of course, since most of these regulations were intended to protect the public, the inspectors feel that the citizens are at risk if the codes go unenforced even "for just a little while until our business becomes successful."

Tax Evasion

In Hong Kong and Taiwan, taxes are much lower than in the United States or Canada. In the People's Republic of China, taxes are often nonexistent; the state receives its income from state-owned businesses without taxing the workers. For at least this reason, many Chinese feel that the tax burden in North America is quite unreasonable. They will often go to great lengths not to pay taxes and feel no guilt about it. Part of the reason many Chinese distrust banks and wish to do business in cash is the desire to hide their income from the government. In fact, it seems many Chinese would rather pay extortion to gangsters than taxes to the government.

Fortune-Telling

Fortune-telling has a valued and respected place in Chinese culture. Although most Chinese will be quick to admit that there are a great many frauds and charlatans posing as fortune-tellers, many believe that it is nevertheless possible to consult with someone who can give advice on the "luckiest" course of action in a given situation. In Chinese culture, there is a great emphasis on luck and ways to improve one's luck. Although this idea sounds absurd on the surface, there is some historical basis for it.

The culture was traditionally nonscientific, and, as such, the Chinese took many observations about things that were considered beneficial and lumped them together as "lucky things." Conversely, things seen as being unlucky often were. Of course, not all of these observations were correct, and there is a great deal of what can only be called nonsense in many Chinese fortune-telling arts.

Nevertheless, the social role of fortune-tellers cannot be ignored. Chinese will often visit a fortune-teller when they are feeling lonely or distraught and need advice; in fact, ironically, there is less stigma attached to this than to visiting a psychotherapist. Also, visiting a fortune-teller can serve as a way to mediate a dispute: for example, to choose a good wedding date that will not offend any of the guests, a fortune-teller will often be consulted.

In many localities in the United States and Canada, fortune-telling is allowed if it is done "for entertainment purposes only." The reason being that many fortune-tellers have taken advantage of their clients, often as part of an elaborate con game, and those who were distraught and easily manipulated have often been bilked of a great deal of money.[2]

DEALING IN ENDANGERED SPECIES

The Chinese record on environmental issues is terrible. The Chinese frequently are involved in buying, selling, and smuggling endangered species and their by-products. There are some reasons for this.

The Chinese are an ancient people, and much of their culture goes back to preindustrial times when the human population was much lower and the wildlife population significantly higher. Many attitudes developed during a period when mankind did not have technology to inflict the sort of damage on nature that occurs now. There was also an attitude that the more scarce and rare something was, the more valuable it was likely to be.

Traditional Chinese medicine evolved out of a complex system of ancient theories combined with a vast collection of recipes for medicines made from natural substances and compounds. Although some of these formulas undoubtedly worked as

Exotic animals and their by-products on display in Chinatown.

described, others had a symbolic rather than a practical basis. Many were based on the idea, for instance, that eating pieces of a strong animal might help make someone strong. Similarly, eating the eyes of an animal with good eyesight was believed to improve vision, and eating the penis of various large, strong animals might cure impotence or infertility.

It's safe to say that, before modern times, such practices did little harm to the environment. Even though it was believed that a soup made from ground-up tiger bones was good medicine, it was no easy feat to kill the tiger with spears and arrows and then transport it to the pharmacy. Therefore, such exotic cures were reserved for the very rich or important.

In modern times, there are far fewer tigers or other large, fierce animals. To make the situation worse, it is much easier to find them, shoot them, and then to ship their by-products to a point where they can be sold for a great deal of money. Furthermore, as the average level of income goes up in Taiwan, Hong Kong, South Korea (where Chinese medicine is widely used), China, and elsewhere, the number of people who want and can afford such products is increasing. Thus, poaching endangered species and smuggling their products is big business. Tigers, rhinoceroses, and perhaps elephants will come close to disappearing from the wild in a few decades, and the Chinese black market for such products is a major cause.

It isn't only Chinese medicine that's to blame for this widespread destruction. Other animal products, notably ivory, are highly desired for their decorative appeal and as rough materials for fashioning objets d'art and jewelry. Some wild animals are sought after to provide delicacies for immoral Chinese gourmets. Since in the holistic traditional Chinese medicinal theory there is no real line between food and medicine, many of these dishes, particularly stews and soups, are supposed to have a medicinal value. But at other times, the only real purpose in eating the animal is for a touch of exotic variety—much valued among Chinese gourmets. Armadillos, bears (particularly the paws), alligator, rattlesnake, tarpaulins (a spiny Asian armadillo-anteater type thing), tigers, and large cats are all eaten from time to time for one reason or another.[3] As a rule, the Chinese eat more of what we consider "normal" food, and most Chinese probably go their entire lives without eating any of these exotic animals. But there are enough gourmets to ensure that a black market will continue and that the numbers of many endangered species will dwindle as a result. The money involved makes it unlikely that the market will dry up soon.

To list just a few examples, the gallbladder of a black bear, desired for traditional medicine, sells for $45,000. In powdered form, it is said to be worth $5,000 a pound in Korea. In Taiwan, powdered rhinoceros horn sells for three times the price of cocaine, or $40,000 a pound for Sumatran horn and $15,000 a pound for African horn (both rhinoceros species are dangerously close to extinction.) A bowl of soup made with a tiger's penis sells for $320 (U.S.) in Taiwan; it is believed to increase sexual prowess in men. The orangutan, another species endangered in the wild, is much desired as a pet and curiosity in Taiwan and elsewhere throughout Asia and fetches extravagant prices.

DOMESTIC DISPUTES

Although Confucianism and Chinese tradition stress the importance of a strong and stable family, the Chinese are only human, and family problems do develop. Occasionally, they grow quite serious and violence breaks out.

It is a Chinese belief that one should not share one's family's problems with the outside world. Instead family problems should be kept quiet or solved within the family. Therefore, those who attempt to intervene in a Chinese domestic dispute or other problem often find it difficult to obtain the information needed to sort out the situation.

Based on Confucian teachings, either the father or the mother can mete out punishment as is seen fit. Harsh punishment, including beating and some other forms of corporal punishment, is believed to be good for children in some cases. Many such punishments are not legally acceptable in the United States and Canada, but then, few Chinese are impressed by the social order or behavior of children and adolescents in American society. Therefore many, particularly older, Chinese prefer to use their traditional methods of child-rearing rather than conform to American ways. Further, as many immigrant Chinese parents see their children become Americanized and/or behave in ways they find immoral, they become frustrated and the temptation to beat them grows.

Although their society emphasizes and teaches the repression of anger, contrary to stereotype, many Chinese have very nasty tempers. When they do become visibly angry, it has often reached a point where they are out of control—often dangerously so!

Those who may have to deal with Chinese families in crisis, with the explosions of long-repressed anger, should be aware of a deep reluctance to speak of the real issues at hand.[4]

Because of this repression of anger, domestic conflicts tend to result in outbreaks of violence and animosity that seem terribly out of proportion to the situation and, in some cases, things can get completely out of hand.

Rape

Although rape is a crime of violence, not passion, and the victim of a rape is, by definition, unwilling, the Chinese traditionally associate a great deal of shame with being raped. For this reason, many Chinese rape victims are quite unwilling to share details of the crime with law enforcement in order to aid with the prosecution. This stems from an ancient Chinese idea that certain behaviors, such as extramarital or premarital sex (at least for women), were sinful in themselves. Whether the woman consented to the act or not was irrelevant. She could, if she were highly honorable, commit suicide to demonstrate her unwillingness to live with the shame. Apparently, this was felt to redeem her in the eyes of all concerned. Although this still happens, these days, a much more common response is for the victim or her family to attempt to hide the act from the outside world and hope that nobody finds out that such a thing occurred.

Law enforcement personnel and others who find themselves dealing with a Chinese rape victim or victims should be prepared to use even more tact and delicacy than normal to get past these cultural barriers.

Embezzlement

Many of the nations of Asia—Taiwan and the Republic of Korea, for example—have never signed extradition treaties with the United States. Therefore, it is not unheard of for a resident of one of these nations to steal large sums of money from his employer if he has made arrangements to immigrate to North America. If he makes it to the United States, there is no way he can legally be forced to return the money.

NOTES

1. Of course, some may find such statements offensive. There are many Chinese who do understand the importance of industrial and fire safety. Nevertheless, based on my experiences—including a stint working at a machine factory where I took it upon myself to try and encourage the management to upgrade safety procedures—the Chinese (at least those who have been raised in Chinese culture) tend to follow the patterns stated and do not exhibit the same concern we do for the same hazards.

2. This sort of thing is not unique to Chinese culture. For good examples of how Gypsy mafia fortune-tellers have conned their clients out of large sums of money in the past, one can read *License to Steal*, by Dennis Marlock and John Dowling (Boulder, CO: Paladin Press, 1994). For a complete description of how spiritualists take advantage of their clients, read *The Psychic Mafia*, by Lamar Keene (New York: Dell Books, 1976).

3. There is no evidence that Chinese restaurants secretly serve cats, despite frequent rumors to the contrary throughout America. An urban legend is a story that is widely told and believed by its tellers but nevertheless is not true. Jan Harald Brunvand, a college professor, has written several interesting books about urban legends in America. In one of these, *The Choking Doberman and Other "New" Urban Legends,* Brunvand examines these stories in depth and fails to find a single case of pets being served at Chinese restaurants that could be substantiated. From time to time over the years, I've also made attempts to track down such stories to a firsthand source. As is typical of unsubstantiated urban legends, the source always seemed to be "a friend of a friend."

4. There are many other reasons, besides respect, that cause Chinese to be reticent about family problems. One is the belief that people should be considerate of one another; adults should not have to be told how to treat each other. If you do not like the way that someone close to you is treating you, it is often enough to indicate that you are unhappy without voicing the exact complaint. If the other party knows you are unhappy, he or she should be able to analyze the offending behavior and correct it. Another reason is that it is considered risky to place all of one's emotional cards on the table and much safer to keep something in reserve.

Although illegal immigration by Chinese is a growing problem in the United States and Canada, estimates as to just how big the problem really vary wildly. According to the official 1992 estimates of the U.S. Immigration and Naturalization Service (INS), 24,000 illegal Chinese aliens were believed to be in the United States, which was only 0.8 percent of the total number of illegal aliens. On the other hand, according to *U.S. News and World Report* (June 21, 1993), 20 different criminal secret societies in Guangdong (Canton) and Fukien provinces are believed to smuggle some 50,000 to 80,000 illegal aliens into the United States each year (Duffy 1994, 26-29, 31). This is two to three times the INS estimate for the entire population of illegal Chinese residents in the country! In any event, no matter how large the problem actually is, it seems safe to say that it is growing in both numbers and seriousness. Some sources state that an estimated 10 percent of all the Chinese in New York City's Chinatown are living and working here illegally.

As stated in Chapter 5, in the United States and Canada, immigration is based on quota systems—only a certain number of people from any given country are allowed admission. Because the slots available are filled quickly, many are left with the desire to immigrate to the United States but little chance to do so legally.

To most working-class Chinese, the motivation to go to the United States or other developing countries illegally and work is simple: money. It is not uncommon for a farmer in China to make less than the U.S. equivalent of $200 a year, and a factory worker often makes less than $400. To such peo-

CHAPTER 10

ILLEGAL IMMIGRATION

ple, the lure of the opportunity to make even a subminimum wage is strong. Furthermore, a surprising number of illegal aliens are paid more than minimum when hired, because for employers there are several advantages to hiring illegal aliens. One is economic. Generally speaking, illegal aliens work for less than legal workers. Although, in many cases, it is necessary to pay the aliens what would actually be a legal wage (in the United States anything over the $4.25 minimum wage is generally legal in most industries), an employer can still see considerable savings by comparing the wages at which illegals are willing to work to what legal residents expect for the same job. Similarly, illegal aliens are often more cooperative and less likely to complain than are legal workers. They generally do not require overtime pay for overtime hours; in fact, many come from countries where such things are unheard of. Frequently they are not as concerned about hazardous conditions as legal employees—or at least when they are, there is little or nothing they can do. And naturally, being illegal, such workers cannot turn to the authorities when mistreated.

Although there are many ways for illegal aliens to enter the country, it generally takes a certain level of knowledge to sneak in. One of the easiest ways to take up illegal residence in the United States is to simply come here on legitimate business and then overstay the welcome. This is done enough so that the United States and Canada both tend to be wary of giving visas to members of certain nationalities. Frequently, these two nations insist that applicants for tourist visas show some sort of guarantee that they will return to their home countries. Examples of such guarantees might be considerable financial holdings in their home countries, the fact that all of their children are not traveling with them, that they are traveling only as part of an organized tour, or other such conditions.

Some classes of people, notably children and young, single women, are particularly suspect when it comes to being granted visas. The fear is that the children will be enrolled in schools in North America, while the women will make an effort to rush into a marriage with a U.S. citizen in order to remain in the country. In fact, one of the primary routes by which women enter the country illicitly is through marriage, sometimes fraudulent. Although the practice is most widespread among Koreans, it is not unknown for women from Taiwan, the Philippines, and elsewhere to marry U.S. citizens for the purpose of engaging in prostitution in the United States, where they can presumably make considerably more at their profession than in their home countries. As for deception in such marriages, there are almost as many variations as there are marriages themselves. Sometimes a male citizen is deceived by a prostitute. Other times, a U.S. citizen deceives a woman with the plan to illegally sell or trick her into prostitution upon her arrival. In some cases, both parties enter with their eyes open, knowing full well that their marriage is merely a transaction to bring a prostitute into the United States. There are also those who seek to recruit brides from otherwise stable and healthy mixed marriages into prostitution. Korean wives of U.S. servicemen are common targets.

Of course, not all marriages of convenience involve prostitution. Many people in developed countries marry foreign-born individuals to obtain citizenship for them. The plan is usually to follow up the acquisition of citizenship for the foreign spouse with a quick divorce. In some cases, the citizen is paid a considerable sum of money for such services. Although this is illegal and carries serious penalties, as long as the two people involved live as husband and wife it is difficult to prove any wrongdoing. Once the alien has gained citizenship, he or she may sponsor relatives.

Such opportunities are open to only a small number of people. The majority of illegal aliens in the United States probably simply sneak in without a visa of any sort and stay here. Although it requires some skill, this is still relatively easy to accomplish for someone with the appropriate knowledge and experience. Throughout the world, there are individuals and organized groups who profit by helping people enter the United States or Canada illegally. Such smugglers work in a variety of ways. A surprising number of illegal Chinese enter the United States through Mexico. Chinese are aware that if they get into Mexico with a legitimate visa, they can then enter the United States by the same routes illegal Mexican immigrants use. Border smugglers—called "coyotes" by both Mexicans and Americans—are not picky. They will generally try to bring in anyone—Central American, Mexican, Asian, or even an outlaw U.S. citizen who wishes to visit home—into the United States for a fee. Often such operations are surprisingly small in scale, and the primary service offered is the preparation of a small, leaky boat to cross a carefully chosen stretch of the Rio Grande River. Fees for such crossings are high, and generally speaking, at least part of the fee goes to bribe the Mexican authorities.

A surprising number of Chinese aliens also seek to use Canada as a jumping-off point for illegal entry to that of the United States. One reason for this is that Canada has less stringent requirements for transit visas than it does for tourist, immigrant, or visitor visas. In other words, if you merely claim to be "passing through" on your way to somewhere else, the Canadians are more apt to let you into their fine country. Of course, once you are in it's often difficult for the relevant authorities to find you and throw you back out, particularly if you've gone south to take up illegal residence in the United States.

Interestingly, although Canada provides asylum for refugees in a manner similar to the United States, some Canadian sources claim that four out of 10 Chinese given Canadian refugee status proceed to cross the border and live illegally in the United States.

Illegal aliens often travel under false documents and passports, which do not necessarily have to be those of the United States or Canada. There are many other nations that will do. For example, Portuguese passports are considered to be one of the documents of choice. Genuine Portuguese passports can sometimes be acquired fraudulently in Macao, the Portuguese colony on the southern coast of China that will revert to Chinese rule in 1999. If the genuine article cannot be obtained, then counterfeit Portuguese passports are often manufactured covertly and sold in Thailand and other Southeast Asian countries. Also, since it is widely recognized that Japanese citizens, who come from a highly developed country, have much less incentive to overstay their visas and obtain illegal work in the United States, there have been cases of smugglers putting a Chinese person's picture on a counterfeit Japanese passport and then applying for a visa for the "Japanese tourist" through the normal channels. Some smugglers have succeeded in placing the counterfeit passport among a large number of legitimate Japanese passports being processed by a legitimate Japanese tour group. Because it is not uncommon for such passports to be given only a cursory check before visa approval, it is not known how many visas have been issued in this manner.

Of course, almost any passport from almost any developed nation can be of use to people smugglers in obtaining an immigration or tourist visa. In most cases, however, smuggling illegal Chinese aliens is a much longer and more complex process that often involves corrupt officials of many nations, various criminal gangs at different points along the way, specially owned smuggling boats, and long, strange networks of contacts that crisscross the globe, designed to facilitate the clandestine illegal transport of small groups of people from one place to another.

Because life in China is difficult and most people are poor, large numbers of people have an interest in not only leaving China to work themselves, but also in encouraging others to do so. To have a relative abroad sending money home can make a major difference in the income of a family. Similarly, to have a family receiving such income living in one's village will help the economy of the village as a whole. One problem with stopping illegal immigration of Chinese is that few Chinese local officials have any desire to do so, for the very reasons just given.

The INS estimates that 25 percent of people smuggling is handled by various Chinese crime groups, the most important of which is the Fuk Ching gang.[1] Smuggling operations involve worldwide networks shipping humans by many clandestine routes, and it is not uncommon for the illegal aliens to be passed from gang to gang as they make their way to America. Groups cooperate and work together for their mutual profit. At times, the groups involved are using their networks to smuggle in associates who can be of use to them in their criminal activities. Also involved are the 14K, the Sun Yee On, the Three Mountain Association,[2] the Green Dragons, the Big Circle Gang, the Vietnamese Born to Kill gang, the Chinese Freemasons (the Chi Kung Tong), the Hip Sing Tong, the Wo Hop To, the On Leong Tong, the Tung On, and the Viet Ching. These groups are frequently assisted at some point along the line by individual entrepreneurs and groups with no formal connection to organized crime, who, in many cases, are involved simply because of profits that it can generate. At times, however, the organized crime groups are using their networks for the purpose of smuggling in criminal associates who can be of use to them in their criminal activities.

Gangs charge their customers high fees for illegally transporting them abroad and setting up work for them. In most cases, the Chinese who work in the United States illegally are not from among the poorest classes of China: the poorest could not afford the fees. Instead, they tend to be young men from the working class who have saved long and hard to make the money needed for the fees. In many cases, family, friends, and neighbors have chipped in, hoping that the illegal immigrant will make enough money to send back periodically, reimbursing them with interest for their investments.

Most smuggling gangs who do the initial recruiting and collection of data are based in Fukien province in southeastern China. There are a few explanations as to exactly why Fukien is the premier source of such gangs. The Fukienese have a history of going overseas to seek opportunity and wealth. Fukien's coast and harbors give access to shipping. Like Canton, it is close to the south, but unlike Canton it lacks the wide special economic zones designed to create jobs and develop industry by taking advantage of wealth and investment from nearby Hong Kong. In terms of economics, Fukien has the appropriate level of development: out of China's 30 provinces, it ranks 15th in terms of per-capita income, which leaves it with a significant amount of poverty but enough wealth so that individuals can manage to save and scrape together enough to leave.

The charge to the average illegal Chinese alien is the U.S. equivalent of $30,000; in some cases, it can reach as high as $50,000 per person or even more. For these fees, smugglers promise to find a way to sneak the workers into the United States, locate and obtain employment for them upon arrival, and give them cursory lessons on how to survive in the United States without attracting attention. Such lessons can include advice on how to deal with the authorities if caught and what is required to qualify for refugee status under the laws of the United States. One is often left with the impression that not all of this coaching is accurate.

Even with the pooling of resources by families and outside investment, few Chinese can obtain the sort of wealth needed to pay the fee. For this reason, among others, the smugglers will often agree to accept partial payment up front, while making arrangements to receive additional payments out of the aliens' expected earnings in North America. The gangs often look to the aliens' families if those smuggled here renege on their contracts or abscond without fulfilling their financial obligations.

There are a variety of shipment routes (see table, page 183). Normally, those who pay the smugglers the most are given in return the most prompt and direct routes to the United States. On occasion, aliens are asked or forced to assist in smuggling heroin, opium, or other contraband as a part of their fee.

A major aspect of the strange and illegal trade of people smuggling seems to be sending the aliens via roundabout routes. On occasion, U.S. embassies obtain information on a shipment of illegal human cargo apparently en route to the United States. The intent of such monitoring is to intercept the aliens and return them home. But because shipments often take roundabout routes, even if they are tracked it is easy to lose track of the people involved, particularly if they disembark or change transportation routes. When smugglers realize that the authorities are carefully monitoring a particular route then they will simply utilize a new route. The latest routes seem to involve smuggling illegal Chinese on boats, with their ultimate destination being either the U.S. Virgin Islands or Puerto Rico. Once the aliens surreptitiously enter these territories, they may take domestic flights (which are less closely monitored by the INS) to the U.S. mainland. A November 1, 1994, *New York Times* article entitled "After Crackdown, Smugglers of Chinese Find New Routes" quoted one coast guard official as saying, "It's like if you squeeze a balloon, it just pops out around your hand. If we tighten up they're gonna look where we have a weak link."

Although there are attempts to prescreen those traveling to the

United States from abroad, often these efforts meet with difficulty. Many INS personnel abroad are overworked, and when they attempt to enlist the help of private citizens, they occasionally run into difficulties. For example, the Bangkok employees of both Northwest and United Airlines were threatened by Asian organized crime figures when they began complying with a U.S. government request to copy travel documents and pass the information on to INS personnel.

Once in the United States through whatever means, the illegal aliens are normally housed—some would say imprisoned—in facilities maintained by the gangs. The gangs seek to find jobs for them and then often even take them to and from their places of work. Work is normally found in either the garment or the restaurant industry, although some aliens enter criminal professions, working either as prostitutes or "soldiers" for the gangs. Often, gangs will offer their services as "labor brokers" to potential employers, who are normally Chinese, ensuring them a steady stream of hard-working, docile workers at low cost. Although many—maybe most—employers refuse these services, the temptation is always there. Ironically, when employers do hire illegal aliens, they often find that it is not the happy picture the gangs painted: the employees may work hard for low wages, but the gangs have a handle on anyone who accepts their services. If the employer decides to stop using gang-controlled illegal aliens as a source of labor, the gang may attempt to blackmail him into continuing—which they typically accomplish by threatening to report him to the labor or immigration authorities! In other cases, a gang might simply threaten him or his business with retribution, so often the employer decides that the simplest thing to do is to continue using illegal labor to avoid the many problems that come with angering a gang. Even if such employers do comply with everything their gang-affiliated labor brokers ask, the gangs are often likely to blackmail them anyway, simply out of greed.

For the illegal aliens themselves life is often no bed of roses. Besides being forced to work long hours and live in substandard housing, their already low wages are frequently garnisheed by the gangs. Often, after being shipped to a job somewhere, they find that they have been deceived and that their new employer has no intention of paying them their promised wages or honoring the contract agreed upon. It is common knowledge that illegal aliens rarely call the authorities if they are kidnapped, held prisoner, tortured, or abused. Women are often sexually exploited by those who see the opportunity: it is not uncommon for women who have been promised restaurant jobs to find themselves imprisoned in a brothel and forced to provide sexual services for a large number of men before being given their freedom.

On occasion, illegal aliens are apprehended by the U.S. authorities, but this does not mean that the trip is over for the aliens. Under U.S. law, if such aliens are caught by immigration authorities, they are allowed to contest the deportation. If they can show a strong reason why they should be allowed to stay in the country, such as on humanitarian grounds, then often they are allowed to remain. Chinese citizens can apply for refugee status and obtain it, for instance, if they can show that they are being persecuted in their home country due to their religious beliefs, racial background, or membership in a political organization, or that they will be punished or made to suffer because of the People's Republic of China's population control policies.

The U.S. immigration policies are much abused. When the illegal aliens are apprehended by U.S. authorities, they routinely apply for refugee status whether they are actually refugees or not. If they can convince the authorities that their lives would be endangered if they were returned to China, then often they are allowed to stay.

The INS is extremely overworked, and often its policies seem a bit strange or impractical. For example, upon capturing an illegal alien, the INS is supposed to detain him and return him to his native country only after giving him an opportunity to present arguments against his deportation. Surprisingly often, though, the INS simply has no detention cells available and is forced to release such people on their own recognizance after setting a date for a hearing to determine whether they should be deported. Naturally, since aliens expect to get deported after such a hearing, many of them simply don't show up. If they don't appear in court, the INS will then try to find them and send them home, but it was already trying to do this anyway.

In many such cases, after convincing the authorities that they should be treated as refugees or else released on their recognizance prior to a hearing, the aliens are turned over to "relatives" who pick them up at the INS office. Often these "relatives" are members of same smuggling ring that brought them to the United States in the first place.

It is widely understood that the presence of large numbers of illegal aliens in the United States encourages crime, but nobody is sure what to do about it. Finding and deporting all illegal aliens is simply not feasible.

Illegal immigration causes several problems in the Chinese restaurant industry. Restaurants that strictly follow immigration laws and pay legal wages must compete with those that use illegal labor and pay subminimum wage, and so must find other ways to cut costs. The quality of food used declines, for instance. When food quality goes down, business goes down as customers begin dining at restaurants that can offer the same quality food for a lower price. As this happens, the employers are forced to cut wages. As the workers' pay goes down, their dissatisfaction rises—and more problems set in, producing a vicious cycle.

As can be imagined, it can be extremely frustrating working day after day under harsh and exploitive conditions. Furthermore, particularly, in the Chinese restaurant industry, these conditions spill over into mainstream America as Chinatown workers, particularly illegals, are often recruited to work for very low wages at Chinese restaurants throughout the United States. Often the recruiting takes place in Chinatowns; contracts and conditions are specified and agreed upon, only for workers to find that they've been transported long distances to their new work sites. Trapped in a strange location without transportation or the ability to speak the local language, they have few options for rectifying the situation—which is exacerbated when workers are in the country illegally and owe money to the gangsters who smuggled them in (see Chapter 13). It is not uncommon for these frustrations to build up until a fight breaks out between the employer and the employees.[3]

In the garment industry, too, those who do not hire illegals often must compete with those who do.

As stated, the smuggling of illegal aliens is a big business and involves a wide variety of different crime groups. Few would deny, however, that the Fuk Ching is the premier group involved in moving illegal aliens. This group, whose membership consists primarily of Chinese from Fukien province, has branches on both sides of the Pacific, and its activities, which also include smuggling and transporting heroin, span the globe. Unlike the majority of Chinese crime groups in North America the Fuk Ching, which appears to have been formed in the early 1980s, has little use for the Kuomintang and the government of Taiwan. Instead, it tends to support the People's Republic of China (although, curiously, its one-time parent body, the Fukien American Association, is a member of the CCBA in New York City). In fact, its activities are often aided by corrupt government officials, particularly in China.

In the United States, the group recruits from among Fukienese immigrants in the Chinatowns. It has been known to use illegal aliens frequently as "soldiers" and enforcers in its various operations, who are quite young, often aged 15 to 25, and often it brings in specific groups of tough, desperate young men to provide "muscle" as needed for its various activities. Despite being illegals themselves, these toughs generally show little or no sympathy for their fellow Chinese. The Fuk Ching gang still practices the usual blackmail, kidnapping, extortion, and torture of both the illegals and their employers.

Some Sample Routes For Smuggling Illegal Aliens

Smuggling Routes Used by Taiwanese
1. Taiwan via air to Bolivia, by air to El Salvador, by air to Guatemala, smuggled over the border to Mexico, smuggled over the border to Texas, secretly taken by van to New York City, where they were put to work in a brothel.
2. Taiwan to Palau to Guam.
3. Taiwan to Los Angeles.
4. Taiwan to Vancouver to Seattle.

Smuggling Routes Used by Hong Kong Residents
1. Hong Kong to Frankfurt to Caracas to Panama to Montreal to New York.

2. Hong Kong to Amsterdam to Panama to Montreal to New York.
3. Hong Kong to London to La Paz to Panama to Montreal to New York.
4. Hong Kong to London to Caracas to Panama to Montreal to New York.
5. Hong Kong to London to Miami to Panama to Montreal to New York.
6. Hong Kong to Frankfurt to Caracas to Panama to Montreal to New York.

Smuggling Routes Used by Cantonese from China

1. Guangzhou to Bangkok to Istanbul to Paris to Toronto to New York.
2. Guangzhou to Bangkok to Kuala Lumpur to Los Angeles.
3. Shenzhen to Hong Kong to Singapore to Auckland to Tonga to Fiji to Vancouver to Blaine.
4. Guangzhou to Hong Kong to Bangkok to Bucharest to Helsinki to Toronto to New York.

Smuggling Route Used by Malaysian Chinese

1. Kuala Lumpur to Los Angeles.

Smuggling Routes Used by Fukienese
("Northwest Passage")

1. Fuzhou to Hong Kong to Vancouver to Blaine.
2. Fuzhou to Hong Kong to Vancouver to San Francisco.
3. Fuzhou to Hong Kong to Vancouver to Toronto New York.
4. Fuzhou to Hong Kong to Vancouver to Toronto to Niagara Falls to New York.
5. Fuzhou to Shanghai to Vancouver to Toronto to Champlain to New York.

Smuggling Routes Used by Fukienese
("Bangkok Connections")

1. Fuzhou via land transport to Hong Kong, by air to Bangkok, by air to Canada.
2. Fuzhou to Yunnan, smuggled over the border to Burma, smuggled over the border to Thailand and taken to Chiang Mai flown to Bangkok, and flown to the United States.
3. Fuzhou to Bangkok to Colombo to Zurich to New York.
4. Fuzhou to Hong Kong to Bangkok to Tokyo to Saipan to Guam.
5. Fuzhou to Hong Kong to Bangkok to Seoul to Vancouver to Toronto to New York.
6. Fuzhou to Hong Kong to Bangkok to Copenhagen to Newark.
7. Fuzhou to Hong Kong to Bangkok to Moscow to Havana to Managua to Tucson.
8. Fuzhou to Hong Kong to Bangkok to Kuala Lumpur to Singapore to Dubai to Frankfurt to Washington, D.C.

Smuggling Routes Used by Fukienese
("Straits Ways")

1. Fuzhou to Hong Kong to Kuala Lumpur to Frankfurt to Amsterdam to Belize to New Orleans.

2. Fuzhou to Hong Kong to Singapore to Kuala Lumpur to Tokyo to Seattle.

Smuggling Routes Used by Fukienese
("European Gateways—Holland")

1. Fuzhou to Hong Kong to Amsterdam to La Paz to Guatemala to Mexico City to Tijuana.
2. Fuzhou to Hong Kong to Amsterdam to La Paz to Guatemala to Mexico City to Brownsville.
3. Fuzhou to Hong Kong to Amsterdam to La Paz to Belize to Mexico City to Tijuana.
4. Fuzhou to Hong Kong to Amsterdam to La Paz to Belize to Mexico City to Brownsville.
5. Fuzhou to Hong Kong to Amsterdam to La Paz to Panama to Mexico City to Tijuana.
6. Fuzhou to Hong to Amsterdam to La Paz to Panama to Mexico City to Brownsville.

Smuggling Routes Used by Fukienese
("European Gateways—Germany")

1. Fuzhou to Hong Kong to Frankfurt to Amsterdam to Mexico City to San Diego.
2. Fuzhou to Hong Kong to Frankfurt to Amsterdam to Guatemala to San Salvador to Mexico City to San Diego.
3. Fuzhou to Hong Kong to Frankfurt to Amsterdam to Guatemala to San Salvador to Mexico City to San Diego.
4. Fuzhou to Hong Kong to Frankfurt to Bogota to Mexico City to San Diego.
5. Fuzhou to Hong Kong to Frankfurt to Antigua (Virgin Islands) to New York.

Smuggling Routes (Miscellaneous) Used by Fukienese

1. Fukien by land to Hong Kong by air to Moscow, to Cruz, Bolivia, to Managua, smuggled over the border to Mexico, then smuggled over the border to United States.
2. Fukien by chartered ship to Mombasa, by a different ship to South Africa by ship to New York City.

NOTES

1. It is my contention that Chinese crime groups do not grow into the monolithic, monopolistic, underground "illuminati"-type secret societies that they are often perceived to be. Without the complicity of government agencies and law enforcement corruption, there seem to be limits to the control that such groups are able to maintain over the world.
2. The Three Mountain Society is a little-known Fukienese crime group with a branch in New York City.
3. Often when the local police are called to the scene of such a fight in a Chinese restaurant or other location, they are extremely confused as the level of violence is completely out of proportion to the situation. At times, the investigators focus in on the

spark that set off the conflict (i.e., division of tips, access to eating leftovers) or some other trivial issue rather than the underlying pattern of abusive exploitation that might have existed. Those who seek to understand problems and fights involving Chinese employees should be prepared to look for complex, hidden issues rather than superficial causes.

B ecause of the high demand and value of illicit drugs of all sorts, it is only natural that organized crime would be in the drug trade. In Asia and around the world, Chinese crime groups have taken an active role in the production, smuggling, sale, and distribution of illegal drugs. At times, one group appears to dominate the sale and distribution of a particular substance, but more commonly a variety of criminal, noncriminal, business organizations, and individuals work together to profit from the worldwide underground market.

Marijuana from Thailand and Cambodia is smuggled and sold by the Hong Kong-based triads. Amphetamines (including "ice") are produced and sold by a variety of Japanese, Korean, and Taiwanese groups, including the United Bamboo and the Four Seas gangs. The Chinese Big Circle gang has even been known to dabble in the sale and smuggling of *South American* cocaine to the United States.

Nevertheless, if there's one drug associated with Chinese organized crime groups, it is heroin. The bulk of the world's heroin is refined in Southeast Asia from locally manufactured opium, which comes from the opium poppy. It can be smoked in its pure form or refined and treated with chemicals to produce more sophisticated drugs collectively referred to as opiates. Some of the common opiates include morphine, codeine, Dilaudid, and heroin. Some of these, such as morphine, are widely known and accepted as legal but strictly controlled (and addictive) painkillers. Others, such as heroin, have no legitimate medical use (at least not in the United States, though heroin is used as a painkiller in parts of

CHAPTER 11

DRUGS AND DRUG SMUGGLING: THE ASIAN SIDE

Europe), and their use, manufacture, and sale are almost universally banned.

Although opium is grown in southern Mexico, India, and such Southwest Asian nations as Afghanistan and Pakistan, the bulk of the world's opium comes from an area in Southeast Asia known as "the Golden Triangle." Chinese businessmen have proven themselves quite successful in many enterprises throughout Southeast Asia, and the profitable heroin trade of that region is no exception. In fact, for many reasons, it seems that the Chinese were destined to figure prominently in the world's narcotic trade.

see p. 42

PRODUCING AND GROWING GOLDEN TRIANGLE OPIUM

The Golden Triangle was traditionally said to comprise three nations—Laos, Burma, and Thailand—and is increasingly coming to include parts of neighboring areas of China, particularly in Yunnan province. Curiously, however, opium is not native to these regions; its long and strange history begins elsewhere.

The opium poppy comes from the eastern Mediterranean. The ancient Greeks knew of opium's medical uses as early as 5 B.C. The ancient Chinese wrote about its uses in 8 A.D. All of them recognized opium as a powerful drug and believed it to be an important medicine. Due to its medicinal value, opium was cultivated and spread eastward into India and Southwest Asia by Arab traders who sold the plant, its products, and its seeds among their many commodities. By the 16th century, opium was documented as being used for "recreational" purposes by the upper classes of Persia and India. When European explorers and traders came to Asia around the 17th century, they sensed an opportunity for profit and began taking the drug farther east and selling it in large quantities in China.

By 1650 the Dutch were delivering and selling 50 tons of opium a year to the Chinese. Furthermore, they introduced the practice of smoking it in tobacco pipes, further popularizing the use of the addictive drug. In 1729, the emperor of China became sufficiently alarmed that he banned the drug and its use throughout China and outlawed its import. Sadly, this did not end the flow of the drug into China, nor did it stop the use and abuse of opium. Instead, it marked the beginning of the modern era of narcotics smuggling.

At that time, the Europeans were illegally smuggling opium into China, but the process would reverse itself, and one day the Chinese, in their turn, would smuggle the drug and its products into Europe and to the North American nations established by Europeans. Even more ironic is the fact that today the European center for Chinese heroin smuggling and distribution is Holland, the home of the Dutch, who initiated the trade of opium in China.[1]

In the 18th century, the British conquered large sections of India. These territories were managed for the crown by the British East India Company, an organization created by the British government. As long as it remained loyal and profitable, this company was allowed a lot of freedom in its actions, one of which was taking an active role in exporting Indian opium to China, knowing full well that this violated Chinese law.

The Chinese found it virtually impossible to keep foreign opium out. Their customs departments were understaffed, many of their officials were corrupt, and the Europeans (and Americans) were dealing in opium everywhere. This eventually led to the Opium Wars of 1839 and 1856, in which China was defeated by the British (and French in the second war). As a result of their losing, the Chinese were forced to open their country to more goods from Europe and other outside countries; among such goods was, of course, much more British-imported opium.[2]

Opium had long been seen as a legitimate cash crop. Since it was so valuable, its growth spread to other regions of Asia. Seeking profits, the French introduced it into some of their Southeast Asian colonies. Although opium was generally seen as a vice, throughout the 19th century it was nevertheless perfectly legal in most of the world, including the United States and England.

Over the past 100 years, however, there has been a significant change in attitude. Today, the production and use of opium and its derivatives are generally condemned, but the unrestricted growth and sale of the plant continues in many regions where its production was encouraged by Westerners more than 100 years ago! Efforts to stop this growth are met with great resistance among the many peoples to whom the harvesting and raising of opium has become a traditional part of life.

Since trade in opium is condemned by the world community, the product is often grown in areas that are isolated and difficult for the authorities to reach.

THAILAND

In Thailand, a nation with very close ties with the outside world and extensive trade and tourism, the importance and amount of opium grown has been decreasing steadily. The relatively small Thai opium crop is raised mostly by non-Thai hill tribesmen who live in the north near the borders with Burma, China, and Laos. They traditionally have raised small amounts of opium on subsistence farms for personal use and to sell on the open market. Like marijuana farms in the United States, these opium farms are often quite difficult to find. Furthermore, because the opium farmers are usually very poor, authorities are reluctant to enforce prohibitions on its growth completely in the region. To do so would most likely cause starvation and ruin among the farmers and their families. The Thai government, with the assistance of the United States, the United Nations (UN), and other nations, has tried various programs to encourage the farmers to substitute other crops for opium, but these efforts have often been half-hearted and poorly designed. For example, one program encouraged farmers to grow coffee instead of opium. Unfortunately, when harvest time came, the usual round of opium merchants arrived at the villages, but nobody arrived to purchase the new coffee crop. Similarly, a UN program to encourage the hill tribesmen to substitute kidney beans for opium poppies also suffered from the lack of a market for the new crop. The first year of the program, the UN was forced to purchase the entire crop of kidney beans out of its own budget.

The hill tribesmen have generally low literacy and lack much formal education; they have little sense of the value or harm that their product has or causes abroad. Although they themselves suffer from the use of opium, one could make a valid argument that the quantities they grow and use are no more harmful to their society than alcohol is to ours. The tribesmen grow opium to make a living in a traditional way, often the only way they know how.

LAOS *legal of all S.E. Asian to raise opium*

In Laos, a former French colony, a large percentage of the population belongs to ethnic groups that are either closely related to or the same people as the hill tribesmen of Thailand. As in northern Thailand, opium in Laos is an important cash crop in the outlying provinces of Bo Kheo and Luang Nam Tha, which border on Burma. For this reason, travel is dangerous to outsiders because the opium growers often suspect that any foreigner entering the area is a foreign drug enforcement agent.

Post-World War II Laos has not been particularly stable politically, and economically it has many problems, not the least of which is a per-capita annual income that is the U.S. equivalent of $135—one of the lowest in the world. With the government anxious to do what it can to raise incomes, Laos is the only nation in Southeast Asia where it is actually legal to raise opium. The legal sale of the product is then supposed to be monitored and controlled by a government monopoly, but in practice it doesn't always work that way. Like most communist nations, Laos has a thriving black market, and it is estimated that half of the opium crop is smuggled into Thailand and then clandestinely shipped by Thai smugglers. As an increasing amount of opium is being smuggled through China and Hong Kong these days, it seems safe to suspect that a portion of the Laotian opium crop is also making its way to the outside world by this route. Most of the smuggled opium crop is shipped in its raw form, but at least some is refined into heroin in Laos. Although the government of Laos denies any knowledge of heroin refineries within its borders, it is curious that tourism and other foreign travel are strictly forbidden in the region in which these refineries are said to operate.

BURMA

The third source country for Golden Triangle opium is Burma. Burma is a very troubled nation. A former British colony, Burma obtained independence in 1948. Like many former British colonies in other parts of the world, Burma comprised many different ethnic groups that had little in common, no shared history, and no desire to be united in a political state. Although the primary ethnic group is the Burmese (who make up two-thirds of the population and live essentially in the south-central portion of the nation), many of the other groups have sought independence ever since Burma received its own from Britain. When they were unable to obtain it politically, many groups openly revolted against the government. Currently, the Burmese government controls the approximately two-thirds of the country where the ethnic Burmese live; the non-Burmese minorities tend to live mostly in the areas near the borders. The different ethnic groups are frequently in opposition to each other as well as to the government and its State Law and Order Restoration Council (SLORC).

The general consensus about the Burmese government is that it is corrupt, inefficient, cruel, and just plain bad.[3]

The Burmese currency is virtually worthless outside Burma, which makes any sort of foreign trade difficult. An extensive black market thrives and deals in almost anything. With all this, it seems almost tangential to mention that Burma is also the largest producer of opium and heroin in the world today.

The whole northern third of the country is a morass of little fiefdoms, tribal territories, occupied zones, and "liberated zones" that are controlled by a confusing variety of opium drug lords, ethnic nationalist guerrillas, at least one Burmese rebel group dedicated to overthrowing SLORC, and at least one Chinese Nationalist Kuomintang army still roaming the jungle.[4]

One thing all of these groups in Burma have in common, however, is a need for money with which to buy supplies. The overwhelming majority of them has discovered that the simplest way to meet this need is to sell opium or opium products to the outside world. Although all the groups are generally hostile to the central government, they frequently fight among themselves, often over control of the opium-growing areas and the smuggling routes. In many cases, the battle for opium and opium profits has taken on a life of its own, and it is virtually impossible to tell which of the opium-selling groups are idealistic antigovernment guerrillas and which are simply organized crime groups fortunate enough to have established themselves in an area where the anarchy allows their operations to continue unchecked. Despite the opium trade, these rebel groups do not have the support or supplies to overthrow the central government. Similarly, the central government does not have the support or supplies to overthrow them. No real change in the situation is expected soon.

Although the United States has considered increasing aid to the Burmese government in order to assist it in suppressing the growth of opium, this would undoubtedly be quite unwise. The hopelessly corrupt Burmese government has misused U.S. aid in the past, has a reprehensible human rights record, and furthermore, has no strong desire to eradicate the growth of opium within its borders, although it does wish to gain control over the territories in which the opium is primarily grown.

CHINA

Today many people add a fourth nation, China, to the traditional Golden Triangle. China, and Yunnan province in particular, borders on all of these nations and, like them, has a long history of growing opium. When the Communists took over China, however, they made a point of suppressing opium production and commerce. Although that eradication program was one of the most successful antidrug measures in history, no one outside China has expressed an interest in copying it, despite its simplicity. Zealous People's Liberation Army soldiers simply shot anyone who owned, grew, or sold opium. As for China's millions of opium addicts, they were simply rounded up and locked in isolation until they finished their dangerous withdrawal from the addictive drug. The surviving addicts were then sent off to reeducation camps, taught a skill, and given a new start on life. The program was a great success, despite its complete lack of regard for the rights, health, and safety of suspected addicts, dealers, and growers.[5]

The People's Republic of China has always grown a small amount of opium for such legitimate medical purposes as morphine production. There have always been rumors that the Chinese were producing much more than they needed and secretly shipping heroin to the West as part of a plan to destroy and undermine capitalist societies.[6] There has never been hard proof of these claims, the majority of which smack of right-wing cold war propaganda. It is generally accepted, however, that corruption in China has reached a point where the drug can be smuggled overland through China from the Golden Triangle to Hong Kong. Similarly, most observers now believe that opium is being grown illegally for export in China's Yunnan province.

THE ECONOMICS AND LOGISTICS OF THE WORLD NARCOTICS TRADE

It surprises many Westerners that the bulk of the opium grown in Southeast Asia is also consumed there. Nevertheless, there is still plenty left over to be shipped to the United States, and there are many ways in which the opium crop ends up as heroin on the streets of New York City and elsewhere. Collecting, smuggling, distributing, refining, and processing the drug can take many forms and follow strange paths. Some of the processes are long and intricate, involving heavily armed Kuomintang mule caravans, Nigerian organized crime members acting as mules, and the American Mafia distributing the final product throughout the United States. Some heroin smuggling involves large-scale chains of organization in which major organized crime syndicates, and even governments, are links.

One point of controversy is whether there is centralized control of drug production, smuggling, and distribution. Some argue that the entire process is controlled by a hidden organization consisting of an integrated network of tongs, gangs, secret societies, Chinese and non-Chinese business people, politicians, and espionage agents, all working in harmony. These people are said to have set up an international crime syndicate or two designed to make as much money as possible while undermining Western civilization. Proponents of this conspiracy theory often advocate the belief that one organization, the so-called Chinese Mafia, essentially controls the entire heroin trade from a central headquarters.

The second school of thought claims that although there is an intricate network of people and organizations getting illegal opium products to the United States and elsewhere, it was created by the simple economics of supply and demand. No one actually arranged for the opium to get from Asia all the way to North

America in large quantities. In other words, under this supply and demand theory, at every step of the way, people simply did what they felt was the most profitable act until the supply of opium products reached all the places where people were willing to pay enough money to make it profitable to ship the product.

I believe that although a large degree of organization is necessary, the process of getting the product to market is not necessarily controlled by the same group of people at all steps of the way in order to make the maximum profits. In fact, at the lowest (street) level, many heroin addicts are involved in both buying and selling heroin in a completely unorganized way. Even if we assume organizations are involved, it is quite possible that different, competing organizations are doing the same things in slightly different ways at each step of the process. Finally, although organizations do much of the trading, shipping, and distribution of opium, there really is nothing that keeps individuals from trying their hand at heroin smuggling as well.

Experts believe that the typical organizing force behind sending a shipment of heroin to the United States from Asia is a small, loosely knit band of criminals, businessmen, and investors. The criminals use their connections to arrange for successful shipping, smuggling, and receiving of the heroin. The investors buy shares in a particular shipment, and if it makes it to the United States they will be reimbursed many times over for their investment. If the shipment is intercepted or lost, then all who purchased shares will lose. Naturally, since certain losses are expected, this is considered a high-risk investment; but generally speaking, all involved expect to make a profit over the course of multiple shipments. Often the investors are people who would not otherwise be considered criminals, and they normally invest in heroin shipments on a "one shipment at a time basis." It may be assumed that they are recruited through personal contacts.[7]

The economics of illegal markets are very complicated, but the point here is that it is extremely difficult to maintain a centrally organized international crime cartel capable of overseeing and monitoring the sale and distribution of a drug while keeping the process secret from the authorities and competitors.

CUTTING THE DRUG OFF AT THE SOURCE

Many have looked into the possibility of somehow stopping the cultivation of opium, thereby cutting off the flow of heroin at the source. It's my feeling that American politicians and others like to advocate this because it places the blame for the entire American drug abuse situation on foreigners. It also makes it seem as if a fleet of B-52s could solve the entire problem without inconveniencing or alienating any American voters in the least.

But there are many problems in cutting off the flow of drugs, specifically heroin, at the source. Some of the problems are economic and political. The situations in Laos, Thailand, Burma, and China have already been outlined, showing the complex political and economic factors involved in opium raising and trafficking.

Destroying the crops is not a viable option. Aside from the political consequences, a series of bombing runs over the opium-growing regions of the Golden Triangle simply would not eradicate the crop. Dropping defoliants would not necessarily make much difference. Poisonous defoliants were dropped on the marijuana crops in both Thailand and Mexico, and in both cases the farmers sold the product anyway. This resulted in the deaths or illnesses of some users, but little reduction in the amount of the drug actually shipped or grown in subsequent years. Furthermore, the world still remembers all the problems the United States caused by dumping Agent Orange all over Vietnam, causing illness in many Vietnamese civilians and U.S. servicemen.

The levels of official frustration become apparent when one looks at some of the bizarre schemes that have been suggested for eradicating the Southeast Asian opium crops. Among those that have been seriously discussed are a UN Division of Narcotic Drugs proposal to use poppy weevils to eat the opium poppies and a U.S. Army Land Warfare Laboratory proposal to breed large numbers of other opium-eating insects and drop them onto areas where opium exists.

In the end, none of these proposals, even if successful, would actually destroy the world's entire opium supply. Like marijuana, opium (at least in small quantities) is now grown even in the United States.

Preparing and Refining the
Opium Crop for Shipment

In most of the Golden Triangle, opium merchants come to the villages and purchase the crop from the farmers. These merchants are not large-scale drug kingpins but merely low-level buyers. Since the opium is grown far off the beaten track and away from the major highways, it is often packaged and shipped by mule train; motor vehicles simply could not enter the areas (helicopters are too expensive and would attract too much attention). In some areas, such as those occupied by the various Burman insurgency groups, the armed troops of one group or another might collect the opium crop. Particularly in the more backward areas of Burma, the opium caravans are guarded by heavily armed paramilitary guards.

These caravans then ship the opium to refineries in Burma, Laos, or possibly China. Although many refineries were once located in northern Thailand, increased law enforcement efforts have forced their relocation. It is simply much more economical to locate refineries for Thai opium in Burma, as close as possible to the border. In the past, there were heroin refineries in Hong Kong and other major cities, but these were always at risk of discovery, not to mention destruction and injury. The refining process is dangerous, and accidents occasionally happened that resulted in explosions.

Refining opium into various grades of heroin is a multistep process, and it can be carried out at a series of refineries spaced between the opium-growing area and the final market destination. Increasingly, heroin refinery is done on ships with a mobile laboratory setup. Although this reduces the chance of exposure, it does tend to make the results of any accidental explosions more severe (Posner 1988, 169).

The Chiu Chau Syndicates

The most important of the large variety of groups and individuals involved in the international heroin trade are the Chiu Chau syndicates. The Chiu Chau (also spelled Teochiu and Chauzhou) are a relatively obscure Chinese subgroup that originated in a town called Shantou (formerly spelled Swatow) on the southern coast of China. As China opened up to foreign trade and Chinese began to emigrate abroad in ever larger numbers, the Chiu Chau, being a coastal people, began to go abroad seeking opportunity too. Ultimately, they became one of the most important Chinese groups in Thailand, made up a substantial minority in Hong Kong (about 5 to 8 percent of the population), and managed to become extremely important in the opium trade around Shanghai in the 19th and 20th centuries, before the 1949 Communist Revolution.

The rise of the Chiu Chau syndicates was closely tied to the rise of Shanghai, which, like Hong Kong, is a surprisingly modern city. Although Chinese civilization is thousands of years old, traditionally it had little use for foreign trade, and most of its coastal trading cities have grown to prominence only within the last 150 years or so. Prior to the 1840s, Shanghai was a village at the entrance to the Yangtze River whose economy revolved mostly around subsistence fishing and weaving. Although it was walled to prevent attacks by Japanese pirates, Shanghai seemingly had little interest in foreign affairs or trade. But the British forcibly established a trading concession in the town following their victory in the first Opium War. This eventually brought traders and merchants from France, the United States, Russia, and the other nations of Europe, as well as Japan. With foreign investment and an increased demand for services by wealthy Chinese and foreign merchants and residents, the city grew to be one of China's leading metropolitan centers.

There was a dark side to this growth. Shanghai also became a center for vice and corruption. The bustling, lawless center of Shanghai attracted the less scrupulous, more adventurous sort from both the foreign and Chinese populations. A kind of symbiotic relationship grew up between the foreign and Chinese entrepreneurs of the city. This became known as the *comprador system.*[8] Foreign traders found it much simpler to deal with a variety of established Chinese merchants and trading companies, the compradors, which would act as middlemen between the foreigners and the Chinese in the trading ports such as Shanghai and the interior.

TONGS, GANGS, AND TRIADS: CHINESE CRIME GROUPS IN NORTH AMERICA

The Chinese compradors in the Shanghai opium trade were primarily Chiu Chau Chinese. Because there was nothing illegal about the trade following the British-imposed legalization following the first Opium War, the Chiu Chau opium compradors organized themselves into a variety of legitimate companies.

In 1840 the Shanghai Municipal Opium Monopoly was established, which controlled and regulated the use and sale of opium in the city. The monopoly also leased the rights to own and operate opium dens to many Western merchants. They, however, left much of the day-to-day management and policing of the opium dens to the Chiu Chau opium compradors. When European and American attitudes ultimately changed, Western merchants left the opium trade, while many Chiu Chau remained involved.

Today, much of the worldwide opium trade is controlled by Chiu Chau merchants and criminal syndicates. The Sun Yee On, said to be the largest triad in the world, is a Chiu Chau triad, although today many of its members are not ethnic Chiu Chau Chinese. Vincent Jew, former leader of the Wah Ching, was a member of this triad (and most likely the Tung On) as well. W.P. Morgan's 1960 work, *Triad Societies in Hong Kong*, listed more than 20 different criminally linked Chiu Chau organizations as being active in Hong Kong at that time.

NOTES

1. Holland has some of Europe's most lax laws regarding the sale and possession of heroin and other vices. Furthermore, its legal system has traditionally tended to focus on the apprehension and rehabilitation of offenders rather than the punishment of their associates. Furthermore, Holland has thriving vice and sex industries and is fairly centrally located in Europe, all of which tends to make the distribution and sale of hard drugs easier.
2. The second Opium War is occasionally referred to as the Arrow War. The spark that set off the conflict was when the Chinese illegally boarded the *Arrow*, a Chinese ship sailing under British flag.
3. If you would like to know more about Burma's appalling human rights record and what you can do about it, you may contact the following: Amnesty International, 322 8th Ave., New York, NY 10001; and Human Rights Watch, Publications Dept. 485 Fifth Ave., 3rd Floor, New York, NY 10017.
4. It is quite difficult to keep track of who these groups are and which territories they control at any given time. My requests to the U.S. State Department, the Drug Enforcement Agency (DEA), and other government agencies for clarification were

met with the reply that such information is "classified."

5. See Zhang Xinxin and Sang Ye, *Chinese Lives*, (New York: Pantheon Books, 1987) for a fascinating firsthand account of the story of a reformed prostitute and the very positive changes the Communist Revolution made in her life. Like many prostitutes in prerevolutionary China, she was sold into the profession, kept in it against her will, received about 20 clients a day, and became addicted to opium as a way to escape the horrors of her life. She discusses being imprisoned and rehabilitated against her will in this manner and credits the process and the Communist party with saving her life and giving her the chance to start over.

6. For one example of these claims, refer to A.H. Stanton Candlin's *Psycho-Chemical Warfare: The Chinese Communist Drug Offensive against the West* (New Rochelle, NY: Arlington House, 1973). Keep in mind, however, that the claims in this book are not generally accepted, and Alfred McCoy's *The Politics of Heroin* is much more widely believed (Brooklyn, NY: Lawrence Hill Books, 1991).

7. See Ko-lin Chin's *Chinese Subculture and Criminality: Nontraditional Crime Groups in America* (Westport, CT: Greenwood Press, 1990); U.S. Senate hearing notes, *Asian Organized Crime: Hearing before the Permanent Subcommittee on Investigations of the Committee on Governmental Affairs,* 102nd Cong., 1st sess., 1992; and U.S. Senate hearing notes, *Asian Organized Crime—The New International Criminal: Hearing before the Permanent Subcommittee on Investigations of the Committee on Governmental Affairs,* 102nd Cong., 2nd sess., 1992.

8. The original trading center for Europeans in China was the Portuguese colony of Macao on the south coast. The term comprador grew out of a Portuguese term meaning buyer.

The last chapter dealt with how heroin, opium, and other drugs are produced in Asia. In this chapter, we will see how those drugs get to the United States and what happens to them after they arrive.

Drugs produced in the relatively close areas of the world, such as Latin America, the West Indies, and the Caribbean, are often smuggled in bulk. Commonly small private planes or fast boats that are capable of making the trip covertly and quickly are used. After a few such trips, the profits from the drug smuggling have paid for the plane or boat. With drugs from Asia, this is not really feasible, since small vehicles are generally not capable of crossing the Pacific.

Fortunately for drug smugglers and unfortunately for law enforcement, there is a constant flow of legitimate products, tourism, and business back and forth across the Pacific that can be used to mask the flow of drugs and other contraband. For instance, heroin can be smuggled in on a large commercial vessel engaged in otherwise legitimate business. In some cases, a single crew member might hide a small quantity on board without the captain or the crew even knowing about it. In other cases the captain and ship owner are involved, and things become more elaborate. For example, there have been ships with false double bulkheads added so that smugglers can hide drugs in between the twin walls.

Obviously, it can be difficult to notice such changes in the ship's construction, particularly when one realizes that there are only so many customs people and a thorough search of every ship

CHAPTER 12

DRUGS AND DRUG SMUGGLING: THE NORTH AMERICAN SIDE

entering a nation is generally impossible. Even when a customs service has been notified of the presence of contraband, finding it can be a lengthy and difficult process. In *The Triads*, Sean O'Callaghan, a writer whose works have often focused on heroin, opium, and the drug trade in Asia and elsewhere, describes a case where a European customs service had been given definite information that heroin was being smuggled on board a particular ship. Because the exact site and method of hiding the heroin were unknown, it took five full hours of careful and systematic searching by professionals to uncover it (O'Callaghan 1978, 136).

In other cases, the contraband is hidden in the cargo, and generally the vessel's crew will have no idea that they are carrying it. In some instances, the techniques for smuggling such items can be quite ingenious: for example, in one case the heroin was dissolved in water and the water was then frozen and used for packing shipments of frozen shrimp from Thailand.[1] There are, however, simpler and easier methods.

While a large number of ships enter the United States or Canada every day, the number of humans who do so is much greater. Because customs agents and other law enforcement officials devote more time searching for large quantities of contraband than small ones, they often inspect commercial cargoes more thoroughly than tourists' luggage. This is only natural; there are fewer large cargoes than there are tourists' bags entering the United States.

The late Abbie Hoffman, an admitted radical who openly favored drug legalization, once estimated that if the U.S. population uses six tons of heroin a year (before cutting), and if a pair of suitcases can conceal 26 pounds of heroin, then the year's supply of heroin to the United States could be brought in by fewer than 500 of the approximately 500,000 people who enter the country each year on legitimate business or pleasure trips (Hoffman 1987, 39). This estimate admittedly ignored such factors as the possibility that customs people might be able to distinguish at least some of these smugglers. Nevertheless, statistically speaking, the odds favor the person carrying the drugs getting through customs without being caught. (Of course, most people look apprehensive or nervous while doing this, and customs people focus on this, so it is not entirely a matter of statistics.)

Drug couriers are made up of a wide variety of different travelers. When a smuggling ring substitutes a piece of luggage similar in make and model to that of an innocent, unknowing traveler, the traveler passes through customs and takes the risks of smuggling heroin. Because most nations' customs people simply do not have the time or manpower to make a thorough search of every piece of baggage coming in, they depend a lot on such intangibles as whether the traveller fits a "profile," appears unnaturally nervous, strikes the customs person as particularly suspicious, or simply the intuition and mood of the customs officer at any given time. Since those who do not realize that they are carrying contraband are not nervous about it and rarely fit a profile for a drug smuggler, they are less likely to be searched.

There is an on-again, off-again network of people making "milk runs" or trips for the small-scale smuggling of otherwise innocuous items. The trips are normally organized by local Asians who arrange to ship the goods to another country and have someone pick them up upon arrival. For example, a person in Korea might wish to have gold, cameras, and other electronics items from Taiwan. The organizer in Taiwan might wish to receive clothing and textiles manufactured in Korea and heavily taxed in Taiwan.

Foreigners are used as "couriers" in such operations because they obtain visas easily. Also, generally speaking, they have powerful governments that, if not entirely sympathetic, will usually, at the very least, attempt to ensure that their citizens are only arrested and imprisoned for acts that are actually illegal in the nation in which they get arrested. In Asia, if one knows where to look, there is a steady supply of foreigners who are willing to break minor laws and take risks in return for cheap thrills, pocket money, and the opportunity to travel. The easiest source of couriers is the steady supply of young, adventuresome budget travelers, college dropouts, students, and other misplaced Europeans, Americans, Canadians, and Australians, who can be found at budget hostels throughout Asia. They are normally provided with a round-trip ticket to their destination and back, a free hotel room for a night or two, and a small supply of cash (often considerably less than the U.S. equivalent of $150) to cover their expenses while at their destination.

Although it is generally a condition of such milk runs that the carriers insist on the opportunity to inspect all the luggage and items that they carry to their satisfaction prior to making the trip, I have spoken to some who state that they were not allowed the time to do this.

On occasion, desperate misplaced travelers can be talked into doing things they otherwise would not do, including carrying packages or even knowingly risking prosecution for carrying drugs. There are others who look like budget travelers who actually make something of a career out of doing this. The primary requisites of successfully functioning as a drug courier are luck and nerve. Few people can repeatedly carry a load of drugs that could send them away for life without looking at least somewhat nervous while passing through customs.

Europeans and North Americans are not the only ones used for such enterprises. The Chinese syndicates who organize such smuggling runs are quick to recruit from various Asian ethnic groups. In the past, Filipinos and Thais have been used, as have a wide variety of Chinese. The motivations of the Chinese who carry drugs are almost as varied as the individuals themselves. Some are willing to face the risks involved for the opportunity to make money. Some are merely little old ladies who wish to have the opportunity to see relatives and grandchildren in North America and are willing to carry a mysterious package or two for someone who might buy them a ticket. Others are men who have racked up a thousands of dollars in gambling debts and face the possibility of receiving crippling injuries or losing their family businesses to organized thugs. Such men sometimes see the offer to remove their debts by serving as a courier as a God-sent opportunity.

A surprising amount of the worldwide smuggling of Golden Triangle opiates in the past 10 years has been done by Nigerians. Criminal gangs, so-called fraud gangs, from this West African nation have shown a great deal of interest in sharing in the profits of this illicit trade. Apparently, Nigerian smugglers began offering their services as couriers on their own initiative.

Although customs and law enforcement officials seek to keep track of trends and maintain up-to-date profiles on what sort of person is likely to be carrying heroin, this is virtually impossible. In April 1971 Prince Sopsaisana, the then recently appointed Laotian ambassador to France, was refused diplomatic credentials by the French government. In other words, he was not allowed to remain in France, and the Laotians were forced to replace him. The reason for this was quite simple: he was discovered, following an anonymous tip, to be carrying 60 kilos of heroin with a then estimated street value of $13.5 million.[3]

Also in 1971, the son of the Panamanian ambassador to Taiwan was arrested, along with his uncle, for possession of 70 kilos of heroin while passing through Kennedy Airport in New York City. Authorities believe that the pair had been involved in bringing previous shipments of heroin into the United States.

Sometimes smugglers carry the contraband inside a suitcase or other carrier without hiding it. They simply assume that the customs personnel will search someone else. To get an innocent traveler to carry drugs through customs unknowingly, as well as switching similar suitcases on unsuspecting voyagers, smugglers simply ask a helpful-looking person to carry a bag through for them. Such requests are accompanied by some plausible reason why the drug smugglers can't carry it themselves. In some such cases, the smugglers reclaim the suitcase after the good "Samaritan" has risked years in prison. In other cases, the smugglers actually hope that the person is caught, knowing that this will serve as a distraction, allowing them to pass through customs more easily with a larger, more carefully hidden load of drugs.

There is seemingly an infinite number of different ways to hide drugs. It can be done in another piece of luggage or property (for example, with a false bottom, or the tubular frame of a baggage cart). Drugs are hidden inside teddy bears and other stuffed toys, which have an air of innocence. Conversely, smugglers place contraband drugs in items such as large rubber dildos, knowing full well that many people, even in customs, find such items embarrassing or distasteful and don't wish to give them any more than a casual inspection. Almost anything can be hollowed out and have drugs placed inside it, and almost anything has. Smugglers have taken a large D-size battery and placed a smaller AA battery inside. When this is done, the hollowed out D battery can still provide electricity, and drug-containing batteries can then be placed in a portable appliance, which will still run normally. The only way to tell the difference between these batteries and others is by their weight.

Drugs can also be hidden inside people. One of the most common methods is for a carrier to swallow condoms or balloons containing heroin or other drugs. This is dangerous; on occasion the condoms rupture, releasing large quantities of the drug into the carrier's system, which is almost always fatal. Nevertheless, when the pay is good, there is always somebody somewhere willing to take the risks. Smugglers have found ways to hide drugs on their person by using straps and harnesses to fasten drugs inconspicuously to different parts of their bodies. Drugs are put inside the artificial limbs of amputees. There are cases of women being arrested for smuggling while traveling with heroin-in-filled dildos inserted in their vaginas. I have even heard stories about persons who have had small quantities of heroin surgically implanted deep within their legs in order to pass through customs uninspected. Large quantities of drugs are often hidden within larger items of industrial machinery, such as washing machines and refrigerators.

At times, smugglers reduce their chances of being inspected by taking roundabout routes, using false documents and fake visa stamps to conceal their travel from drug source countries. Upon arrival in the United States, the Chinese crime groups normally resell heroin in bulk to other criminals and allow them to handle its redistribution and sale. For this reason, it is generally rare to find Chinese crime groups involved in the street-level sales, which are normally done by the African-Americans, Hispanics, and traditional Mafiosi to whom the gangs sell the drugs in bulk. This still allows for a hefty profit for the drug smugglers while reducing the risks involved.

Even though drug smuggling is more loosely organized than many people think, the criminal contacts that come with belonging to an organized crime group—be it a tong, a triad, or a well-organized gang—are nevertheless invaluable to those who smuggle drugs. For this reason, a great deal of the income that Chinese organized crime receives comes from the illicit drug markets.

NOTES

1. See *DEA Classified Intelligence Reports* (Boulder, CO: Paladin Press, 1988), 38.
2. This "street value" is based on prices in New York City, its probable destination, in 1971. At this time, the famed "French Connection" was operating, with Corsican syndicates in league with the American and Sicilian Mafia smuggling heroin across the Atlantic at a fairly steady pace. Although at present, some transshipping does occur, it is much less likely that shipping heroin from Laos to the United States via France is economically viable. See Alfred McCoy, *The Politics of Heroin* (Chicago: Lawrence Hill Books, 1991), 379-380.

There is a great deal of concern in some circles about the future of the "Chinese Mafia" in North America. Some claim it will grow and become even more powerful than the Italian Mafia is now or ever was. Throughout this work, I have done my best to avoid the term "Chinese Mafia" because it implies that there is a unified, centrally organized, all-encompassing Chinese crime syndicate. Although many of the details of Chinese organized crime remain hidden and unknown, there does not seem to be such a unified central organization, but rather a wide variety of different and competing organizations.

For example, in February 1989, in a combined operation, the FBI and the New York City Police Department arrested 44 persons and confiscated $3 million in cash and 820 pounds of 90-percent-pure heroin. The operation, code-named "White Mare," involved arrests at three separate locations in the city and surrounding boroughs. Among the 44 persons arrested were members of five separate Asian drug-trafficking groups.[1]

In my opinion, Chinese organized crime in America (and virtually everywhere else) consists of a large number of small, autonomous gangs and groups with only marginal connections between them. Although some of these gangs may be part of the same umbrella organization or different chapters of the same groups, their operations are not run from the same central office. Many experts argue that in a country where the government seeks to suppress organized crime activity, organized crime groups cannot grow beyond a certain size without inevitably being noticed or detected and then coming into conflict with the authorities.

CHAPTER 13

THE UNDERGROUND ECONOMY AND THE FUTURE OF GANGS

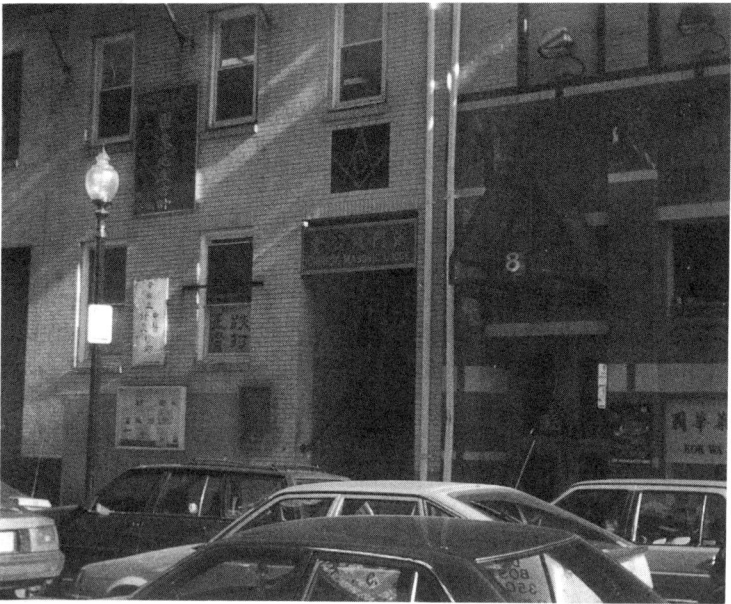

Boston headquarters of the On Leong Tong and the Chi Kung Tong (Chinese Freemasons).

TONGS, GANGS, AND TRIADS:
CHINESE CRIME GROUPS IN NORTH AMERICA

It is important to understand that there are a great many Chinese crime groups of varying sizes and levels of organization within the United States and Canada. An example is the variety of tongs based in the Chinatowns of North America. These tongs originated as self-help organizations for men but are now primarily social organizations. Although many of their members are criminals or involved in crime, the primary concern of the tongs is usually to act for the benefit of their members, to preserve the conservative political situation in Chinatown, and to do so without calling undue attention to themselves from the mainstream American authorities.

Some have argued that the CCBAs of the United States and Canada are, or may soon develop into, a centralized organization that will control the tongs and manage and supervise their organized crime activities in North America. This is unlikely. Although the CCBA includes tongs in its list of member organizations, it is not exclusively tong-oriented. Its purpose since the 19th century has been to serve as a governmental and representative organization for the Chinese in North America. It and its members comprise a mixture of criminal and noncriminal groups and individuals, and it would probably meet with a great deal of difficulty if it were to become more widely identified with criminal activities. This would also make its lobbying efforts on behalf of the Kuomintang more difficult, as its prominent members would be marked as being linked with organized crime and the group would lose much of its legitimacy.

The Chinatown gangs are becoming more developed and organized as their members age and the experience and sophistication of the various groups increase. Nevertheless, their traditional strength has always been their recklessness and impenetrability by law enforcement, and with this increased organization, both are at risk. Traditionally, Chinese gangs have confined almost all their activities to preying on the Chinese community. They will continue to be a threat to Chinese and others in America for the foreseeable future, but it is difficult to see the gangs preying on mainstream American society. Although this could happen, it would pose some serious problems for the gangs who tried it.

Mainstream Americans are much quicker to notify the authorities of threats by gang members than are Chinese immigrants. For this reason, most Chinese gangs simply don't see it as worthwhile to prey on non-Chinese as long as there is a ready pool of Chinese or other Asian victims available. In areas of the United States and Canada where other types of gangs have become a fact of life, the Chinese gangs would have to compete with them, and this would be difficult to impossible. Furthermore, as Chinese gangs become more sophisticated and adapted to North American society, those in law enforcement will become more knowledgeable about their activities and skilled at combating them. As the amount of information available on Chinese gangs steadily increases they become less and less mysterious. In a move that is tellingly American, Nickey Louie, a founder of the Ghost Shadows in New York City, is trying to market the movie and book rights to his life story. Such a move, if nothing else, shows a disregard for the vows of silence of Chinese gang members and will undoubtedly be followed by other gang members exposing gang secrets if it can help them make it in American society. Louie is not even the first Chinese criminal to succumb to the lure of selling his story to an American publisher. Eng Ying "Eddie" Gong, a member of the Hip Sing Tong in New York City, had his story published way back in 1930 under the title *Tong War,* coauthored by Bruce Grant.

As for the inner-city Chinese gangs forming a unified conglomerate and spreading throughout North America, this is unlikely. Although the tongs have some control over the gangs, it is not complete. The tongs simply attempt to ally themselves with a gang and then more or less let it do whatever it wishes. If the tongs need the gang to get involved in a specific situation, then they request or arrange for its assistance. Similarly, if the gang's activities become too troublesome for the community, the tongs will attempt to intervene and tone the gang's activities down to a more tolerable level. (Of course, this is not always successful. On the West Coast the Wah Ching outstripped its parent tong in power, and there was no way the tong could bring it under control.) Other than this, the tongs essentially leave the gangs alone and claim no responsibility for their actions. For the tongs to maintain a tighter degree of control over gangs' activities would probably not be desirable for them and their members. Even though the number of aging, adult gang members joining the tongs is increasing, this does not necessarily mean the two groups are merging. Such a merger would not be in anyone's best interests. The important gang members would become unimportant tong members, and the tong members would suffer image problems as well. They would go from being important men in the community who just happen to have some degree of influence and respect in the gangs to simply the criminals who control the gangs. This would make it difficult for them have the necessary legitimacy and respect to function in the legitimate activities of mainstream American and Chinese-American society.

It is unlikely too that the gangs will unite. First of all, each gang fights internally almost as much as it fights with other gangs. Second, most of the members simply cannot function well in American society; they do not even speak English competently or understand most American institutions. Third, virtually all traditional Chinese institutions would do their best to prevent such a thing. They would undoubtedly be quick to involve the American authorities or law enforcement in disbanding the gangs if the alternative was to see the gangs unite and displace the traditional Chinatown power structure.

Furthermore, the Chinese gang situation is becoming diverse in America. The bulk of the gangs and the tongs were originally composed of Cantonese-speaking immigrants who supported the Kuomintang and the traditional Chinatown power structure. The Hong Kong-based triads have been attempting to establish a source of profits in North America and have been competing against both the indigenous Chinese organizations, various non-Chinese crime groups, and each other to do so. These Hong Kong groups include the Wo group triads, the 14K, and the various Chiu Chau syndicates. Such groups generally consist of a wide variety of different organizations rather than being a single entity. It is unlikely that they would ever unite if they have not done so yet.

There are also nontriad, nontraditional Chinese crime groups active in North America today, including the Fuk Ching, a pro-communist Chinese gang from Fukien; the United Bamboo, a

Taiwanese gang; the Big Circle Brotherhood, another mainland Chinese gang; and many others. Such groups compete with each other for profits, but they must also compete with other crime groups in America: that is, a wide variety of Latin-American, Jamaican, African-American, Southeast Asian, Caucasian American, and Italian-American crime groups of varying sizes and styles, levels of sophistication, and organization already functioning. It is unlikely that a unified Chinese Mafia will somehow develop and displace these existing criminal organizations.

Of course, in today's world of high-tech communication, it is inevitable that there will be increasing levels of communication and cooperation among some of the personalities involved in Chinese organized crime. Nevertheless, such personal alliances and arrangements are often made quite independently from organizational mergers. Many Chinese criminals are members of multiple organizations, and it is frequently quite difficult (and largely irrelevant) to determine if they are arranging a crime as part of an organization or merely as individuals who are recruiting people from among their contacts in a criminal organization.

THE UNDERGROUND ECONOMY, GANGS, AND CRIMINAL ACTIVITY

One of the recurring themes of this work is that commerce and society function simultaneously on two different levels. The first is the ordinary, legal, and aboveboard level where most of us work and do business. Items are bought and sold openly, and their sale, quality, and distribution are monitored and supervised by government and international agencies. Banking is done in a more or less open manner (subject to privacy and confidentiality laws, of course), and the money and goods move reasonably naturally according to the laws of supply and demand. If customers, merchants, or manufacturers are displeased or feel cheated, they may seek intervention by the authorities. Peaceful means of dispute resolution are common; violence is rare. And taxes are generally paid to provide the services necessary to keep society flowing smoothly. At times, however, there are goods or services that the authorities do not want available for purchase, for whatever reasons. However, if there is a demand for the products and if the potential for profit is sufficient, then there will be someone willing to supply the desired contraband service or products. This is how a "black market" or "underground economy" comes into existence. It is often possible for an individual or group to offer prohibited goods or services as part of this economy, but there are inherent risks in doing so.

The authorities have committed themselves to stopping the flow of such goods and services, and this complicates the business a great deal. If customers or dealers are dissatisfied with the quality or type of services received on a black market, they cannot reasonably expect intervention by or redress from the authorities. They therefore must either simply endure the possibility of being cheated or misused or find their own means of convincing those they do business with to deal fairly. Most businessmen prefer to avoid such risks and confine their transactions to legitimate commerce. Although it's not unknown for legitimate business people to dabble in the sale of contraband items, few choose to do so regularly. (In fact, it is fairly certain that a sizable portion of the trade in Southeast Asian heroin is done by otherwise legitimate Asian and Chinese businessmen.) Most members of mainstream society feel that the profits simply are not worth the risks, and many seem to lack the skills and knowledge necessary to do business in the underground economy in the first place. Most of us have heard stories of people who request a receipt when making an illegal transaction or instead call the police to report a theft upon discovering that someone has stolen their valuable cache of cocaine!

By contrast, those who regularly do business in the underground economy often lack the skills or temperament needed to function in the mainstream economy. Although organized crime groups do at times reinvest their profits in legitimate enterprises, this is considered a sign that they have achieved a high level of sophistication and organization. Most newly formed gangs and criminal groups lack the desire or ability to reinvest their funds in legitimate business ventures.

For simplicity, one can look at extortion and "protection" rackets as underground financial transactions. The problem is almost inevitable in some areas, is usually done by gangs, and is often tolerated by the authorities until it reaches a certain level. Then the authorities step in, put a stop to the activities, and arrest those responsible, until another gang of extortionists moves in to take over the territory. Of course, the level of extortion tolerated by the authorities varies widely and depends on a wide range of factors, the most important of which seems to be the amount of time that the police can afford to devote to extortion.[2]

How the Underground Economy Determines Gang Characteristics

This shadow world of the underground economy lies hidden from mainstream society. Although the authorities are aware of its existence, they often lack the detailed knowledge needed to suppress it. In other cases, although those in law enforcement are knowledgeable, the authorities simply feel that it is not worth the effort to devote resources to affect certain parts of the underground economy. When it becomes obvious that the underground economy is flourishing, the authorities will sooner or later intervene in that activity. Authorities can sometimes be corrupted and bought off, but there is no guarantee that such a situation will last. For this reason, much of organized crime is in the form of small, loosely connected or affiliated bands or gangs. Although the gangs sometimes communicate with one another and exchange goods and services, conditions impose limitations on their size and level of organization. Gangs and organized crime groups may export their organization to new locations, but it is often believed that this should be seen as more of an economic process than part of a long-term, organized, strategic plan to gain control over a large geographic area. New gangs are more likely to be run as independent franchises than as subdivisions of a large, centrally organized group.[3]

Leaders of organized crime have a lot of difficulty in maintaining control over their hidden empire. Although they can bring a great deal of violence down on those who offend them, they must be aware of a problem before they can act on it. Since their operations are hidden from public view, this can be difficult. Covert communication remains a constant problem. Few criminals keep accurate records of their operations, and when they do it is virtually impossible for a leader to carefully audit the entire operation. Small- and large-scale embezzlement is a constant problem. Negotiations with other groups must be done with great care. Due to the difficulty in control and communication, a surprising number of major decisions involve face-to-face meetings between the important gangsters involved. Although such meetings often involve many risks, including surveillance and arrest by the authorities or assassination by and violence from rival gangsters, they seem to be a necessary part of running an organized crime operation.

Such "independent franchises," for one reason or another (e.g., corruption, secrecy, concealment), exist outside the societal realm where the authorities are likely to intervene. In other words, the police either don't know or don't care about what the gang is doing. Therefore, a competing franchise can take advantage of this and attempt to drive out the existing franchise through violence or intimidation and replace it with a franchise of its own.

A potential competitor's attempt to drive out and replace an existing provider of black market goods or services can be part of a conscious strategic plan or else an unconscious result of economic conditions.

In such a situation, where the use of violence is actually economically beneficial, then it is likely to be a frequent or continuing feature of such markets. In the underground economy, the sort of violence that is typical is what can loosely be called "gang warfare" or "gang violence." Although all violence is inherently ugly and uncertain, this sort of violence is especially so. Gang warfare is characterized by little strategic movement, unexpected ambush, assassination, and large amounts of inefficient and unskilled marksmanship at close ranges. For this reason, there is no real way one can protect oneself from the effects of such violence by superior skills and strategic planning.[4]

How the Underground Economy and Gang Characteristics Influence the Gang Life-Style and Membership

Most people will do what they can to avoid such a "gangster" life-style. Although some might find the thought of "life on the edge" briefly appealing, most people change their minds quickly after facing death a few times. Those who participate time and time again in gang violence (e.g., the hard core-gang members) generally feel that they have little in the way of opportunity in the legitimate mainstream society. They are, in effect, trapped in a cycle of violence. Society has little use for undisciplined youths lacking skills or education and—as is often the case with Chinese and Vietnamese gang members—English-language skills. The economic prospects for the gang members are made even worse if they have obtained a criminal record.

This is not to excuse or justify the actions of many gang members: the violence that is so often used with little thought for the consequences or possibilities of hurting innocent bystanders; torture and rape practiced when there is nothing to be gained from them. Such acts are often committed more as an outlet for pent-up, unfocused anger than for any rational purpose.

Those who find themselves trapped in such a violent life-style with little way out seek to use certain rationales to justify their actions and involvement. Often, it seems they are not only trying to rationalize their involvement in such a self-destructive and predatory life-style, but also to seek emotional compensation for the problems that led them to become involved in the first place.

Time and time again, while reading accounts of gangs and gang activities, I have run across certain cross-cultural parallels that show a surprising uniformity. The following curious facts seem to arise again and again where with gangs and gang violence are concerned:

1. Gangs claim to be protectors of the ordinary people in their communities, when actually they prey upon them. Although on occasion they may do something good to assist their community (as they see it), the majority of their actions are not in its best interests (i.e., extortion).

2. Gangs are seen as a surrogate family by their members, although actually there exists little sense of stability among their members. Despite this, gang members receive great emotional rewards from seeing themselves as part of such a group. They frequently speak of being close-knit. In reality,

intragang violence is often as prevalent and deadly as inter-gang violence.

3. The majority of hard-core gang members are people who lack the skills to be doing something else. If they leave the gang, often they have little opportunity to find a decent job in main-stream society. To some extent gang society functions as a parallel society in which the members can achieve positions of prestige and power.

4. Gang members like to see themselves as nonconformists who are free from the constraints of society. Although they tend to dress and behave in a manner distinct from that of society at large, within their own subculture they conform to standard codes of dress and behavior to an astonishing extent. This out-ward style often includes tattoos and other essentially perma-nent markings that show a willingness to commit to the gang-ster life-style rather than mainstream society. It is ironic that this is done, because it increases the gang members' notice-ability and the attention that they will receive from the author-ities. The advantages to such easily recognizable styles are recognition from others involved in the gang's life-style and the emotional bond of belonging to such a group.

5. Gang members are not revolutionaries. Instead they tend to be archconservatives. They generally have little desire to change society but instead want a greater share of the material rewards that mainstream society has to offer. They are often quite opposed to those who wish to change society. Sociologists suggest that since crime and crime groups offer a "counterculture" within the larger culture, those involved do not feel much need to change the overall structure of society. And since leading gang members have already obtained wealth, fame, and power within the criminal subculture, they do not feel much need to change society in order to improve opportunities for such people as themselves. Ironically, on the rare occasions when most unsophisticated gang members show any interest in politics at all, they often support conser-vative law-and-order candidates!

6. Gang members and criminals often settle disputes with vio-lence because they lack the skills or education to settle them

differently. Much gang violence is not in anyone's best interests, including those of the person committing it. Too often the response to an act of violence is another act of violence, which results in the never-ending cycle of violence that marks gang relations.

Gangs, gang violence, and organized crime all exist as part of the same underground economy. They all gain income and power from their dealings in such prohibited commerce as drugs, prostitution, or contraband, including guns, pornography, and products made from endangered species. Although there are important differences between gangs, all normally evolve to fill similar niches in the overall society and recruit similar people who are attracted to the group by the same emotional needs. Many economic transactions by the gang, such as robbery and extortion, do not involve an exchange of goods and services but are instead predatory and one-sided, and it is possible to see them as just another variant of capitalizing on an economic opportunity.

SPECIAL CHARACTERISTICS OF CHINESE GANGS

Chinese gangs differ from other gangs not so much because of culture but because of conditions. For example, North American Chinese gangs function primarily in the Chinese communities of the continent's large urban areas. When Chinese gangs commit crimes outside Chinese neighborhoods, they still tend to target people of Chinese or Asian descent.

With so many Chinese living and working in North America illegally and, therefore, functioning as part of the underground black-market economy, it is only natural that the Chinese gangs have involved themselves significantly in that economy.

What characterizes many Chinese gangs in particular is their relationship with the tongs. As noted before, the old-style tongs have been seeking to become less and less involved in openly criminal activities while keeping much of the prestige in, and power and influence over, their communities while utilizing violence and criminal acts as instruments of power. There are tongs that have close relationships with street gangs. The relationships serve to stabilize the power of Chinese gangs within their community. Although it is not unheard of for a tong to actively found a Chinese street gang and train its members, only some of the Chinese gangs have such a tong sponsorship. Many Cantonese gangs, such as the Ghost Shadows, the Wah Ching, and others do have a close relationship with a Cantonese-speaking tong, but others, such as the Taiwanese United Bamboo, the Fukienese Fuk Ching, and the mainland Chinese Big Circle gang do not.

The code of conduct that Chinese gangs conform to is part of what identifies them as individuals who have cut themselves off from society at large and entered the criminal Chinese jiang hu subculture. Jiang hu is not an organization but rather a life-style, just as in our society, for example, a person becomes a biker but joins the Hell's Angels—not the other way around. So in Chinese society in North America, one becomes a jiang hu but also a member of the Ghost Shadows or the Hop Sing Benevolent Association or the Heaven and Earth Society.

Different Chinese gangs and criminal groups have widely differing levels of organization and sophistication. At the higher levels of sophistication, they have a mix of people who can function in mainstream society and those who function best in the underground economy, and members will not be quick to identify themselves as belonging to the gang. This is, of course, a matter of evolution and necessity; more sophisticated gangs come into contact with the authorities and mainstream society more often, and cannot be blatant in their style or operation if they hope to survive. Because most of the Chinese criminal groups are able to make this adjustment smoothly, they will not grow without coming into serious conflict with rival gangs and, ultimately, the authorities.

NOTES

1. See U.S. Senate hearing notes, *Asian Organized Crime: Hearing before the Permanent Subcommittee on Investigations of the Committee on Governmental Affairs,* 102nd Cong., 1st sess., 1992, 307-308.
2. Curiously enough, it seems that the police become accustomed to certain levels of illegal activity in certain places. See Bernard Cohen, *Deviant Street Networks* (Lexington, MA: Lexington Books, 1980), 111-130. Bernard Cohen describes how

certain groups seem to get established on certain street corners in New York City. For example, some corners regularly have a large number of panhandlers. Others might have heterosexual prostitutes, and still others have homosexual prostitutes. Although the police periodically harass those involved, arrests are only occasional and obviously not enough to discourage the serious malefactors. However, when those involved in the criminal activity attempt to set up shop in the wrong neighborhood (e.g., panhandling in an area of prostitution), then police generally try to stop the spread of the wrong activity into the wrong place by harassing, or arresting, as many of those involved as possible until they return to areas where such activities are tolerated.

3. Some may argue that the Italian Mafia is a large, centrally controlled, international crime group and feel that I have ignored it. Actually it is debatable just how tightly the Mafia controls crime in America. For a detailed study of this view one may see *Disorganized Crime: Illegal Markets and the Mafia*, by Peter Reuter.

4. To some extent, knowledge of tactics, weapons, and martial arts might be of help in surviving gang violence, but in reality, all such skills are irrelevant when a 14-year-old with a pistol starts firing at a person's back at a range of 10 feet with no warning.

well   that's just the context!

Chinese gangs don't exist in their own vacuum. What follows is a brief description of some of the criminal groups in America that are often associated with the gangs.

VIETNAMESE GANGS AND CRIME GROUPS

There is a close association between Vietnamese and Chinese gangs, but despite this, there are many important differences between the two.

Vietnamese gangs have a reputation for being tough, vicious, and much more likely to resort to immediate violence than are Chinese gangs. In part this is because of the harsh background of many Vietnamese. A large percentage of the Vietnamese in America are refugees of either the war or the events following the war. In the aftermath of the U.S. pullout, a large number of people left Vietnam, many as refugees or "boat people." In their way, these experiences were almost as horrible as the war itself. Many of the boat people were robbed, killed, raped, or preyed upon by pirates and other criminals. Others were detained for years in the large refugee camps of Thailand, Hong Kong, Malaysia, and elsewhere. Often, the bulk of the economic activity in these camps consisted of illegal black market transactions, and violence was not uncommon. Children raised in such places learned to compete, fight, and suffer, and they learned to do whatever it took to keep their heads above water on a day-to-day basis while protecting themselves from their neighbors. Many learned little else, and they now find themselves without

CHAPTER 14

OTHER ASIAN GANGS

the means to make an honest living in a new country. Like the hard-core Chinese gang members, the Vietnamese gang members often have little opportunity for legitimate advancement in mainstream American society.

A problem peculiar to many Vietnamese gang members is that they really do not mind being jailed very much. The temporary loss of freedom is something they grew accustomed to in the refugee camps. The level of violence in jail is no worse than much of what they've experienced elsewhere, but the food and a warm place to sleep come much more freely and easily than in the outside world. (Incidentally, those admitted to the United States as refugees, unlike most classifications of new immigrants, cannot be deported for committing a serious crime.)

It has been pointed out that many Chinese gangs are kept at least somewhat in check by the Chinatown tongs, but Vietnamese society in America does not have the same cohesive and long-established tongs. Most Vietnamese gangs are more loosely organized and less controlled by their gang superiors than Chinese gangs. For example, the government estimates that Orange County, California, has more than 80 different Vietnamese gangs.[1] From this one may assume that even though Vietnamese gangs are a serious problem in this area, many are small and poorly organized. In fact, although there are some long-term, permanent Vietnamese gangs with staked-out territories, many of the most violent crimes by Vietnamese are committed by temporary bands of youth who often only get together specifically to commit their crimes. The latter are more unrestrained in their actions, and their crimes appear more random.

Since gangs receive more attention from the authorities as they become more violent, extremely violent gangs tend to have trouble surviving for long periods and becoming organized and established.

Vietnamese gangs tend to consist of three to 10 individuals who range in age from 11 to 30. In keeping with their poor organization, the gangs often do not have names. Similarly, they often have no formally chosen leader. A typical Vietnamese gang often travels across the United States from one Vietnamese community to another, stopping along the way to commit house break-ins, armed robberies, and other crimes. Although this means that the size of the gang is limited by the transportation available, it's not uncommon for two or three carloads of Vietnamese gang members to go on a trip in "caravan" style. They may stop in certain places, particularly where Vietnamese-Americans live, and take a break from the hard work of preying on their fellow countrymen. At such points, some gang members may leave and others might join.

Although the Vietnamese gangs, like the Chinese, prefer to prey on their own countrymen, when they cannot find Vietnamese victims they seem much more likely than the Chinese to prey on people of whatever ethnic group is available. In cases where the Vietnamese gangs have become more organized, more stable, and less mobile, they have staked out their own turf and often use violence to defend themselves and their control over their territory from rivals. In other cases, where a Vietnamese gang has established itself in a given territory, it will provide logistical support and intelligence to another Vietnamese gang that is passing through town on a crime spree. For example, the local gangsters will put up and hide the out-of-town gang members and then suggest a target for a robbery that the former will help to plan. The out-of-town gang members do the robbery, and the locals receive a share of the take. The victims have no idea who the gangsters were or where they came from, and catching them is that much more difficult.

While such loose organization has been the rule with regard to Vietnamese gang structure, there are, increasingly, exceptions. There is a trend among Vietnamese gangs toward improving levels of organization and becoming more permanent. There are Vietnamese gangs that are fairly formalized in numerous cities throughout the United States. Some of them have reached a point where they rival Chinese gangs for control of their own territories. For example, the Born to Kill gang originated in New York City but has chapters throughout the major cities of the Northeast and Canada. It is a long-time rival of the Chinese Ghost Shadows gang. This rivalry has resulted in a series of violent incidents, the most notable being the one in 1991 in Linden, New Jersey, when a number of Ghost Shadows shot up the funeral of a Born to Kill member.

Unlike the Chinese gangs, there are many Vietnamese gangs composed entirely of women and girls, and such are likely to be a growing problem in the future.

Older, more established Chinese gangs have attempted to set themselves up as umbrella-style organizations with a structure that includes many independent gangs under a loose sort of control within their territories. Such "member" gangs are usually more or less free to do as they wish up to a point, but the "boss" organization can call on their services from time to time if need be. This sort of structure seems to be more common on the West Coast. It has been suggested that many Vietnamese (and Cambodian) gangs are often quite proud of being associated with one of the leading Chinese gangs or tongs because they feel it lends a certain prestige and legitimacy to their organization. For example, the Hung Pho (Red Fire) gang is said to be loosely affiliated with the Wo Hop To triad in the San Francisco area. In Southern California, this same group and its rival, the Vietnamese V Boys gang, have both had links with the United Bamboo.

Although the Vietnamese have their own gangs, it is not unusual for them to be fully initiated members of Chinese gangs as well. In fact, as the Vietnamese Communists heavily discriminated against Vietnam's Chinese community (who were often successful businessmen), a large percentage of the "Vietnamese" refugees and immigrants in America and Canada are actually Chinese whose ancestors had settled in Vietnam centuries ago.

Although many of the Vietnamese refugees are either freedom-loving people who found life under communism intolerable or ordinary people who had too many ties to the former government or the capitalist system to be tolerated by the communist government of Vietnam, there are exceptions. Like Cuba, the Socialist Republic of Vietnam simply allowed many of its petty and minor-league criminals and other undesirables to leave if they wished, thereby saving the cost of incarceration and causing problems for the United States in the process.

Other Vietnamese in America are Vietnam War combat veterans. They are often too old to be active in Vietnamese gangs at present, but many were active in such groups in the past and, in some cases, have passed skills on to the newer members.

THE BORYOKUDAN OR JAPANESE YAKUZA

There is currently very little Japanese immigration to America, so there is not much of a problem with Japanese youth gangs in the United States. There simply are not the large numbers of Japanese youth without skills, hope, or a future that make up the bulk of hard-core Chinese and Vietnamese gangs. There is, however, an increasing concern in many quarters about the expanding North American activities of sophisticated Japanese organized crime groups.

Japanese gangsters have been known as *yakuza*. In Japan, outlaw gangsters have a long history of association with the legendary gamblers who roamed from place to place eking out a happy-go-lucky, rags-to-riches, riches-to-rags life-style in games of chance. The term yakuza itself comes from gambling. Ya-ku-za, or 8-9-3, is the worst possible combination of cards in the Japanese game *hanafuda*. For this reason, when one is referred to as an 8-9-3, it means that he is a born loser, and the yakuza, showing a lack of self-esteem typical of many gangsters throughout the world, have taken it to heart as their name. Other yakuza groups are descended from associations for street cart vendors rather than gamblers, but all have the same traditions. According to legend, the yakuza were a group of noble outlaws who helped the common people and resisted corrupt government officials.

Although yakuza is a traditional term used for many centuries in Japan, there is a move by the Japanese government to replace it with the term *boryokudan*, meaning "the violent ones." This is because many feel that yakuza implies a respectable and noble tradition and that this is hardly the image modern Japan should use for its leading organized crime problem. Since the newer term has less in the way of positive connotations and implied respectability, it is now preferred in law enforcement circles, although both terms are still common.

The yakuza are a fact of life in Japanese society. Because the Japanese have traditionally seen organized crime as just one of many unpleasant facts of life, for many years the yakuza were essentially accepted by the powers that be as long as they kept their activities to a reasonable level, stayed within certain unspoken boundaries and limits, and did not disrupt society too much. The yakuza form part of a secretive subculture made up of those who have no place in polite Japanese society. In post-World War II Japan, the yakuza groups often functioned in an astonishingly open manner with many of the same sort of trappings and emblems used by the legitimate Japanese corporations. Things have reached the point where different yakuza groups operate out of clearly marked offices and their leading members are dressed in suits and ties, with their yakuza group affiliation clearly identified by a tie, pin, or other emblem.

Traditionally, there has existed a stratum of Japanese society known as the "floating world," which includes most of the vice, prostitution, and entertainment industries. In its time and place, the floating world is accepted, yet its boundaries are defined as the loose conglomeration of industries and companies shunned by polite society. Although it would be unseemly for society to focus too much attention on the floating world, it was commonly believed that the services it offered provided an escape for some people from the stresses and expectations of mundane life and were necessary for society to function smoothly. Within the floating world, the yakuza were accepted in their roles as procurers, enforcers, regulators, and even extortionists and, as such, were able to attain a great deal of sophistication and organizational skills, without coming into serious conflict with the authorities.

These gangsters are generally adults, born and raised in Japan, and although some manage to play a role in many activities of American life, they only rarely come to America planning to live here. The heart of the traditional yakuza group organization was the relationship between the *oyuban,* or leader and teacher/mentor, with his *kobun,* or follower and student/apprentice. The oyuban would bring the kobun into the group and teach him how to survive, prosper, contribute, and fit in. In gratitude, the kobun was expected to follow, serve, and obey his oyuban. An oyuban might be called upon to fight to the death or serve a prison term for his kobun.[2] Of course, such ideals are not always followed, but they are followed enough to be frightening.

Discipline is strict in the yakuza groups. If a member makes a serious mistake, he is called before his superiors. If these superi-

TONGS, GANGS, AND TRIADS: CHINESE CRIME GROUPS IN NORTH AMERICA

ors are sufficiently offended, then they will request that the yakuza cut off his own fingertip and present it to them, accompanied by an apology. Such requests are always complied with. In fact, one way to recognize experienced yakuza is that they are frequently missing the tips of one or more fingers. Some have even worn false fingertips as part of a disguise. Another distinctive yakuza tradition is acquiring large, ornate Japanese tattoos all over the body. This apparently grew out of a traditional Japanese practice of tattooing criminals in order to mark them. Being tattooed is expensive and painful and takes great discipline to endure. Due to the expense and impracticality of the procedure, today it seems to be going out of style. The traditional weapon has been the sword, so the yakuza spend a great deal of time studying kendo, or Japanese fencing. These days, however, many of the traditions are in decline, and the yakuza are becoming more and more like the gangsters of other nations. As the flamboyant tattoos are becoming less popular, so the swords are often being replaced by guns.

In Japan, the yakuza are traditionally involved with extortion, prostitution, gambling, loan sharking, debt collection, illegal weapons importation, the drug trade (particularly the manufacture and sale of amphetamines), and other vice. In America, the yakuza are most likely to be involved in these same sorts of activities, but primarily in the areas and environments frequented by Japanese tourists. They have trouble expanding their operations into mainstream American society because of cultural and linguistic problems. Nevertheless, they cooperate with traditional American crime groups in such activities as money laundering and importing Asian-manufactured amphetamines into the United States.

Many Japanese tourists, businessmen, and other successful Japanese come to the United States mainland and Hawaii for a variety of reasons and for varying lengths of time. A sizable number prefer to relax and do their shopping for souvenirs and other goods among businesses that cater specifically to Japanese customers. The tourists often have an appetite for vices and activities that are not easily available in Japan, among which are American (particularly blonde) prostitutes and the opportunity to shoot pistols at firing ranges. The yakuza often are involved in arranging such opportunities, as well as choosing the shopping plazas that the organized tours stop at (in return for a small consideration, of course). At times, Japanese businesses in America are subject to extortion by yakuza.

The yakuza also come to America to acquire items for illegal export to Japan. The items they desire the most are firearms, particularly handguns, hard-core pornography, and prostitutes, particularly Caucasians. The importation of firearms to Japan (where their private ownership is outlawed) is prohibited except in very rare circumstances, and the weapons must be smuggled in ingenious ways.

Japan has very strange pornography laws. In magazines, it seems, no pubic hair is allowed to be shown. Of course, if you were to leaf through some Japanese pornography, you would soon get the feeling that everything else is allowed. For example, one might find a photograph of an attractive Japanese woman hogtied and chained in a humiliating position but with her pubic hair somehow "tastefully" covered. In "manga," the genre of popular comics for adults, virtually any sort of rape or misogynistic portrayal of women is allowed. Nevertheless, American-style hardcore porn magazines with photos of folks actually engaging in sexual acts are strictly banned by the Japanese government. Naturally, a black market in pornography has sprung up, and the yakuza are involved.

Caucasian women who are able to work as hostesses, dancers, erotic performers, or prostitutes are much in demand in Japan. Although a small number of Caucasian women go there of their own accord to seek work in these professions, the demand still far outstrips the supply. Some Japanese, frequently yakuza, have been known to stage very professional-appearing auditions for "models" or "actresses" in order to lure Western women to Japan. Upon arrival, their passports are seized, the terms of the contract are ignored, and the women are frequently forced, tricked, or otherwise pressured into working in these less respectable professions. Because technically, nothing illegal has happened in the United States, the U.S. Embassy can do very little to assist its citizens who find themselves in such a plight.

Taiwan was a Japanese colony from 1894 to 1945, and Korea was a Japanese colony from 1904 to 1945; therefore, there is often close cooperation between the organized crime groups in Japan, Taiwan, and South Korea. The large and heavily discriminated-against Korean minority population living in Japan today serves to further strengthen these links. The yakuza often have close ties with Taiwanese organized crime groups, including the United Bamboo gang, which has branches in America. Yakuza and the United Bamboo have worked together to manufacture and sell amphetamines and to acquire Taiwanese prostitutes for work in Japan, and it is possible that such cooperation exists in North America as well.

An old yakuza debt collection technique is to force victims to take out life insurance policies and name the yakuza as their beneficiaries. If a debtor then refuses to pay, the yakuza simply kill him and collect the money from the life insurance company. In 1984, a Japanese citizen attempted to flee to Los Angeles to avoid payment on some gambling debts. Although it is believed that he was killed by yakuza, his life insurance policy (from an American carrier) awarded the U.S. equivalent of $315,000 to a beneficiary in Taiwan.

Today in Japan there is a continuing problem with "hot rod" and motorcycle gangs. These violent, lawless groups often serve as a source of recruits for the older, more sophisticated yakuza. As a point of curiosity involving U.S./Japanese crime links, in the mid-1980s one of these groups petitioned the American-based Hell's Angels for permission to incorporate themselves as an official Japan-based chapter of the international motorcycle gang. Although the notorious motorcycle club did have official chapters in Australia, New Zealand, Great Britain, continental Europe, Brazil, and Canada, this would have been an unusual move. Not only are its members frequently involved in committing criminal acts, they are also generally known to be white supremacists. In 1985, two officers of the Hell's Angels went to Japan to give serious consideration to the request and to inspect the situation firsthand. Not surprisingly, the Japanese request to form the first non-Caucasian chapter of the "club" was ultimately turned down (Lavigne 1987, 52).

Although Korean organized crime activity in the United States is currently not nearly as serious as that of Chinese or Vietnamese groups, in some places it is nevertheless a problem. In Korea, as in China, there is a tradition of sworn brotherhoods, but, unlike China, Korea does not appear to have the same variety of traditional secret societies these days. This is probably largely a result of repressive conditions under the Japanese in colonial times and in both the North and South Korean postwar governments. In the United States, there are Korean organized crime groups and youth gangs, however, and in some areas they are growing in power.

In Hawaii and elsewhere, Korean organized crime groups work in close cooperation with the Japanese and others to import large quantities of methamphetamines, including one known as "ice." Other criminal activities of the Korean organized crime groups include extortion, illegal gambling, illegal debt collection, and extensive involvement in indoor prostitution ("call girls"). In some parts of America, Korean gangs such as the 24K, Korean Power, the Korean Killers, and the Korean Fu Ching, among others are competing with Chinese street gangs for power and territory. Furthermore, in some areas, notably Queens in New York, it is not uncommon for Koreans to join Chinese gangs.

One large-scale U.S. crime problem uniquely involving Koreans is a nationwide prostitution network using Korean women. These women normally enter the country as the wives of U.S. servicemen stationed in Korea. Although many of these marriages are fraudulent and arranged for the express purpose of bringing prostitutes to the United States to work, other Korean prostitutes are recruited upon arrival. On occasion, brides in otherwise healthy marriages are recruited deceptively by being told initially that they will be hired to give back massages and similar services only. Upon their recruitment, hiring, and frequent relocation, they are forced into performing sexual acts for money. Some of these Korean prostitution networks are international in scope, and some are believed to have ties with organized crime groups based in Taiwan.

In 1986, the FBI and law enforcement agencies in New York

City worked together in an undercover operation to gather evidence about a large network of Korean criminals who were extorting lots of money from more than 40 Korean-owned bars and restaurants in the metropolitan area. The extortionists covered themselves by "selling" their victims overpriced herbal medicines and house plants in return for the extortion payments.

NIGERIAN FRAUD GANG

Nigerians are surprisingly active in smuggling drugs, as well as committing a variety of fraud and other crimes within the borders of the United States. According to officials of both the U.S. State Department and Customs Service, worldwide Nigerian drug smuggling networks import 35 to 40 percent of the heroin that enters the United States. Naturally, much of this is produced in Southeast Asia and then illegally collected and sold by Chinese. The smugglers are believed to be carrying both heroin and cocaine on a free-lance basis at the request of large networks of Nigerian smugglers. Although little is known, the role of Nigerians and Nigerian gangs in the worldwide crime scene should not be underestimated.

The gangs are said to be involved in car theft, as well credit card and insurance fraud schemes, among others, in the United States, and they are said to be involved in smuggling ivory to Asia.

THE ITALIAN MAFIA AND
TRADITIONAL AMERICAN CRIME GROUPS

Some experts in law enforcement believe that there are Chinese organized crime groups with increasingly strong ties to the Italian Mafia. Many believe that in the past the Italian Mafia had a virtual monopoly on the importation and distribution of heroin in America. Prior to the Vietnam War, the bulk of heroin sold in America was refined from opium grown in Turkey or the Middle East and was brought into the United States by the Mafia through ties with its Sicilian and Corsican syndicates. The drug was apparently distributed throughout the United States by various Mafia "families" that controlled different regions of the

United States. In the past 20 years or so, there have been many changes in the situation. During the post-World War II period, the bulk of the heroin entering the United States was produced in Turkey and neighboring Southwest Asian nations and then shipped from these nations through a variety of European countries, including France. Ultimately, however, with the smashing of the "French connection" and a Turkish government crackdown on the illegal growth of opium, Southeast Asian opium has become much more important in the U.S. narcotics trade.

Today, a great deal of drug smuggling and distribution within America is done by so-called nontraditional crime groups, including various outlaw motorcycle gangs, Jamaican, Latin American, African-American, or Asian (specifically Chinese) groups. However, some speculate that this widespread drug importation and distribution must be done with the awareness and perhaps compliance of the Italian Mafia. Even when drugs are brought into the United States by the Italian Mafia, they are largely sold wholesale and then distributed by other crime groups.[3] For example, although the bulk of heroin in America is of Southeast Asian origin and is imported by either the Italian Mafia or the Chinese, in my area the last major bust of a heroin ring resulted in the arrest of mostly African-American drug dealers.

LAW ENFORCEMENT AND CHINESE CRIME IN THE UNITED STATES AND CANADA

In North America there has been a variety of responses to Chinese crimes and gangs. For instance, many major urban centers with large Asian populations have designated special units to deal with Chinese and Asian crime. In some areas these units have been found to be more efficient when they work in conjunction with social services workers. In some cities there is a police gang unit that spends a great deal of time dealing with Asian gangs. Among the cities in the United States and Canada with special units designated to monitor or combat Asian crime are New York; Arlington, Virginia; Dallas; Toronto; Vancouver, British Columbia; Garden Grove, New Jersey; Westminster, California; and Seattle. The Toronto Metropolitan Police Force has gained a reputation as a clearinghouse for Asian organized crime information.

In some major cities, Chinese-run nightclubs have a tendency to hire retired police officers as security guards. Since many of these nightclubs have ties with organized crime, some feel that the security guard situation leads to a conflict of interest that may discourage some officers from actively investigating and prosecuting Chinese organized crime groups.

LAW ENFORCEMENT AND
CHINESE CRIME IN HONG KONG

In Hong Kong there has been a problem with Chinese police officers having ties to or even being active members of one of the triad societies. At times this problem has become quite serious, and several important police officers have been brought up on corruption charges. Many of these managed to avoid trial by fleeing to Taiwan, and a few quit or retired and immigrated to the United States or Canada before being punished.

The situation has apparently improved since the formation of the Internal Commission against Corruption (ICAC) in 1974, an agency with branches throughout Hong Kong whose duty is to seek out and prosecute corruption among government bodies. The Royal Hong Kong Police are also known for their professionalism and experience in dealing with Chinese organized crime groups, although there has been a great deal of apprehension expressed in some circles about how the 1997 Chinese takeover of the city will affect the police force. It has been announced that all members of the Royal Hong Kong Police, including non-Chinese, will be allowed to keep their jobs following the Chinese takeover. This has alleviated some of the apprehension surrounding the unknowns of the future.

THE GOVERNMENT OF TAIWAN

Very few nations of the world have extradition treaties with Taiwan. In the past, the government of Taiwan has given shelter to some of the most notorious gangsters from Hong Kong. The government of Taiwan has shown no desire to turn such people over to foreign governments so far, and one may safely assume that it will show little desire to do so in the future. It may be presumed that elements of its intelligence service profit too much off the opium trade and that they value their ties to Chinese organized crime groups in hopes that such links may prove valuable in the future.

THE PEOPLE'S REPUBLIC OF CHINA

Within China there has been a growing problem with opium smuggling and the spread of organized crime groups. The People's Republic of China has shown an openness toward some forms of cooperation with international law enforcement agencies in order to combat the problem. Unfortunately, these experiments have met with mixed results.

In one peculiar incident, the United States and the Chinese authorities had worked in close cooperation to arrest a number of Chinese involved in a plot to smuggle opium from China into the United States and arrested a large number of suspects. When the Chinese government allowed one of the key witnesses in the case to fly to the United States to testify in court, it was seen as a great sign of closer ties between the two nations in the future. Unfortunately for all concerned, when the witness arrived in the United States he claimed refugee status. When the United States decided that the witness was in fact eligible for classification as a refugee, the Chinese government was furious. Naturally, the Chinese have expressed much less willingness to cooperate with American agencies following this incident.

NOTES

1. See U.S. Senate hearing notes, *Asian Organized Crime: Hearing before the Permanent Subcommittee on Investigations of the Committee on Governmental Affairs,* 102nd Cong., 1st sess., 1992, 124; and U.S. Senate hearing notes, *The New International Criminal and Asian Organized Crime,* report prepared by the permanent subcommittee on Investigations of the Committee on Government Affairs. 102nd Cong., 2nd sess., 1992, 27.
2. It is interesting to speculate about a possible link between the structure and organi-

zation of the northern Chinese Ching, or Green, societies, where the primary relationship copied is the one between a teacher and his students and the yakuza oyuban-kobun relationship.

3.   There is a theory that organized crime in America is largely a matter of ethnic succession. As immigrant groups enter American society, they use several means to advance. One of these is organized crime, and it is often used either in conjunction with or separately from other methods. Once the ethnic group in question achieves a certain level of success and integration in American society, its involvement in organized crime becomes distinctly less than it once was. Organized crime activity is then taken over by another new ethnic group. For example, some of the oldest gangs and organized crime activities in America involved such groups as the Irish and the Jews, which were apparently succeeded by the Italians. Today, however, the bulk of organized crime activity in America involves newer immigrant groups, such as Asians, Latin Americans, and Jamaicans. (This is, of course, a simplified view of the theory, but it serves to communicate the main idea.)

As already discussed, Chinese gangs tend to be locally based predatory crime groups made up of young men who range in age from their very early teens to their early 30s. Theirs are often crimes of opportunity. When plans are made, as in extortion, armed robbery, and breaking and entering, little in the modus operandi of the crimes themselves would indicate that they are insolvable and beyond the reach of a well-trained law enforcement agency. Although some groups are, of course, more sophisticated and organized than others, their crimes still tend to follow the same general patterns as those of other ethnic organized crime groups.

It could be argued that the greatest difficulties most law enforcement agencies face when dealing with Chinese crimes and Chinese crime groups often center around the Chinese culture itself.

FINDING AN INTERPRETER

Many Chinese in America do not speak English. Few police in America speak Chinese. Obviously, there are potential communication problems. Although many large police agencies are actively hiring Chinese-speaking recruits from within the Chinese community, this is really only of use in areas with large Chinese populations. In most other areas, when police find themselves facing someone who speaks only Chinese, they need an interpreter. Outside of the major urban areas, few law enforcement agencies have much need for a full-time Chinese-language inter-

CHAPTER 15

DEALING WITH CHINESE CRIME: SPECIAL LAW ENFORCEMENT CONSIDERATIONS

preter. Nevertheless, from time to time, police departments need one working part time—preferably a willing volunteer.

Finding and acquiring an interpreter can be a special skill in itself. First of all, the interpreter must have a good working command of both English and the foreign language. Although some non-Asian Americans and Canadians speak excellent Chinese, they are few and far between, and under normal circumstances a police force is unlikely to simply bump into one by accident and know it. A local university, particularly one with an Asian studies department, or returning missionaries are possible sources of interpreters. Quite often the more zealous religious groups tend to be the most determined to send missionaries abroad for long periods: the Mormons are quite prevalent in Taiwan, and, as a rule, their missionaries to that island have undergone extensive training in spoken Mandarin Chinese. Fundamentalist Christians, Roman Catholics, mainstream Protestants, and others all have trained missionaries who speak Chinese.

Despite the fact that some non-Asian-born interpreters exist, the overwhelming majority of Chinese-to-English interpreters are Chinese, which only makes sense since most educated people in China have studied some English, and there are more Chinese immigrants in North America than there are students going abroad to study Chinese.

Often, hospitals keep a list of which of their employees have skill in a certain language in case interpreting is needed in providing medical care. In many large towns and metropolitan areas, there are special clubs or community centers for Chinese people. Often these groups are quite anxious to prove that Chinese are productive, helpful, law-abiding members of the community, in which they live (as most are, of course) and some might be willing to assist with emergency interpreting.

Of course, there are also commercial translation agencies, but for some reason, to the best of my knowledge, none of the police departments in my area have used them to overcome language barriers.

There are some important considerations when seeking an interpreter, the first of which is to determine whether the interpreter can speak the required dialect of Chinese (as discussed in Chapter 1).

If, for example, there is a need to listen in on a conversation between Chinese speakers, for example during a wiretap, without knowing the dialect spoken, it can be extremely hard to find the right interpreter.

Chinese is, of course, a written language. However, it does not use an alphabet like English does. Instead, it is written with a wide variety of symbols, and each symbol represents a word or a part of a word. These symbols were universal and could be understood by educated people throughout China, regardless of their native dialect. (Although they might pronounce the written messages in different ways, they could all understand the underlying meaning.) For better or worse, the Communists simplified these characters to speed up education, and now there are often two different styles of writing—the new simple characters (which are also used in Singapore), and the old complex characters (which are still used in Hong Kong, Taiwan, and most overseas communities). Some people can understand both; many others cannot. In fact, many from Taiwan will make a great show of how they cannot understand the "corrupted Communist writing." Although there is an element of self-congratulatory propaganda in these statements, there is also some truth in them.

If an interpreter in the native dialect cannot be found, keep in mind that most Chinese can speak either Mandarin or Cantonese to some extent. For this reason, if one wishes to simply communicate with a Chinese speaker then it can be done about 90 percent of the time.

If this method is used, then all concerned should keep in mind that the Chinese person can communicate in another language or dialect that cannot be understood by those handling the case. This may be significant if the person wishes to pass on secret messages to his family and friends, and those concerned with the case should keep that in mind.

As a last resort, one should be prepared to attempt communication using lateral thinking. Many Chinese who cannot communicate effectively in English verbally can read and write English to some extent. (Their education system often emphasizes reading and writing a foreign language over speaking it.) Others who cannot read or write English can read or write Chinese symbols. Of course, it is often those who are the least educated who speak only their own local dialect and cannot speak Mandarin, and these are often illiterate in all languages, including their own. I've even met a surprising number of Chinese who speak something other than Chinese or English (e.g., Spanish) as their native language.

As if seeking an interpreter were not complicated enough, caution should be used in accepting the first one qualified who comes along. It should be determined just why the person is willing to serve in this capacity for a law enforcement investigation. There are many who simply wish to do their bit to help their community, but there have also been cases where Chinese organized crime figures have actually sent volunteers to serve their local police as interpreters. This provides them with an inside source about the intelligence the police have on organized crime progress in a Chinese community.

In other cases, particularly in incidents involving Chinese restaurants, it could be dangerous to have people with underlying grudges or personal conflicts interpreting for each other's cases. There is a risk that someone might take advantage of the opportunity to cause trouble for or eliminate a business rival or other enemy. As with so many other things in Chinese culture, always be alert for the hidden agenda. Seek to understand the motivations and hidden desires of anyone who volunteers as a Chinese translator.

On the other side of the coin, many people who could make competent interpreters might hesitate for some reason. One quite understandable concern is for their personal safety if they are known to be working with the police. This fear needs to be addressed to some extent, and perhaps the best way is to assure the translator that his or her anonymity will be preserved to the fullest extent possible. The extent to which this may realistically and legally be assured should be determined and explained prior to the translation if possible. Translators should be assured of anonymity but be told that it depends to a large extent upon their own actions and that if they wish to preserve secrecy, they should tell as few people as possible.

USING AN INTERPRETER

Communicating through an interpreter is an art in itself. In some cases it is possible for a highly skilled translator to engage in "simultaneous translation," but engaging the services of a makeshift untrained interpreter is much more likely. In fact, trained translators simply don't exist for many of the more obscure dialects of Chinese.

In investigations or interrogations, you will have to pause periodically to allow the interpreter time to restate your questions and tell you how the subject answers. The interpreter will have to remember and restate the questions asked. If there are too many of them, the interpreter or the subject may easily become confused. Obviously, an interpreter must be able to communicate clearly and easily in two different languages, or the entire interrogation session will fall apart. Be forewarned that there are some people who cannot do this, buckle under pressure, and become highly nervous around authority figures. Such people will often seek to respond too quickly and in too favorable a manner to the law enforcement officials or others who seek to use their services. They don't really mean to lie or contradict themselves; it just happens as they seek to appease or calm down an angry questioner. Dealing with such a person in the role of an interpreter can be very frustrating, and it is best to avoid it if there is another option.

Interpreters should be carefully instructed not to insert their own questions without first clearing them with the interrogator. It is also recommended that, following the session, the police interrogator ask whether the interpreter feels the subject is being truthful or hiding something and if the interpreter recommends any further questions to ask the subject. If the interpreter is allowed to ask his or her own questions, these should be understood and cleared by the officials present

WITNESSES AND A CODE OF SILENCE

Chinatowns throughout America are often seen as closed communities, with those who live in them rarely interacting with mainstream American society. Chinatowns developed and continued because of mutual antipathy between the Chinese and mainstream American societies.

Although there have been some notable attempts to change this, the bulk of the Chinatown population has been surprisingly

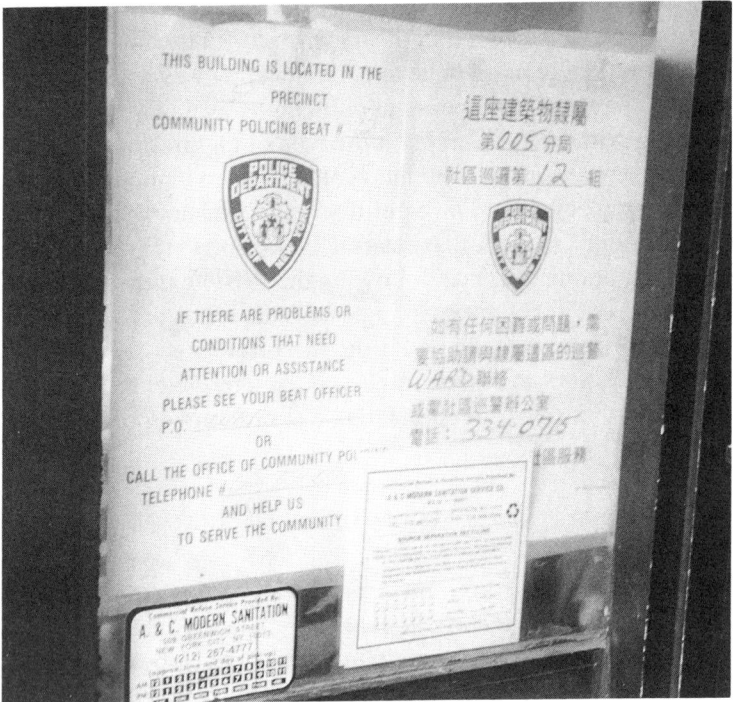

Signs of police involvement in Chinatown.

TONGS, GANGS, AND TRIADS:
CHINESE CRIME GROUPS IN NORTH AMERICA

passive about the social injustice, crime, exploitation, and poverty that still exist in their communities. This passivity becomes most evident when a crime occurs in Chinatown and almost nobody steps forward as a witness despite the fact that dozens of people may have seen it. Similarly, continuing criminal or illegal activity, such as extortion by gangs, the routine payment of sub-minimum wages to workers, and unsafe working conditions often go unreported even by the victims. There are reasons for this passivity.

In Chinatowns, there is a small elite consisting of the tongs, the CCBA, the heads of the family associations and other traditional organizations, and a small number of wealthy businessmen and restaurateurs which, in effect, runs a neighborhood wherein the bulk of the residents are low-paid laborers who struggle to make ends meet.

The old-style Chinatown elite does not see much need to change the situation. The more isolated the community, the more the Chinatown upper class has traditionally stood to benefit.

This situation is compounded by the very nature of Chinatown. Immigrant laborers, many of who are working or living in their new country illegally, wish to avoid the attention of the authorities. They are quite unlikely to offer themselves as witnesses if they happen to spot a crime, particularly if it involves people they do not know. The legal immigrants often do not understand the way the government and the bureaucracies in this country work.

Even when it comes to reporting a serious crime, many Chinese show surprisingly little interest in doing so, not only for the reasons stated above. There are many uncertainties inherent in the criminal justice systems of the United States and Canada in comparison with the systems often used in Asia. For example, I recently ran across a report concerning the capture of a serial killer in rural China. The killer, a butcher by profession, was capturing people, killing them, and then eating their brains. When the Chinese police captured him, there was a great deal of evidence, such as human body parts left in the back of his butcher shop. What is most surprising about the case from an American point of view is that on the same day the man was arrested, he was also tried and then executed—all within a 24-hour period. Apparently there were no bail hearings, no lengthy legal discussions as to the admission of evidence or other matters, no strong interest in whether the man's actions should be excused due to mental health problems, and no appeals.

In the United States the system is much slower and much less black and white. This is particularly true in large urban areas where the system is overworked and stretched beyond its limitations. There are several steps in the process that make Asians uncertain. In order to arrest a person, evidence must be collected. Generally this includes collecting witnesses' statements. Following arrest, bail is often set, and the accused is allowed to go free if he meets his bail requirements. Unfortunately, the negative side of this is that it gives a dangerous criminal or gang member a chance to go out and assault or intimidate witnesses if he can determine who they are. Therefore, a Chinatown storekeeper knows that if he presses charges against a gang member who is attempting extortion, the gang member will be out on bail shortly, most likely within 24 hours. Even if the gang member is locked up, he may have the opportunity to tell his fellow gang members who pressed charges against him.

Even if witnesses are found and the criminal is convicted, often the punishment is absurdly inconsequential due to overcrowding in the jails and prisons. Chinatowns are located in the heart of most of the urban centers of North America, which are precisely where the criminal justice system has the most problems.

NAMES

Many Americans have a great deal of difficulty with Chinese names. This is understandable; they can be quite confusing. In Asia, Chinese, Vietnamese, and Korean names are usually three syllables long. The Asian custom is for the family name to appear before the person's given name. Most family names are one syllable long. Therefore, Mao Tse-tung is also known as Chairman Mao or Mr. Mao. The Western custom is, of course, to put the family name last. Often when Asians go to Western countries they attempt to conform to this custom. Therefore, someone named

Wu Li-chong in Asia (aka Ms. Wu) might tell people in Canada or elsewhere that her name is Li-chong Wu. This way most North Americans would identify her more easily as Ms. Wu instead of misidentifying her as "Ms. Chong." Unfortunately, Asians only do this some of the time, and it is often impossible to tell if they have done this or not.

Many Asians use an English name because they are easier for Westerners to remember. For example, although someone might be named Liu Yi-liang in China, while traveling or visiting in America he could identify himself as Henry Liu. Generally speaking, such names are chosen in a haphazard manner, taken from books or songs or simply assigned by an English teacher. Often they can be quite strange; I have met Chinese in Taiwan who have had names such as Swen, Voltron, Inga, Nein, and MacGyver, among others. Generally speaking, these names have no real legal or social standing and can be changed either on a whim or to conform to some current fashion if the person so desires.

As in many other ethnic gangs, Chinese gang members often use nicknames. Sometimes these are designed to appear fierce or intimidating, sometimes they are simply based on a childhood incident or other source. For example, the founder of the United Bamboo is nicknamed "Dry Duck" because the members of the organization took animal nicknames and he is unable to swim. (Other members were Green Snake, White Wolf, and Yellow Bird.)

PROPER ETHNIC TERMS

In most minority groups there are some people who are quite sensitive about the terms that are used to refer to them. Generally speaking, people who come from China should be referred to as either Chinese, Chinese-American, Asian, or Asian-American (or, of course, Chinese-Canadian or Asian-Canadian). Oriental is an older term, and although sometimes it can be used with no problems or offense taken, some Asians find it offensive. Most members of the minority group will not take offense if such obsolete terms are used as long as they know that no offense was meant. Nevertheless, some people among the group might seize upon them as offensive, particularly if they are already upset over something else, and most would expect that an educated or important person could keep up to date on the proper terminology.

"Chinaman" is very offensive to many Chinese in America because when the term was commonly used, the Chinese were treated very badly.

One may also run across references to "ABCs," which stands for American-Born Chinese. The term simply means a Chinese-American. As stated previously, there are people in Southeast Asia who insist on describing themselves as Chinese, despite the fact that they were actually born and raised in a Southeast Asian nation and their families have not even visited China for generations. Such people often insist that they are "not really Vietnamese" (or whatever country they are from), despite the fact that they were born and raised in that country.

CORRUPTION AND APPARENT CORRUPTION

Many Asians and Chinese in America come from countries where corruption is rampant. In Chapter 1 it was stated that in traditional Chinese culture, morality and behavior often emphasize loyalty to one's friends and loved ones over duty to abstract moral concepts. The importance of having personal connections in important places was also discussed. For this reason, many Asians would like to have a friend among the police. They often assume that having such a connection could prove quite useful since a good friend among the police might bend the rules for them.

Human beings everywhere love to brag, and as anyone who has spent much time among Asians can testify to, some Asians have been known to exaggerate the importance of their guan-hsi, or "important connections."

Police officers and others should be wary about letting themselves be seen as developing friends with particular individuals in an Asian community. On one hand, such friendships can be good for all concerned; on the other, it is also possible that such individuals may begin to expect a favor from their friend. Although they may not see this as immoral, and in fact might be quite willing to repay the favor, it is also quite possible that a favor might not be on the up and up. In Chapter 1, I told about a Chinese man who assumed that by having a friend in the New York State Department of Motor Vehicles he could have the results of his failed road test changed behind the scenes. Police officers and others in authority should be quite careful about allowing their picture to be taken with Asian acquaintances, particularly those who may have criminal connections. When Asians display such photos, often framed, in their place of business, the underlying message can be, "This policeman is my friend. If you cause me problems, then I can ask him to help me." Although this might convey a powerful message to extortionists, it may work both ways. A criminal might use a picture of himself and a policeman to let an extortion victim know that "the policeman in this picture is my friend. He will not arrest me, and he will not help you if you report my actions to him. It is best if you simply pay me money and do not go to the police." Although this may sound strange, not too long ago some major figures in a large tong in a major American city began a campaign of attempting to have their pictures taken with police officers. The intention was presumably to use such photos to improve the prestige (and perhaps image) of the tong in that city's Asian community.

Similarly, those in positions of power should be wary about receiving gifts from Asian immigrants if they suspect that they will be asked to reciprocate in an unnamed way in the future. At times, such gifts might not be given directly to the officials but instead will be intended for their families or to "help with their children's education" or some other pretense. Not only might some Asians misunderstand if such gifts are accepted, they might further misunderstand if they attempt to collect on the favors in the future and find that the official refuses. Such actions will surely lead to bad feelings.

THE BIG PICTURE—PUBLIC POLICY AND ASIAN CRIME GROUPS

Asian crime organizations are a growing problem in America. They prey most on their own ethnic groups, and in their communities, the drain on the local economy is very real. Gangsters and criminals come to America to live, and many of the disaffected youths who fail to make it in their new country find themselves involved in gang life. Small businesses and immigrant entrepreneurs who are seeking to establish themselves in a new country suffer from extortion, the frequent threat of kidnapping, and constant competition from the low-cost labor of exploited illegal aliens. Finally, there is the threat that heroin importation presents to society at large.

Realistically, no policy or set of policies is going to be 100-percent effective in dealing with these problems. Nevertheless, there are ways to improve conditions and reduce Asian crime in America.

Immigration policies must be reassessed carefully. The two extremes of completely open and completely closed immigration must be seen as faulty. An open immigration policy would result in chaos and overload all available services and jobs for Chinese speakers. A completely closed immigration policy would not end Asian crime and would hurt the American economy. It would also result in a further alienation of a large minority and increased illegal immigration. As noted elsewhere, illegal immigration increases crime because illegals frequently are forced to avoid all contact with law enforcement or face deportation. Thus illegals are more likely to become criminals or vigilantes, and much, much more likely to become crime victims than other immigrants.

Although the immigration services should receive increased funding for detention facilities and personnel to screen immigrants, there is probably little need to change immigration policies drastically. Instead, it would seem much more efficient to direct efforts to making the current policies work better.

One potential source of improvement is in the way visas are issued for immigrants and visitors in their home countries. In Taiwan, for example, there is no official U.S. Embassy, because there are no official ties between the government of the United States and the government of Taiwan (Republic of China). Instead, there is a poorly funded institution known as the American Institute in Taiwan (AIT). The staff of AIT consists of U.S. diplomatic personnel "on leave" at the upper levels, while locally hired Taiwanese manage the actual day-to-day affairs of the institution. In effect, it is a U.S. government bureaucracy staffed and run by people who are only experienced in the ways of Taiwanese bureaucracy. The result is a nightmare. The Chinese personnel frequently issue visas based on clearly inconsistent standards and often play power games with the applicants. Although I know of no instances of actual bribery, favoritism and guan-hsi play an integral part in the issuance of visas by the United States in Taiwan.

There is no way that anyone whose first taste of the American government is exposure to this institution can walk away with much respect for bureaucracies in America. Furthermore, it reinforces the Chinese stereotype and assumption that the United States is run in a manner similar to that on Taiwan and in China.

When those who do come to America get into serious trouble, deportation should be considered. In many cases, Asian immigrants are more fearful of deportation than jail time, and thus it makes a better deterrent. Efforts should be undertaken to establish an extradition agreement with Taiwan. Although such efforts are hampered by the lack of official relations between the two governments, several important trade agreements have been established between the United States and the Republic of China on Taiwan. There is no real reason why an extradition agreement could not be established if both sides desired one.

On the local level, efforts should be made to improve police presence in Chinese neighborhoods. Such police should have specialized training or familiarity with Asian customs and their special crime problems. In areas without Chinese or Asian neighborhoods, I believe that law enforcement officials should make a special effort to keep an eye on Chinese restaurants. Although this may at first sound racist, I feel the effort is justified for the following reasons. First of all, Chinese restaurants frequently employ and mistreat illegal aliens and thus are likely candidates for labor violations (i.e., they "fit a profile"). Second, even when law-abiding, many Chinese restaurants and their owners' families are high-profile targets for robbery, extortion, or kidnapping by Asian gangs. Such gangs will often drive hours from their home city to target and hit a particular restaurant.

If we wish to reduce the presence and dangers of Asian gangs in America, we must realize that social programs can do as much to reduce gang membership as law enforcement initiatives. Since the typical hard-core Asian gang members are those who have been unable to assimilate properly into American society and lack the skills to make a future for themselves, there should be more programs in place to help them find opportunity, preferably before they get into trouble with the law. Bilingual education is one part of this. Although many oppose bilingual education in principle, stating that previous immigrants managed to assimilate without it, they are ignoring the obvious fact that large numbers of immigrants did not assimilate well to American culture but instead eked out grim lives filled with poverty and crime while living in ethnic neighborhoods—and the same thing is happening today.[1] Perhaps Chinese- or Vietnamese-language vocational training schools with a minimum level of English as a graduation requirement (enough to sell and describe their services to non-Asians, for example) would be appropriate. I will leave the details of potential programs to the experts, but the important thing is to provide alternatives. Such programs cost money, but prisons, increased crime, and increased law enforcement cost more.

There should be increased opportunities for English-language classes for immigrants who want them at prices they can afford. When I visited the CCBA headquarters in Boston, I was quite pleased to see that they were offering English classes for Chinese speakers, although I thought that the cost of $50 a month was somewhat high. (This is a third to a half week's pay or more for some people in Chinatown.)

The Chinese are known as being among the most entrepreneurial and hard-driven people anywhere. If given the slightest opportunity to get ahead, they will take it. Nevertheless, there are potential programs that could assist them in doing this. Property values are frequently outrageously high in Chinatowns, and so is rent. Open-air or sidewalk markets with reasonable or free rents, such as exist in some cities, should be established, regulated to a reasonable extent, and encouraged. Providing the opportunities for legitimate entrepreneurs lacking large amounts of capital to establish themselves in business will help to reduce poverty and encourage the integration of Chinese immigrants into American society.

Labor laws and working conditions should be enforced more carefully in Chinatowns. Violators should be given punishments that will deter future violations. Ensuring that workers are paid legal wages and work reasonable hours would help to reduce the cycle of poverty common among new Chinese immigrants and allow parents to spend more time with their children to reduce the number of potential recruits for Asian gangs. Enforcing labor laws would make it much more difficult for employers to hire illegals. Reducing the demand for illegal labor would inevitably reduce illegal immigration, which would, in turn reduce the crimes by illegals and, more important, those perpetrated on illegals. This would reduce Chinese organized crime groups' profits from smuggling and exploiting illegal aliens, thus reducing the importance of the groups.

Finally, in regard to heroin smuggling, my admittedly radical suggestion is that heroin be legalized for sale and consumption with a complete ban on advertising. The product could then be taxed heavily and regulated. The regulation would reduce immeasurably the chances of accidental overdose or poisoning, and the money raised through the taxes could be used to fund rehabilitation programs for the resulting addicts. And legalization would virtually destroy the illegal and dangerous traffic and, consequently, the power of the criminals engaged in that commerce. Conversely, I most certainly do not think that the United States should fund corrupt dictatorships such as that of Burma, in order to prevent our small population of heroin addicts from abusing their own minds and bodies. I do not even think such a government would have any desire to end opium production under such conditions. I suspect that as long as they are being given money to "fight" opium production, they will find ways to encourage it surreptitiously so that they can continue to receive money in order to "fight" it.

CONCLUSION

Chinese and Asian organized crime groups present a growing problem in the United States and Canada today. Nevertheless, they are a human problem, and their effects can be greatly reduced. Furthermore, Chinese and Asian criminals are only a small part of a large minority group, and, in fact, the problems they cause are greater among their own people than in mainstream society. In attempting to combat Asian crime in North America, seeking to understand Asian cultures is a good place to start. This in itself can be a highly rewarding experience.

NOTES

1. Although there are many books that describe the struggles and harsh living conditions of immigrants coming to America, for two quite readable ones see Herbert Asbury, *The Gangs of New York* (New York: Old Town Books, 1928) and *The Barbary Coast* (New York: Old Town Books, 1933).

[Editor's Note: * indicates a work that is highly recommended by the author for further reading.]

Asbury, Herbert. *The Barbary Coast.* New York: Old Town Books, 1933.

———. *The Gangs of New York.* New York: Old Town Books, 1927, 1928.

*Badey, James R. *Dragons and Tigers.* Loomis, CA: Palmer Enterprises, 1988.

Beach, Walter G. *Oriental Crime in California.* Stanford, CA: Stanford University Press, 1932, reprinted 1971.

Benson, Ragnar. *Gunrunning for Fun and Profit.* Boulder, CO: Paladin Press, 1986.

Billingsley, Phil. *Bandits in Republican China.* Stanford. CA: Stanford University Press, 1988.

Bing, Leon. *Do or Die.* New York: Harper Collins Publishers, 1991.

Bo Yang. *Golden Triangle: Frontier and Wilderness.* Hong Kong: Joint Publishing Co., 1987.

*Bond, Michael Harris. *Beyond the Chinese Face: Insights from Psychology.* Hong Kong: Oxford University Press, 1991.

Booth, Martin. *The Triads: The Chinese Criminal Fraternity.* London: Grafton Books, 1990.

Boucard, André and Louis. *Burma's Golden Triangle.* Hong Kong: Asia 2000 Ltd., 1988.

Bresler, Fenton. *The*

SELECTED BIBLIOGRAPHY

Chinese Mafia. New York: Stein and Day, 1980.

Brunvand, Jan Harald. *The Choking Doberman: And Other "New" Urban Legends.* New York, London: W.W. Norton and Co., 1984.

Buck, David D., ed., *Recent Chinese Studies of the Boxer Movement.* Armonk, NY: M.E. Sharpe, 1987.

Campbell, Anne. *The Girls in the Gang.* New York: Basil Blackwell, Inc., 1984.

Carr, Caleb. *The Devil Soldier.* New York: Random House, 1992.

Chan, Wing-tsit. *A Source Book in Chinese Philosophy.* Princeton, NJ: Princeton University Press: 1963.

*Chesneaux, Jean, ed. *Popular Movements and Secret Societies in China: 1840–1950.* Stanford, CA: Stanford University Press, 1972.

*Chin, Ko-lin. *Chinese Subculture and Criminality: Nontraditional Crime Groups in America.* Westport, CT: Greenwood Press, 1990.

Chow, David, and Richard Spangler. *Kung Fu: History, Philosophy, and Technique.* Burbank, CA: Unique Publications, 1977.

Christensen, Loren. *Skinhead Street Gangs.* Boulder, CO: Paladin Press, 1994.

Clearly, Thomas, translator and editor. *Mastering the Art of War: Zhuge Liang and Liu Ji's Commentary on the Classic by Sun Tzu.* Boston and Shaftsbury: Shamballa.

Clements, Allan. *Burma: The Next Killing Fields?* Berkeley, CA: Odonian Press, 1992.

Cohen, Bernard. *Deviant Street Networks.* Lexington, MA: Lexington Books, 1980.

Connor, Michael. *Sneak It Through: Smuggling Made Easier.* Boulder, CO: Paladin Press, 1984.

Conover, Ted. *Coyotes: A Journey through the Secret World of America's Illegal Aliens.* New York: Vintage Books, 1987.

Daraul, Arkon. *A History of Secret Societies.* New York: Carol Publishing Group, A Citadel Press Book, 1961, 1989.

Dillon, Richard H. *The Hatchet Men.* New York: Coward-McCann, Inc., 1962.

Draeger, Donn F., and Robert W. Smith. *Comprehensive Asian Fighting Arts.* Tokyo and San Francisco: Kodansha, 1969.

Eberhard, Wolfram. *Guilt and Sin in Traditional China.* Taipei, Taiwan: Rainbow Bridge Book Co. Ltd., 1967.

Elliot, Alan J.A. *Chinese Spirit Medium Cults in Singapore.* London: London School of Economics, Department of Anthropology, 1955 (reprinted by Southern Materials Center, Inc., Taipei, Taiwan, 1982).

Fried, Morton H. *Fabric of Chinese Society.* Taipei, Taiwan: Southern Materials Center, 1953, 1985.

Gong, Eng Ying, and Bruce Grant. *Tong War!* New York: Nicholas Brown, 1930.

Goodrich, L. Carrington, and Chaoying Fang. *Dictionary of Ming Biography: 1368–1644.* New York: Columbia University Press: New York, 1976.

Gronewold, Sue. *Beautiful Merchandise: Prostitution in China 1860–1936.* Binghamton, New York: Harrington Park Press, 1985.

Gross, K. Hawkeye. *Drug Smuggling: The Forbidden Book.* Boulder, CO: Paladin Press, 1992.

Hail, William James. *Tseng Kuo-fan and the Taiping Rebellion.* New Haven, CT: Yale University Press, 1927.

Hartzell, Richard W. *Harmony in Conflict.* Taipei, Taiwan: Caves Books, Ltd., 1988.

Heaps, Willard A. *Riots U.S.A. 1765–1970.* New York: Seabury Press, 1966, 1970.

Hoffman, Abbie. *Steal This Urine Test.* New York: Penguin Books, 1987.

Hogshire, Jim. *Opium for the Masses.* Port Townsend, WA: Loompanics Unlimited, 1994.

Houston, Jean Wakatsuki. *Farewell to Manzanar.* New York: Bantam Books, 1973.

Howard, Michael. *The Occult Conspiracy—Secret Societies—Their Influence and Power in World History.* Rochester, VT: Destiny Books, 1989.

Hsu, Francis L.K. *The Challenge of the American Dream: The Chinese in the United States.* Belmont, CA: Wadsworth Publishing Co., 1971.

*Kaplan, David E. *Fires of the Dragon: Politics, Murder, and the Kuomintang.* New York: Atheneum, 1992.

*Kaplan, David E., and Alec Dubro. *Yakuza: The Explosive Account of Japan's Criminal Underworld.* New York: Collier Books, 1986.

Keene, M. Lamar. *The Psychic Mafia.* New York: Dell Books, 1976.

*Kinkead, Gwen. *Chinatown: A Portrait of a Closed Society.* New York: Harper Collins Publishers, 1992.

Knox, George W. *An Introduction to Gangs.* Berrien Springs, MI: Vande Vere Publishing Ltd., 1991.

Kwon, Peter. *The New Chinatown.* New York: The Noonday Press, 1987.

Llaughlin, Burgess. *Black Markets around the World.* Port Townsend, WA: Loompanics Unlimited, 1981.

Lavigne, Yves. *Hell's Angels: Three Can Keep a Secret if Two Are Dead.* New York: Lyle Stuart, 1987.

Leung Ting. *Skills of the Vagabonds.* Hong Kong: Leung's Publications, 1983.

———. *Skills of the Vagabonds II: Behind the Incredibles.* Hong Kong: Leung's Publications, 1991.

Li, Peter S. *The Chinese in Canada.* Toronto: Oxford University Press, 1988.

*Lillius, Aleko E. *I Sailed with Chinese Pirates.* Hong Kong: J.W. Arrowsmith, Ltd., 1930 (reprinted by Oxford University Press, 1991).

*Liu, James J.Y. *The Chinese Knight Errant.* London: Routledge and Kegan, 1967 (reprinted by Southern Materials Center, Taipei, Taiwan, 1979).

Marlock, Dennis, and John Dowling. *License to Steal.* Boulder, CO: Paladin Press, 1994.

*McCoy, Alfred W. *The Politics of Heroin.* Brooklyn, NY: Lawrence Hill Books, 1991.

Moore, Joan W. *Homeboys: Gangs, Drugs, and Prison in the Barrios of Los Angeles.* Philadelphia: Temple University Press, 1978.

*Morgan, W.P. *Triad Societies in Hong Kong.* Hong Kong: The Government Printer, 1960.

Nee, Victor G., and Brett de Barry Nee. *Longtime Californ': A Documentary Study of an American Chinatown.* Stanford, CA: Stanford University Press, 1972, 1973, 1986.

O'Callaghan, Sean. *The Triads.* London: Star, 1978.

O'Neill, Hugh B. *Companion to Chinese History.* New York: Facts on File Publications, 1987.

*Pan, Lynn. *Sons of the Yellow Emperor.* London: Mandarin Paperbacks, 1990.

Polner, Rob, and Paul Schwartzman. *New York Notorious.* New York: Crown Publishers, Inc., 1992.

Posner, Gerald L. *Warlords of Crime: Chinese Secret Societies: The New Mafia.* New York: Penguin, 1988.

Quinn, Peyton. *A Bouncer's Guide to Barroom Brawling.* Boulder, CO: Paladin Press, 1990.

Reisner, Marc. *Game Wars: The Undercover Pursuit of Wildlife Poachers.* New York: Viking Penguin, 1991.

*Reuter, Peter. *Disorganized Crime: Illegal Markets and the Mafia.* Cambridge, MA: MIT Press, 1983.

Rolfe, Peter Lars, and Zelma E. Greeson. *Gangs USA.* Boulder, CO: Paladin Press, 1992.

Sandmeyer, Elmer Clarence. *The Anti-Chinese Movement in California.* Chicago: Illini Books, 1939, 1973.

Schirokauer, Conrad. *A Brief History of Chinese and Japanese Civilizations.* New York: Harcourt, Brace, Javanovich Publishers, 1978.

Shapiro, Sidney. *The Law and Lore of China's Criminal Justice.* Beijing: New World Press, 1990.

Siegel, Ronald K. *Intoxication.* New York: Pocket Books, 1989.

Spencer, Jonathan. *Chinese Roundabout: Essays in History and Culture.* New York: W.W. Norton and Company, 1992.

Stanton Candlin, A.H. *Psycho-Chemical Warfare: The Chinese Communist Drug Offensive against the West.* New Rochelle, NY: Arlington House, 1973.

Sun, Haichen. *The Wiles of War: 36 Military Strategies from Ancient China.* Beijing: Foreign Languages Press, 1991.

Thompson, Hunter. *Hell's Angels: A Strange and Terrible Saga.* New York: Ballantine Books, 1966, 1967.

Wakeman, Frederic, Jr. *Strangers at the Gate: Social Disorder in South China, 1839–1861*. Berkeley, CA: University of California Press, 1966.

Ward, J.S.M., and W. G. Stirling. *The Hung Society or the Society of Heaven and Earth, Three Volumes*. London: Basherville Press, 1925 (reprinted by Southern Materials Center, Taipei, Taiwan, 1977).

Werner, E.T.C. *Chinese Weapons*. Singapore: Graham Brash, 1932, 1989.

Wolf, Arthur P. *Studies in Chinese Society*. Stanford, CA: Stanford University Press, 1978.

OFFICIAL DOCUMENTS

National Narcotics Intelligence Consumers Committee, *The NNICC Report 1992: The Supply of Illicit Drugs to the United States* (Washington, D.C.: GPO, 1992).

Padavan, Sen. Frank, Chairman, New York State Senate Committee on Cities, *Our Teeming Shore: A Report on Federal Immigration Policy and Its Impact on the City and State of New York, with Proposals and Recommendations for the Future* (New York, 1994).

Royal Crown Colony of Hong Kong. Police Report of the Current Triad Situation (untitled). 1994.

Royal Crown Colony of Hong Kong. Press Release on the Big Circle Gang. 1994

United States Department of Justice. Office of the Attorney General, *Attacking Organized Crime, 1991 National Strategy, 1990 Annual Report* (Washington, D.C.: GPO, 1991).

United States Department of Justice. *Legal Activities 1993–1994* (Washington, D.C.: GPO, 1994).

United States Drug Enforcement Agency Intelligence Division. *Source to the Street, Drug Intelligence Report* (Washington, D.C.: GPO, 1993).

United States Drug Enforcement Agency. *Southeast Asian Heroin Trafficking: Emerging Trends* (Washington, D.C.: GPO, June 1994).

United States Drug Enforcement Agency. *Worldwide Heroin*

Situation Report—1992 (Washington, D.C.: GPO, 1994).

U.S. Senate Committee on Governmental Affairs. *Asian Organized Crime: Hearing before the Permanent Subcommittee on Investigations of the Committee on Governmental Affairs.* 102nd Cong., 1st sess., 1992.

U.S. Senate Committee on Governmental Affairs. *Asian Organized Crime—The New International Criminal: Hearing before the Permanent Subcommittee on Investigations of the Committee on Governmental Affairs.* 102nd Cong., 2nd sess., 1992.

Senate Committee on Investigations of the Committee on Governmental Affairs, *The New International Criminal and Asian Organized Crime,* report prepared by the permanent subcommittee on Investigations of the Committee on Government Affairs. 102nd Cong., 2nd sess., December 1992.

PERIODICALS AND NEWSPAPERS

Abrams, Jim, "Chinese held for ransom—63 illegal aliens smuggled into Maryland house," *The Daily (Schenectady, NY) Gazette*, Associated Press, 7 April 1994, sec. A-4.

Bendsten, Robert D., "I Was There—Gunshop Shootout," *Soldier of Fortune* 16 (December 1991): 16, 73-75.

Border, Jake, "Battle at Three Pagoda Pass—Burmese Renew Attacks on Mon Army," *Soldier of Fortune* 12 (August 1987): 38-45, 77-78.

———, "Battleground Burma," *Soldier of Fortune* 13 (January 1988): 44-51, 92-93, 96-97.

———, "Burma's Unlikely Alliance," *Soldier of Fortune* 12 (December 1987): 40-45, 108,113-114.

Brown, Cailin, and John Mahoney, "Robbery stuns posh neighborhood,"*(Albany, NY) Times Union,* 21 June 1994, sec. B-1, B-3.

Caher, John, "2 admit East Wok kidnapping," *(Albany, NY) Times Union,* 6 July 1994, sec. A-1, A-9.

"Chinese Americans dominating heroin trade, Congress told," *China Post, Taipei, Taiwan, Reuters,* 7 November 1991.

Coyne, Jim, "The Last Battle? Will U.S. Aid to Burma Kill the

Republic of Kawthoolei?" *Soldier of Fortune* 9 (June 1984): 66-73.

"The Curse of China White," *Newsweek* Asian edition (14 October 1991): 12-18.

"Death Is the Best Deterrent," *Newsweek* (14 October 1991): 14-15.

Duffy, Brian, "Coming to America," *U.S. News & World Report (21 June 1993):* 26-29, 31.

Dunn, Ashley, "After Crackdown, Smugglers of Chinese Find New Routes," *New York Times,* 1 November 1994, sec. A-1, A-24.

"F.B.I. says Asian syndicates, gangs a major threat," *China Post,* Taipei, Taiwan, Reuters, 15 October 1991.

Golden, Daniel, "The Lost King of Chinatown," *Boston Globe Sunday Magazine (*13 November 1991).

Gorman, Peter, ed., "High Times Travel Guide: Exotic Pot Spots," *High Times* (September 1994): 47-49, 52-53, 62-63.

Haas, Alain, "Killed in Action," *Soldier of Fortune* 14 (November 1989) 52-57, 83-84. (Note—article deals with the tragic death of *SOF* correspondent Lance Motley while reporting a story in Burma.)

Harris, James, "Back to Basics Plus: A View from the Drug Enforcement Side," *The Police Chief* (October 1993): 73-75.

Henican, Ellis, "Getting Oriented," *Penthouse* (June 1988): 145-152.

Holley, David, "Filling a void with 'qigong' in China: Millions have turned to the practice which mixes exercise and meditation—officials fear unpredictable political consequences," *Los Angeles Times,* 16 October 1990, sec. H-8.

Hood, Marlowe, "Mystics, Ghosts, and Faith Healers: Forces of China's Past Re-emerge in a New Occult Craze," *Los Angeles Times Magazine* (19 April 1992): 20.

Huston, Peter, "Trying to Understand Traditional Medicine," *Skeptical Inquirer* 18 (Winter 1994): 207-108.

"International Assistance for U.S. Police," *The Police Chief* (October 1993): 40, 45-46, 48, 51, 54-55.

Jackson, Vincent, and Jay Jochnowitz, "Restaurateur tried to deal with kidnappers alone," *(Albany, NY) Times Union,* 2 January 1994, sec. A-1, A-8.

Johnson, Mark, "Rebellion in Burma," *Soldier of Fortune* 11 (January 1986): 64-67.

———, "Resisting Rangoon—Burmese Rebels A-Z," *Soldier of Fortune* 10 (90-95, 130-131).

Krieger, John, "Holiday in Hell: SOF Staffer Caught in Jungle Attack with Karen Freedom Fighters," *Soldier of Fortune* 16 (January 1991): 36-43.

Kurtz, Paul, and James Alcock, Kendrick Frazier, Barry Karr, Philip J. Klass, and James Randi, "Testing Psi Claims in China: Visit of CSICOP Delegation." *Skeptical Inquirer* 12 (Summer 1988): 364-375.

Li, Jane H., "Week in sweatshop reveals grim conspiracy of the poor," *The New York Times, 12 March 1993, 1,40.*

———, "Last Stand in Manerplaw," *Soldier of Fortune* 17 (May 1992): 54-59, 70-71.

Maas, Peter, "The Menace of China White," *Parade* (18 September 1994): 4-6.

Massarella, Linda, "Chinatown rapist exploits shame, fear and silence," *New York Post,* 28 May 1994.

Neumeister, Larry, "U.S. witness faces deportation to China," *Daily (Schenectady, NY) Gazette, Associated Press,* 6 July 1994, sec. B-4.

"The Nigerian Connection," *Newsweek* Asian edition (14 October 1991): 19.

Peters, John, "Combat and Caring," *Soldier of Fortune* 17 (August 1992): 30-33, 66-68. (Note—article deals with medical relief in Burma.)

Peterson, Tom, "Bad Day at Thingannyinaung," *Soldier of Fortune* 15, (February 1990): 28-33.

———, "Karen Kill Zone," *Soldier of Fortune* 15 (March 1990): 26-35.

Polachanin, David, "Chinatown residents kidnapped," *Boston Globe,* 10 November 1994.

"The Poppies of Colombia," *Newsweek* Asian edition (14 October 1991)*: 17.*

Ricciuti, Edward R., "Guns n' Rhinos." *Wildlife Conservation* (January/February 1992); 26-36.

Sabbay, Robert, "Lost in America," *Rolling Stone,* (1 March 1995) 56-61, 72.

Scholing, Elaine, "State Sept. report labels Nigeria major trafficker of drugs to U.S." *New York Times,* 5 April 1994, sec. A-1, A-11.

Scott, Jim. "The China Syndrome," *Soldier of Fortune* 15 (February 1990): 70-72, 79-82.

Seagrave, Sterling, "Betrayal in Burma," *Soldier of Fortune* 9 (August 1984): 28-31.

————, "Burma: The Battle Continues," *Soldier of Fortune* 9 (July 1984): 26-27.

————, "Burma's Golden Triangle," *Soldier of Fortune* 9 (May 1984): 38-43).

————, "Karen Rebels in Burma," *Soldier of Fortune* 9 (April 1984): 58-66, 101-102.

Surovall, Harriette, "Chinatown Cosa Nostra," *Penthouse* (June 1988): 40-44, 96-100.

"Tiger, Tiger, Fading Fast," *Time* (28 March 1994): 44-51.

Turnbull, P.E.X. Lt. Col. "Burma's Battle of the Box," *Soldier of Fortune* 12 (January 1987): 86-93, 109-110.

Williams, Mike, "Gutsy Karens Continue to Bloody Burmese Butchers," *Soldier of Fortune* 15 (February 1990): 34-35.

Winchester, Mike "Losing Ground in Burma—Karen Resistance Drags On," *Soldier of Fortune* 11 (April 1986): 52-55, 89-93.

Witkin, Gordon, "The New Opium Wars—The Administration Plans to Attack the Lords of Heroin." *U.S. News and World Report* (10 October 1984): 39, 44.

Yu, Winifred, "Chinese restaurateurs more likely to be victims," *(Albany, NY) Times Union,* 21 June 1994, sec. B-3.

Peter Huston has a degree in Asian studies, lived in Taiwan for more than three years, and has traveled extensively throughout Northeast Asia. While living in Taiwan, he taught English as well as working as a business assistant to a Taiwanese machinery factory. He continues to add to his knowledge of Asian culture whenever possible through both reading and hands-on experience. In Taiwan, he wrote the screenplay for an English-language publicity film for Taichung, the third largest city in Taiwan, as well as pieces for the Taiwanese magazines *New Taipei* and *English Excellence Monthly.* He has spoken on conducting business in Taiwan at Union College.

Huston also has an extensive background in emergency medical care and security. He has been an ambulance attendant, volunteer firefighter, taught first aid and CPR for Red Cross, and was once a member of the Albuquerque Mountain Rescue Council. He has worked rock concert security for more than seven years, as well as a variety of other security related positions, including work in the Albany inner city housing projects. He is a New York state certified advanced emergency medical technician. While living in Taiwan, he appeared on the nationally syndicated ICRT radio as a member of a panel of experts to discuss problems with emergency and prehospital care in Taiwan.

ABOUT THE AUTHOR

Huston has also worked as a newspaper correspondent, grant researcher, environmental activist, mental health residence counselor, hospital orderly, and fast food cook. He once competed nationally in skeleton sledding, a sport related to bobsledding. He volunteers as a supervisor at court-appointed family visitations. His hobbies include studying the martial arts and cooking. Huston has lived among the Navajo Indians in New Mexico and also in Argentina. He speaks Spanish, Mandarin Chinese with a strong accent, a little Korean, and he can spit out a steady stream of obscenities in Navajo.

One strong interest of his is the way science and paranormal claims interface. He is admittedly quite skeptical about most paranormal and supernatural claims and feels that the bulk of such reports can be explained by an understanding of scientific laws, human perceptions, belief systems, psychology, folklore, and hoaxing. He has explored and investigated such phenomena as the Lake Champlain Monster, sleep hallucinations, Satanic cult fears, Taiwan spirit mediums, Chinese chi gong masters and their alleged powers, and more. He has written about such things in *The Skeptical Inquirer, Skeptic,* and had a column dealing with such claims in the short-lived yet nationally syndicated science fiction magazine *Expanse.* His piece on sleep paralysis was translated into German and appeared in the book *Mein Paranormales Fahrrad (My Paranormal Bicycle).* He has spoken at science fiction conventions and made radio appearances on this subject.

Tongs, Gangs, and Triads: Chinese Crime Groups in North America is his first book.

INDEX